PERSONALITY
LINGO

Use the Power of Personality to Transform Relationships,
Improve Communication and Reduce Stress

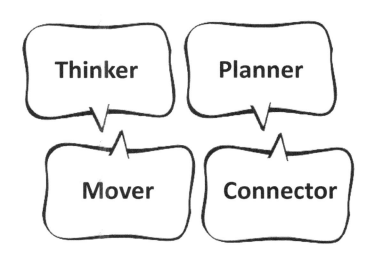

Mary Miscisin

illustrated by Jeff Haines

positively publishing

Author Contact:

Mary Miscisin

7485 Rush River Drive
Suite 710
Sacramento, CA 95831

LearnMore@PersonalityLingo.com
www.PersonalityLingo.com

Illustrated by Jeff Haines
Cover Design by Ed Redard

www.PositivelyPublishing.com

ISBN: 978-1502718389

Library of Congress Control Number: 2014918148

CreateSpace Independent Publishing Platform, North Charleston, SC

**Dedicated with love
to my daughter
Crescentia**

Contents

Acknowledgments

There are so many people whom I would like to thank for their contributions to this book, beginning with the pioneers in the field of typology, from its roots to its many branches. They have paved the way for those who have carried on to explore, expand, and evolve the original methods and theories.

Ed Redard, my best friend and soul mate for his incredible curiosity about human nature and his outstanding capacity to come up with solutions to complex problems. His ever-expanding tech expertise has accelerated my capacity to reach hundreds of thousands and saved me tons of frustration. Thank you for putting up with the piles of papers and books in the office, late night typing, and numerous revisions. Thank you for supporting me through thick and thin, helping me reach my goals, accepting my different methods, and finding ways to help me increase my knowledge, grow in my skills, and foster my self-expression.

A special appreciation goes to Don Lowry for his genius in developing the True Colors concepts. Beyond his brilliance in distilling personality temperament theory to the pure essence and putting it into the hands of the general public, I am deeply touched by his continuing friendship. His enduring quest to enhance the lives of children and adults is heartfelt and sincere.

Erica Echols-Lowry for her devotion to excellence. She is not one to back down from a challenge when her intelligence, intuition, and savvy eye for aesthetics informs her otherwise. Erica's tenacity and talent in developing the True Colors model to various next levels of application is beyond measure. I cherish her friendship, spiritual connection, passion, kindness and intellect.

Cres Jaeck for her ongoing exploration into Jungian Psychology. Deep gratitude for the countless conversations and endless insights about human behavior and consciousness.

My never-ending gratitude goes to Cindy Holmes who believed in me before we ever met. Once we did meet, we connected quickly, deeply, and permanently. I have been gifted not only with her incredible friendship, but her exceptional editing expertise. Her boundless enthusiasm for sifting through pages and pages of manuscript and spotting the tiniest detail that most eyes would miss is truly remarkable.

A heartfelt thanks to the thousands of participants in my various workshops who have supplied the fuel for the material in this book, and especially those who asked, "Okay, I know my personality style, now what?"

Joe and Elaine Sullivan, along with Fred Leafgren, who brought True Colors into my life via the National Wellness Conference.

Cliff Gillies, who from the beginning provided enthusiasm, motivation, and words of encouragement.

Larry Barkdull for his steadfastness, Jennifer Adams for her finesse in refinement and editing talents, and Brian Carter for his contributions.

Jeff Haines, whose artistic flare is truly remarkable. Thank you for your patience and diligence in working with my demanding and detailed requirements for the illustrations that make the words of this book come alive.

John Butler for being helpful, patient, and kind. Mike Berry and Michael Church for their creative talents. D.S. Fields for his artistic contributions.

John Valdez for his innovative panache and continued patronage to my success throughout the years and many phases of my career. His artistic expertise and willingness to keep diving into projects have supplied vital fuel to keep the dreams alive.

Mom (Jean Marie) and Dad (Ron) and my sisters and brothers: Evelyn, David, Therese, Martin, John, Michelle, Karen, Matthew, and Michael for providing a plethora of experiences that have helped to form who I am. Manuel, who is like a son to me.

Those who read sections of my several manuscript versions: Cres Jaeck. Gina Snyder, Michael Viola, Sande Roberts, Dave Manahan, Michael Peart, Joanie Stephen, Helen Scully, David Lee, Tim Schmidt, Paul McKay, Bobbie Lewis, Teresa Gibson, Jackie Mead, and Cherrise Knapp.

And others who contributed stories, ideas, or advice: Dave Roberts, Lisa Konarski, Martin Brady, Lyle Groen, Rick Jenkins, Karen Martins, Steve Steuart, Nikki Lynn Ahrens, Jessica Dolge, Janice Whiting, Tanya Harris, Nancy Henriksen, and Nina Olson.

Thank you Emily Hine for your sincere exploration, insightful coaching and steadfast support.

I would also like to acknowledge you, the reader, for your willingness to learn and expand your appreciation of human behavior.

Part I
Introduction

EVER WONDER...
ABOUT
HUMAN BEHAVIOR?

I know I do! For instance, have you ever noticed that some people are very punctual? They make it to places on time or even early. Yet others have a tough time being on time. It doesn't seem to matter if they give themselves an hour or five hours to get ready - they still end up being five minutes late. What is it that makes someone very uncomfortable if they are running late, while others take it in stride and actually find it stimulating to race the clock?

Or, have you ever observed how some people speak their mind even before they know what is on it, while others are more reserved and think before they

1

speak? Why do some people speak out spontaneously, and others hold their thoughts in?

It is interesting to watch the behaviors of people on the highway. If someone is driving slower than us, we may think to ourselves, or even out loud, "What a slowpoke!" Or if someone happens to be driving faster than us, we might think they are a "crazy driver." No matter the posted speed limit, we seem to have an internal gauge for determining the "right" speed for us to drive.

Philosophers have been pondering human behavior for centuries and researchers have been studying it for decades. People have different preferences, communication styles, and ways of behaving. Although there are certain laws that govern what is "right" and "wrong" within different societies and cultures, as *individuals* we often judge the world by what *we* would do in a particular situation. If another person's way of doing things differs from ours, there is a natural tendency to regard it as the "wrong" way.

As social beings, we have an innate tendency to try to understand and regulate the behaviors of others. And if we admit it, we have all tried to get another person to behave differently. Sometimes we have been successful and other times not. Many fields of Psychology promote that "one cannot change the behaviors of others, they can only change themselves." Yet consider the fact that we've been shaped, formed, and sculpted by the influence of others practically since the day we were born. Our parents tried their best to guide us; teachers attempted to educate and train us; relatives, friends, and even society as a whole have an influence on our behaviors and choices almost constantly. No wonder we try to change others too!

Specific habits or manners *have been* conditioned into people to a certain extent. This conditioning has had a tremendous influence on our personality. However, even with all the poking, prodding, and encouraging, our natural behaviors will keep emerging. When we get comfortable around friends and others we know and trust, we have a tendency to relax and reveal more of our innate preferences. Often in times of joy and

especially during times of stress (when it can be difficult to concentrate), our conditioned behavior gives way to what comes more naturally - our inborn temperament.

Our personality style is a combination of these external influences (nurture) and our inborn temperament (nature).

Our Inborn Nature

Modern research indicates that our temperament is set at birth, it is coded into our DNA. We are born with a predisposition that acts as an internal compass that tugs us toward our own personal values, needs, and preferences.

It's Apparent!

I often ask parents if their children's personalities are more similar or different. I usually get a resounding, "different!"

As the second oldest child in a family of ten children, I was often intrigued that although the same parents raised us, we all seemed to have distinct personality traits early on in life. As an infant, my sister, Evelyn, loved to be held, cuddled, and rocked. I, on the other hand (my mother reports), would buck and kick when picked up and would squiggle about unless I was held facing outward. One of my brothers, John, was always fascinated with money. He found ways to earn it, count it, and save it.

My sister, Therese, was quite proper and neat. She would sort her sock drawer according to colors, arrange her toys in their "correct" places, and always waited her turn.

3

Then and Now

Nearly fifty years later, times have changed, but some things have not. Evelyn still loves to be hugged and held, I squiggle and kick if I am in one place too long, John is a successful banker, and Therese is a homemaker with everything in its place.

Certain traits from childhood still appear in our behavior as adults. The ability to recognize our inborn personality temperament enables all of us to realize that other people are not "wrong" for having different preferences or doing what comes naturally. They are simply pulled in a different direction by their own distinctive set of values, needs and approaches.

Navigating Life

We are all navigating life guided by our own unique compass. While one person may be pulled toward intellectual pursuits and secure surroundings, another person may be drawn in the direction of spontaneous adventure and high stakes risk-taking.

Keeping in mind that our overall personalities can and do shift with our life experiences, our temperament remains in our nature. It can be hidden, stifled, influenced, *or* adaptive to your circumstances and fully expressed. Because this innate predisposition is coded into your DNA it remains there throughout life whether you choose to follow its guidance or not.

Knowing your personality style and understanding the personality styles of others helps us recognize our similarities and differences as gifts and unique contributions. This self observation and resulting awareness helps you follow your own path in life. It accelerates your individuation process and improves your personal and professional effectiveness.

Using these powerful insights we are more able to head off conflicts, reduce stress, increase respect, open up lines of communication and bring out the best in everyone!

Chapter 1
THE HISTORY OF
PERSONALITY LINGO

"It is more important to know what sort of person has a disease than to know what sort of disease a person has." - Hippocrates

Hippocrates (460-370 BC)

Often referred to as the "Father of Western Medicine", Hippocrates is credited as being one of the originators of temperament theory. He observed that people in general seemed to have one of four approaches to life: Phlegmatic, Choleric, Melancholic, or Sanguine. Each correlated with a body fluid or "humor".

He theorized that a preponderance of one of the four humors was a strong predictor of personality type as follows:

Yellow bile (Choleric) strong-willed

Black bile (Melancholic) serious

Phlegm (Phlegmatic) calm

Blood (Sanguine) buoyant

5

The number of notable contributions and remarkable distinctions since the time of Hippocrates are too numerous to name them all here. Instead, I will highlight some of the most popular models that have impacted our modern personality lingo.

Carl Jung (1920's)

"Everything that irritates us about others can lead us to an understanding of ourselves." -Carl Jung

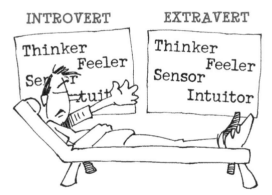

Renowned psychologist Carl Jung is best known for his theory of psychological types. From years of observation and research, he proposed and developed the concepts of Introversion and Extraversion. He defined the two attitudes of Introvert (I) and Extravert (E), as whether our psychic energy was focused inward or outward. Although these terms have remained in our modern vocabulary, the way the words are typically used by the average person today differs from Jung's original intent (see chapter 3 *Introvert does not Mean Shy* for more details).

Later in his extended research, Jung noted that people further displayed "functions" or particular psychological patterns that remain the same in principle under varying conditions.

Sensing (S) Concrete information gathering by the way of your 5 senses

Intuition (N) Perception of meaning and possibilities by way of insight or hunches

Thinking (T) Decides from a detached standpoint of logic, cause and effect, and objective criteria

Feeling (F) Comes to decisions by associating with the situation and considering the values and needs of the people involved

After endless deliberation over descriptors, Jung published his pioneering work *Psychological Types* in 1921.

Myers-Briggs (1950's)

"I dream that long after I'm gone, my work will go on helping people." -Isabel Myers

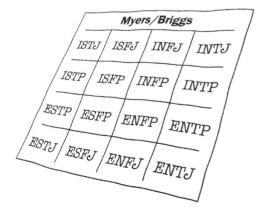

Fascinated by the research of Jung, Katherine Briggs and Isabel Myers (mother-daughter team) developed the famous Myers-Briggs Type Indicator (MBTI). One of the many ways they expanded the work of Jung was to add two more functions:

Perceiving (P) Those with an orientation towards this function spend more time gathering information as their circumstances unfold. They are most comfortable leaving options open and undecided as long as possible.

Judging (J) Those with an orientation towards this function move quickly through the information gathering stage in order to reach conclusions and closure as quickly as possible.

This addition of these two functions doubled the personality types designated by Jung: (8 x 2 =16 personality types). Recognizing that using the four-fold combination of traits as descriptors for each type style would be quite a mouthful, they used specific letter combinations as a shortcut lingo for understanding their system.

Keirsey Temperaments (1970's)

"Our attempts to reshape others may produce change, but the change is distortion rather than transformation."
-David Keirsey

Embracing the two functions added by Myers and Briggs, Educational Psychologist, David Keirsey returned to classifying personality into four

temperament types. In 1978, David Keirsey and Marilyn Bates published *Please Understand Me* using descriptors based on Greek Gods to represent each type: Apollonian, Promethean, Dionysian, & Epimethean.

Continuing to investigate personality differences and refine his theory of the four temperaments, Keirsey updated his terms in 1998 with the release of his expanded book, *Please Understand Me II*. For ease of identification, Keirsey often refers to the letter abbreviations of the MBTI in conjunction with his updatd personality temperament terms:

Idealist (Apollonian) NF
Intuition, Feeling

Rational (Promethean) NT
Intuition, Thinking

Artisan (Dionysian) SP
Sensing, Perceiving

Guardian (Epimethean) SJ
Sensing, Judging

Lowry (1970's)

"When you know what your core values are, and feel good about them, you can perform at your highest potential in every area of life."
-Don Lowry

In the years that followed, a variety of four quadrant systems emerged using different descriptors for the personality temperaments. Author, educator and playwright, Don Lowry popularized the use of the colors blue, gold, green, and orange with his True Colors model.

Gold (SJ) Practical, dependable

Blue (NF) Spiritual, emotional

Green (NT) Inventive, analytical

Orange (SP) Active, hands-on

What began as a theater production by Don Lowry dramatizing each of the four dominant types, grew into widespread use of color terms. This popularity brought the concepts into the hands of the general public and caught the attention of other four quadrant personality models.

Recognizing the practical benefits of using colors to trigger associations, even systems that had entirely different personality vocabulary started using color along with their descriptors (such as the DISC system, Herrmann Brain, and Keirsey). Other common colors used today in correlation with personality temperaments include red, yellow, and white.

Mary Miscisin (2000's)

"How do we bring out the best in each other instead of driving each other crazy? That is the power of knowing your personality."
-Mary Miscisin

As an avid personality researcher, with degrees in psychology, health education and communication, I wrote the book *Showing Our True Colors*. In response to the demand for more insights and applications of the personality principles, the book was first published in 2001 with several editions and translations that followed throughout the years.

Ever-evolving Applications

As a recognized leader in the health and wellness field, university instructor and master practitioner of Neuro-Linguistic Programming (NLP), I continued to study, field test, and teach the personality temperament concepts to a wide variety of audiences. In order to convey different nuances or answer specific participant questions, I found myself presenting the temperament concepts using colors, letters, numbers, and other descriptors.

"...a science is never made by one man, but by many. The individual merely offers his contribution, and in this same sense I dare to speak of my way of seeing things." -Carl Jung

Realizing I had become multi-lingual in several personality systems, I decided to officially open up my personality approach to include distinctions, research and data I collected throughout the years. I took the next logical evolutionary step in the teaching and training of communication dynamics by blending the technologies of personality theory, NLP, and Cognitive Psychology. The result is the Personality Lingo® system!

The Compass Metaphor

"The four functions are somewhat like the four points of the compass; they are just as arbitrary and just as indispensable..." – Carl Jung

In studying the work of Jung, I resonated with the way he likened the temperaments to a compass that provides us with direction with which to navigate our lives. Just as a compass contains all four directions yet the needle points towards "True North", each of us has all four styles within us yet we are naturally drawn in a specific direction towards the values of our most dominant style.

By following the guidance of our personality compass we can tap into our inborn strengths as well as our learned behavior traits to lead us in the right direction to feel the most alive, on path, and motivated throughout life.

The four Personality Lingo® styles described in this book are:

Connector: connects their world with relationships, possibilities & meaning

Planner: plans their world with consistency, responsibility & following rules

Thinker: thinks about their world with keen logic, questions & innovation

Mover: moves about their world with spontaneity, adventure & risk-taking

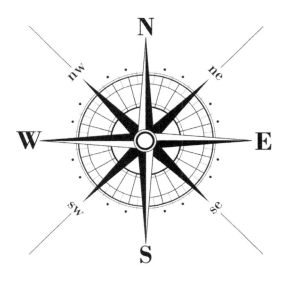

Approximate Comparison of Systems

Personality Lingo	Connector	Thinker	Planner	Mover
Don Lowry's True Colors	Blue	Green	Gold	Orange
Color Lingo	Blue	Green	Gold	Orange
Personality Dimensions	Blue	Green	Gold	Orange
Insight Learning	Blue	Green	Gold	Orange
Four Lenses	Blue	Green	Gold	Orange
Four Windows	Blue	Green	Gold	Orange
Real Colors	Blue	Green	Gold	Orange
Personality Resources	Blue	Green	Gold	Orange
Living Your Colors	Blue	Green	Gold	Orange
Color Code	Blue/White	Red	N/A	Yellow
Herrmann Brain	Red	Red	Green	Yellow
Birkman	Green	Blue	Red	Yellow
Myers-Briggs	ENFJ,INFJ ENFP, INFP	ENTJ, INTJ ENTP, INTP	ESTJ, ISTJ ESFJ, ISFJ	ESFP, ISFP ESTP, ISTP
Keirsey Temperaments	NF	NT	SJ	SP
Keirsey/Bates	Apollonian	Promethean	Epimethean	Dionysian
Keirsey (current)	Idealist	Rational	Guardian	Artisan
Ancient Greek	Fire	Water	Earth	Air
Hippocrates/Galen	Phlegmatic	Choleric	Melancholic	Sanguine
Carl Jung	Intuition/ Feeling	Intuiting/ Thinking	Sensing (/Judging)	Sensing (/Perceiving)
Diet Styles	Diet Connector	Diet Thinker	Diet Planner	Diet Mover
Inner Hero	Helper	Thinker	Planner	Doer
Helen Fisher	Estrogen/ Oxytocin	Testosterone	Serotonin	Dopamine

For additional comparisons (including DISC and Enneagram) visit our web site at:
www.PersonalityLingo.com/personality-systems-compared/

Chapter 2
UNIQUE AS A FINGERPRINT

You Truly Are One Of A Kind

Sometimes when people first learn about their personality they are surprised (if not downright skeptical) that there are only four basic styles. How is it possible to distill the endless variety of traits and characteristics a person could have into four basic styles? Since there are billions of people, it stands to reason that there are probably billions of variations in personalities, right?

Absolutely! We are all unique and different, each of us remarkably individual - just like our fingerprints! Our fingerprints are so unique in fact, they are used to confirm our identification. No two fingerprints have ever been found to be exactly alike. Even those of identical twins are different.

Interestingly, an expert can look at a fingerprint and identify three basic patterns: loops, arches and whorls. Every fingerprint, as unique and special as it is, can be characterized as having a combination of only three basic patterns (and I thought four personality styles was incredible)! The proportion of these characteristics and how the patterns are arranged provides you with your unique "print".

Similarly, people are a blend of characteristics from all four of the basic styles mixed in a variety of ways to form endless combinations. The style that is most abundant for you is said to be your dominant personality style.

Don't Put Me in A Box

As children, we may or may not have grown up in environments that encouraged us to follow our true nature. Some parents may have admired and fostered creativity, imagination, and self-expression. Some supported conventionality, while others promoted risk-taking. Still others taught the cultivation of competence in intellectual pursuits.

It is common for parents, teachers, and even communities to attempt to instill their own values in others. If they are not aware of the importance of supporting an individual's own gifts and preferences, these individuals or groups may end up rewarding the behaviors they label as "good" or "appropriate" and punishing behaviors they do not understand or approve of. When children think they have not lived up to their parents', teachers', or community's expectations, they may feel inadequate or even defective. As adults we can have more control over the behaviors we choose. However, some of us still believe the old labels and behave accordingly. Many of us have held jobs we hated—just to make a living. Some of us were criticized by our spouses, family members, bosses, or friends for behaving or not behaving in manners they deemed appropriate. We may have even felt we must pursue activities or causes that others considered suitable, enjoyable, or worthwhile. Many of us have lived up to–or down to–our labels. Fortunately, many people have at least some family or friends that they can "be themselves" around. Others are not that lucky. They may never have been validated for their own unique values, abilities, and preferences. Now it is your opportunity to shine–to be esteemed for being who you are and to foster self-expression in others so they may shine too.

What? More Boxes?

It is important to discern the difference between stereotyping people, which is

restrictive, and identifying commonalities and differences, which expands possibilities for more understanding and appreciation.

Sometimes people misuse personality typing as a way of labeling others or putting people into boxes. Because the benefits of knowing and using the personality concepts are so tremendous, it is tempting to try and use them to explain or "fix" challenges by constantly putting people or situations into neat little labeled boxes. This is both the beauty and the shortcoming of type watching. It is easy, fun, and revealing to identify people's personality styles, yet, if taken to the extreme, it can become restrictive. Attractive as it may be, take care not to oversimplify your entire world by boxing it all up into four rigid stereotypes.

Contrary to stereotyping, which is a "fixed conventional representation," Personality Lingo recognizes that all people are a unique blend of characteristics. There are four categories in our model but these four styles blend in a variety of ways to form endless combinations.

We do generally refer to people as being dominant in one of the four styles for ease of identification. However, this is not stereotyping. It is just identification. What category people are identified with is determined by the characteristics they have in common. Think in terms of automobiles. A Chevrolet Corvette and a Toyota Corolla are not the same, yet both are put into the category

of "cars." Similarly, dogs and elephants are both "animals," but nobody would mistake one for the other. Every noun in the English language is essentially a label—a way of identifying what we are talking about.

Knowing a Little Can Tell You a Lot

Just as with being able to identify certain characteristics of animals or cars, the benefits of identifying certain characteristics of people are endless. For example, if you know someone is a vegetarian, how is this information of benefit to you? What do you know about this "category" of people? The number one thing you could be sure of is that they do not eat meat!

Simply knowing this one thing–someone does not eat meat–provides you with a variety of information. However, take heed to make sure you are not simply stereotyping.

Would it be safe to assume that vegetarians would choose whole wheat bread over white bread or that they enjoy eating sprouts?

Could you conclude that they own a comfortable pair of blue jeans? Would you expect to find that they recycle?

Although the probability is higher that these things are also true, one could not assume so with 100% accuracy.

All vegetarians are not "sprout eatin', blue jeans wearin' recyclers." This is stereotyping.

However, just knowing that a person is vegetarian does give you specific information about that person. For instance, if you are inviting vegetarians over for dinner and really want to impress them and make them feel welcome, would you cook a roast for dinner? During conversation, how interested would they be about the butcher sale at the local grocery store? How much rapport will be built if you talk about the "delicious" taste of a good steak or the "scrumptious" recipe you have for meatballs or lamb chops? How much would they be able to contribute to the conversation? How much do you think they would want to contribute?

Now, if you are one of those people who really enjoy making your guests as uncomfortable as possible, you could still choose to serve meat and make it your topic of conversation throughout the evening. Although your guests will have to forego the roast at dinner, and may be polite enough to listen to the conversation about meat, they will probably not have much of a chance to be themselves.

Just knowing your dinner guests are vegetarian gives you plenty of information to assist you in knowing how to make them feel as comfortable and welcome as possible. You can either ignore this information because you feel calling someone a vegetarian is labeling them, or choose to use it because you know it can assist you in building rapport, opening lines of communication, and increasing self-expression.

So, when people are not comfortable with the use of personality temperament systems because they don't want to be labeled, it is for a good reason. They just want to be sure that people are not getting unfairly stereotyped. Just like any tool, it can be used to destroy or build.

Identifying your personality is a way for you to break out of boxes!

Learning the language of personality is a powerful way to recognize your gifts as just that–gifts! It's also a way of acknowledging that others are distinctive individuals with different gifts to contribute; and different does not mean wrong. Understanding your personality using a four quadrant system is one of the easiest, most convenient methods for understanding and appreciating human behavior.

Don't miss out on the benefits because you might not understand it yet. You will. Once you harness the power of Personality Lingo, you can use it to build self-esteem, enhance relationships, and bring out the best in everyone.

Chapter 3
DOES YOUR STYLE SHOW

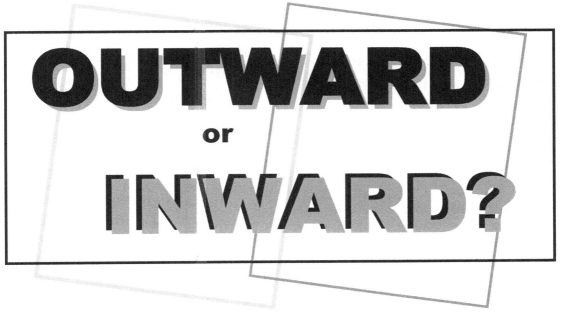

A Note about Introversion and Extraversion

Some people's most dominant personality style is obvious. One could say they wear their style on their sleeves for everyone to see. Others may not show their personality style as readily. For this reason, we might not recognize our most natural temperament style immediately or may sometimes misinterpret the style of others. As you will learn, many Movers are very loud and straightforward. You

definitely know when they are in the room. But some Movers are quiet and don't call attention to themselves. That is what is usually expected for Thinkers. Typically a Thinker doesn't like to be in the limelight. However, some Thinkers are energetic, enthusiastic, and take the initiative to motivate others to action. So why the difference? The difference is whether their energy is generated outward or inward.

15

Renowned psychologist Carl Jung is credited as pioneering the terms "introversion" and "extraversion". Through his research he noted that children in their earliest years displayed two unmistakable attitudes of introvert or extravert.*

Extraverts:

Think and process out loud

Prefer to bounce ideas off others

Enjoy attention from others

Speak readily in many situations

Outwardly focus on surroundings

Seek activities involving many people

Pursue breadth of experiences

Introverts:

Process internally before sharing

Explore options independently

Avoid attention from strangers

Pause and think before speaking

Inwardly focus and ponder

Seek solo, intimate experiences with select individuals

Pursue depth of experiences

Although the alternative spelling "extroversion/extrovert" is typically used by the general public, I will stick with Jung's original terms using an "a" instead of "o".

Understanding the importance of parental influence, Jung's studies showed that in spite of the greatest possible similarity of external conditions, children will assume one attitude or the other. Unless extreme "abnormal" circumstances were present to alter these attitudes, the preferences for introversion or extraversion prevailed throughout adulthood.

Introversion DOES NOT Mean Shy!

The way the word "introvert" is typically used today differs from Jung's original intent. When the average person is asked for their definition of *extravert* they are described as "sociable and likes people". *Introverts* are often depicted as "anti-social or shy". However, being shy has little to do with introversion. Shyness is the fear of social judgment. Although someone with an attitude of introversion *can be* shy, there are plenty of shy extraverts as well. Individuals that are struggling with shyness experience anxiety around their desire to interact with others but their fear of being judged, evaluated or embarrassed holds them back. Introverts are COMFORTABLE being alone. Introverts have a tendency to conserve their social energy, not wanting to drain it, thus preserving their strength.

Extraverts in contrast, do not typically function at their best in solitude. They gain strength and energy from interacting with others. A person can overcome or outgrow shyness but people do not outgrow their predisposition for introversion or extraversion. They can strengthen their access to their less preferred function, but their innate strength trait remains in their nature.

"Just as the lion strikes down his enemy or his prey with his forepaw, in which his strength resides, and not with his tail like the crocodile, so our habitual reactions are normally characterized by the application of our most trustworthy and efficient function; it is an expression of our strength." – Carl Jung

Muddled Meanings

Although it is customary to refer to someone as an "introvert" or "extravert", Jung was careful to declare that no one is exclusively extraverted nor introverted. Everyone is affected by the stimuli the outside world provides and we all process thoughts internally (if we didn't we would not be able to function in the world). As you read forward for further distinctions, keep in mind the terms are used in general to describe someone with a preference or strength for introversion or extraversion.

Outward – Extraverted

Extraverts are generally fairly easy to spot. They are usually very approachable–if they haven't approached you first. They typically are comfortable meeting new people and will readily talk to strangers. They enjoy interaction with others and gain energy from it. The more they talk and share, the more energetic they become.

Extraverts will ask others for their opinions and take pleasure in sharing their own. They have a tendency to get bored if they are not contributing to the conversation. In fact, if some extraverts don't self-regulate they may end up dominating the entire conversation. Given the opportunity, extraverts will speak before or as they think. They can blurt things out without much thought. Some extraverts can have an entire conversation with themselves while you are in the room and thank you for your input, when in reality you didn't say anything!

HI BOB! WHAT DO YOU THINK OF MY PEARLS, AREN'T THEY WONDERFUL, DON'T YOU JUST LOVE THEM! ME TOO! BYE!!

Another way to look at extraverts is to say that their style is expressed outward for the world to experience. Their attention is focused on the external environment of people, activities, and things.

Inward – Introverted

Introverts choose solitude to gain their energy. They prefer to think and reflect before sharing their opinions with others. They cherish their privacy and therefore honor the privacy of others. They are often thought of as good listeners because they typically wait to communicate until they have given the topic at hand some consideration.

Although, introverts usually turn inward to gather their energy and focus much of their attention on the inside world of thoughts, ideas, and reflections, this does not mean that introverts are never social or interactive. Some introverts are most comfortable socializing with individuals that they have known for a while. Other introverts muster up the resolution to be more verbal because they know it can help bolster rapport with extraverts. In addition, if an introvert finds a person or topic fascinating they can effortlessly bubble with enthusiasm and become quite talkative.

Marla was working on a project in her home office when she heard her introverted husband James greeting the satellite dish serviceman at the front door. As she typed at her computer she could hear them chatting. Within a few minutes she heard them laughing. Marla knew James had a keen interest in satellite technology and surmised he was asking questions and observing how the serviceman was wiring certain connections. Trying to concentrate on her project, she was intrigued by how loud the two were talking and laughing. The serviceman worked as James accompanied him from room to room. Their conversation and laughter was so loud at times, she wondered what they were finding so funny. The discussions and laughter continued for the entire two-hour service call. Finally she heard James bid the serviceman goodbye and close the front door. James immediately walked into her office and said, "That guy sure knew what he was doing. I learned all kinds of things."

However talkative or social they are, a great amount of interaction can be draining to an introvert who eventually needs private time to recoup energy. Even a long commute from work can be enough "alone time" to reenergize introverts by the time they arrive home.

Outside, Inside, In Between

Keeping in mind there are degrees of extraversion and introversion, an introvert can seem to be an extravert to someone who does not know them and vice versa. We all have times when we behave more introverted or extraverted, depending on our mood, experiences, and phase of life.

Sometimes people may question themselves and think that it is better to be one way or the other. For instance, many people find extraverts refreshing and entertaining and may wish they had the same ease with words. On the other hand, there are extraverted individuals who berate themselves for not pausing before speaking and admire the independence of introverts, wishing they had the ability to be content and comfortable when alone. Neither way is the better way to be. Introversion and extraversion are simply characteristics pertaining to the way a person gathers their energy.

Insights into Extraverts

"When I am socializing and others are not contributing to the conversation I feel almost a burden or obligation to liven up the conversation by asking questions or getting others involved. If I don't keep talking there is all of this awkward silence. I feel as if they are relying on me to provide all of the entertainment. Sometimes I can get so frustrated I just give up and find other people to talk to."

—Judy, an extravert

Tips for Introverts to Relate to Extraverts

Silence is agony to Extraverts. They rely on outside stimulation for energy so they get bored quickly when it gets quiet.

Extraverts want some indication that you heard their question or they are likely to ask again. A simple "hmm…" or head nod will do.

Just because you rehearsed something in your head does not mean you shared it out loud. When you are ready, use your "outside voice" to share your inside thoughts.

If you are worried that extraverts will drain your brain with their constant chatter on a long car ride, encourage them to bring an MP3 or something to listen to while you take a breather from conversing.

Extraverts think out loud so their thoughts can at times be incomplete. Bouncing them off of you/others is the way they process and finalize.

Extraverts can be like puppies when they see another person in their path. Eye contact, smiling or a simple "hello" can make their day.

It does not mean you are not special because extraverts want to spend time with other people. They need to get out and interact to get recharged.

Insights into Introverts

Howard was eating lunch with several other students after class. He was quietly content, listening to their banter. When a topic was discussed he would find his mind drifting from the conversation at the table to a conversation in his head. Suddenly one of the students paused and asked, "Hey Howard, what do you think?" Startled back to the presence of five other students staring at him for his response, Howard struggled to fit the dialogue he had going on in his head into their current conversation. He could tell from the confused looks on their faces that he had pondered the topic in an entirely different direction.

Tips for Extraverts to Relate to Introverts

Introverts actually enjoy sitting back and listening during conversations.

Even though introverts may appreciate the effort of trying to include them, they can feel put on the spot to share. It works better to simply pause for a few moments to allow them the opportunity to verbally participate if they want.

Just because introverts like space to observe and think, doesn't mean

they want to be ignored altogether. Check in with them but don't hover.

When you ask them a question, give introverts time to go inside their heads and ponder before expecting a response.

Related to the above, their silence does not mean they did not hear you, are ignoring you, or that they agree with you.

Introverts need time alone to recharge. It's not because they don't like you, it's the way they regroup and recoup.

When introverts are riding in the car with you it is not necessary to fill every moment with conversation. They enjoy your company and appreciate the refreshing pleasure of a pause.

If introverts don't return a smile and a wave immediately when you encounter them, don't assume they are unfriendly. It can take them some time to get out of their heads to respond.

Extra attention is needed to determine the top personality style of someone who tends towards introversion. What is visible to others may not be what is going on inside. Because introverts typically use their dominant personality traits to process more internally they may communicate and behave in manners more indicative of their second style. One really needs to pay attention to tell which is which!

Chapter 4
IDENTIFYING YOUR PERSONALITY STYLE

In the chapters that follow, I will be using the *Personality Lingo* terms Connector, Planner, Thinker and Mover. As you will learn, people usually have various characteristics from all four of the styles in their personality. However, one style is typically more dominant. So when we refer to someone as a "Connector" for instance, they wouldn't necessarily have all the characteristics of that style, just more traits than the other styles.

The descriptions on the following pages will help you determine the order of your personality from your top most dominant style to the style least like you.

To begin, quickly read through all four pages so you get a general idea of each style.

Then go back and identify the style that you resonate the most.

This is the style that best describes you.

Write a "1" in the RANK box in the bottom left hand corner of that page to indicate that this your most dominant style.

HINT: *If you follow your gut, you will be able to recognize your style more easily than if you try to scrutinize each one too closely.*

The next easiest to identify is usually your last style, the one you relate with the least. Mark a "4" in the corner of that page.

Then read through the remaining two styles again to figure out which ones are your second and third styles and record their ranking in the corresponding boxes on those pages.

Should you prefer an online version, go to our website and take the quiz there:

www.PersonalityLingo.com

21

CONNECTOR (NF-Blue)

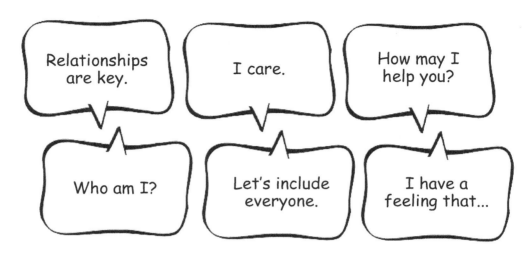

Supportive	Caring, kind, and cooperative, I have a positive attitude and like to bring out the best in others.
Thoughtful	
Empathetic	I desire meaningful, personal connection and cherish relationships. I seek authenticity and acceptance.
Inspiring	
Accepting	
Passionate	I value diversity, teamwork and harmony. I am most comfortable when everyone is getting along.
Creative	
Friendly	I rely on my emotional wisdom and keen intuition to help me make decisions that feel good.
Helpful	
Peacemaker	I have a creative imagination and enjoy self-expression. Validating and affirming, I like to include others.

I aspire to find my purpose in my life and develop my unique identity. I am passionate about all the possibilities life has to offer.

PLANNER (SJ-Gold)

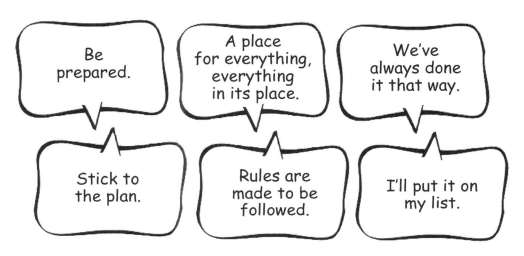

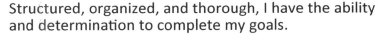

Respectful
Organized
Accountable
Timely
Consistent
Traditional
Law-abiding
Hard working
Responsible
Loyal

RANK

Structured, organized, and thorough, I have the ability and determination to complete my goals.

I desire respectful, stable relationships and prefer people to follow the rules. I believe in loyalty and duty.

I value consistency, security and commitment. I am most comfortable with clearly defined roles and expectations.

I rely on my sound judgment of what is right and wrong to make decisions. I like having a plan and sticking to it.

I work hard and derive great satisfaction from crossing items off my "to-do" list. People can depend on me.

I aim to create a life that is safe and secure. I enjoy the consistency of maintaining traditions, protocol and daily routines.

MOVER (SP-Orange)

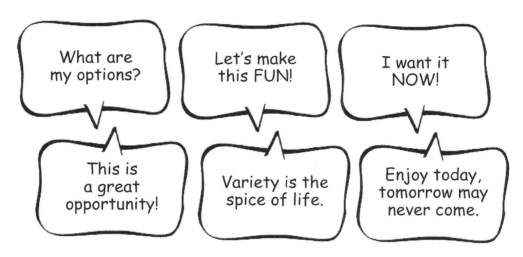

What are my options?

Let's make this FUN!

I want it NOW!

This is a great opportunity!

Variety is the spice of life.

Enjoy today, tomorrow may never come.

Playful **Spontaneous**	Daring, mischievous, and adventuresome, I crave excitement - especially a sudden adrenaline rush.
Expedient **Risk-taker**	I desire fun-loving, active relationships and like the freedom to be playful and engaging.
Negotiator **Charismatic** **Straightforward**	I value the here and now. I am most comfortable when people welcome my flexible nature and spontaneity.
Hands-on **Tangible**	I rely on my instincts to decide in the moment which is the best action to take. Competition drives me to win.
Physical	I am direct and quick and want to charge ahead with decisiveness and confidence.
	As a lover of variety and new experiences, I enjoy a challenge and have a voracious eagerness to live life to the fullest.

RANK

THINKER (NT-Green)

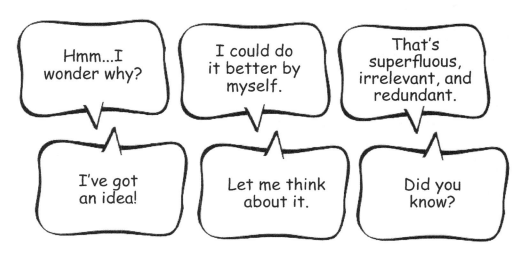

Knowledgeable	Curious, questioning and complex, I have diverse interests and an insatiable appetite for knowledge.
Questioning	
Private	I am independent and able to work alone quite proficiently. I like to keep my personal life private.
Independent	
Analytical	I value objectivity, intellect and problem-solving. I am most comfortable thinking "outside the box".
Innovative	
Strategic	I rely on my logic, having time to think, and investigation of the facts to help me make decisions.
Dry Humor	
Abstract	I can be a fountain of information as I generally know a little something about everything.
Tenacious	
	I seek competency in my life. When presented with an idea, it is irresistible to evaluate, analyze and improve upon it.

What Is Your Ranking?

As mentioned, most of us have a combination of characteristics from each style. If you read the descriptions and feel you are equally strong in two or more styles, this is natural. We each have the capacity to excel in various areas exhibited by the different styles. As you continue to read the other chapters of this book, you will gain further clarifications. Most people find the more they learn and use the personality concepts, the more obvious their top style becomes.

Looking back at the numbers you placed in the boxes of the previous pages (or the results of your online quiz), record your personality style ranking in the blanks below starting with the style that best describes you in the #1 blank and continuing until you have ranked all four styles ending with your least preferred style in the #4 blank.

1. _____

2. _____

3. _____

4. _____

1 Your Primary, Most Dominant Style

The style listed for this #1 top position indicates your "True North", the most dominant style that guides, directs, pushes and pulls you

throughout your life. These are the traits you access when you are being your most natural self. These behaviors seems to happen almost "automatically". Similar to being right handed or left handed – we don't usually think about it consciously, we just naturally use our preferred hand.

2 Your Second Style

This second ranking represents your next best "go-to" style. This is the copilot that supports the actions of your most dominant style. This second style will have a major influence on your first. Many people report feeling as though they seamlessly operate between these two styles. Those individuals with a preference for introversion may in fact use their most dominant style to process and make decisions internally so externally they use their second style to relate to the outside world. Take this into consideration if you are confused about your own or another person's behaviors. Some consider their second style to be interchangeable with their first.

3 Your Third Style

You may or may not recognize very many traits of this style in your personality. Many times these traits will not be as obvious as the more dominant ones but will come in handy when needed. It is most likely you will access these characteristics in certain social settings when the situation demands it. You may also consciously or subconsciously exhibit these traits when no one else is accessing them, as if you sense that there needs to be a balance of personalities under that particular circumstance.

4 Your Last/Least Style

This last style in your personality combination is significant. Because these traits are the least natural to you, you may admire them in others. In fact, there is a tendency for people to attract a mate of their last/least style (you know the saying: opposites attract). However, because these traits are the least natural for you, chances are they are also the characteristics you least appreciate or understand. This lack of understanding can cause criticism and conflicts with others possessing these traits. Therefore this is the area with the most opportunity for growth for you.

How Can I Be Sure?

The descriptions for each style were written in general terms to that you can use your own imagination to try on each style trait to see how well it fits you. This quick ranking is only a starting point to begin exploring your personality. Don't worry if you are not absolutely certain about the order of your styles at this stage.

It may require you to live through some life experiences before you are certain of your own personal preferences and innate approaches. Sometimes the behaviors we learn in order to survive in life (adaptive traits) can become "second nature" to us, making it less easy for us to tell which one is actually our natural preference.

What About Ties?

Everyone has traits from all four of the styles, usually in differing amounts. On occasion some people feel their traits are evenly distributed - one style not any more dominant than another. This very well could be true. Some people who have had a lot of life experiences, such as those in the military, have had the opportunity to develop many aspects of their various personality traits and therefore may appear to be quite balanced in their characteristics. Others have consciously gone about strengthening their ability to use traits from all four styles so they feel comfortable operating from any one of them.

Common Reasons for Reporting "False" Ties

Many personality experts agree, "Thinkers" are the most likely to report equally spread personality traits. Because of their keen ability to extensively analyze, their ever-busy brains can come up with examples of situations in which they have used each trait. However, as they continue their research, it becomes obvious that a majority of their preferences are consistent with the Thinker style.

Another reason individuals may not be able to clearly discern their top personality style is because they are in a transition period in their life. Divorce, death, changing jobs, moving to a different town or other major stress inducing circumstances can shift us into the use of our less dominant preferences.

Perhaps you or someone you know wasn't able to truly "be themselves" for one reason or another. Learning and applying the concepts in this book can help individuals discover their true nature and clear up "false" ties.

Part II
STYLE
WATCHING

What Style am I?

Now that you have your preliminary ranking of your styles as a starting point, the remainder of this book is devoted to elaborating upon each and depicting the characteristics in contextual situations.

As I mentioned earlier, you will notice that as I describe the trait patterns for each style, I often refer to someone as being that style. For instance, those individuals with a majority of

29

characteristics associated with the Planner style are referred to as being a "Planner". Keep in mind that one does not need to possess all of the traits of that style to be considered dominant in that style.

In addition, because for many of us, our second style has such a major influence on our choices and behaviors, I also may refer to someone as their first and second style such as "Planner-Mover".

What Style are You?

Identifying your own style is usually easier than figuring out someone else's, especially if you only interact with them in certain contexts. For instance, some people find it quite natural to access their Planner traits at work, yet as parents they seem to shift into their Connector style. With friends, the Mover in them is brought forth. That same person when playing chess, seems to cross over into their Thinker style. If the only interaction you have with them is in a single context, you may not have all the pieces to their personality puzzle.

Even though the people we encounter and situations we find ourselves in definitely have an influence on our behaviors, our basic temperament remains in our nature. Therefore, to get a clearer personality perspective when observing others, it is important to look for the underlying motivation for the behavior. If a person is following the rules because it is the appropriate and responsible thing to do, it is different than someone following the rules to keep harmony or to

be liked and accepted by others. Notice the action is the same but the motivation behind it is different.

Moving Forward

As you read the information in the chapters to come, you will likely find some context in which you can relate to the story. You may find yourself reading along thinking, "Oh, yes! I do that!" Or you may pause and remember a time you interacted with someone else who behaves that way.

You could resonate with most of the stories in a chapter, then find other chapters that have you pause and ponder. That's terrific! You are looking for patterns and general trends. We are all a blend of a variety of traits. Amazingly enough, many people find several, if not all, of the attributes in their most dominant style apply to them in one way or another.

The stories and examples I use are only a representation of the some of the most common ways the different personality traits might be demonstrated. Notice as you read, who you know that fits the various descriptions. Pay attention to the ways they are similar to or diverse from each other. And most importantly, realize how you can use this information in your life and relationships.

If you want even more clarification, ask a friend, relative, or co-worker to read the style you think applies to you. Whether they agree with your perception or not, you will receive valuable feedback on your journey to discovering your personality style.

Chapter 5

THE
CONNECTOR
STYLE

Friendly, kind, and understanding, this style places high value on relationships. They are drawn to connect, associate and unite with others. Individuals with this style also naturally connect meaning to actions and events, connect concepts to each other as well as to the bigger picture. They may seek spiritual connection to a "higher power", nature, their communities, and tribes. This unique inclination for connection makes them the glue that bonds families, organizations, and relationships.

If you've ever seen the movie Dead Poets Society, starring Robin Williams, then you have experienced the motivating enthusiasm of a passionate Connector. In the movie, the character acts as a mentor to lead his students down the path of their own calling. He stimulates their imagination through his assignments and encouragement. He acts as a catalyst to thrust them in the direction of being the best they can be at being true to themselves.

The character that Robin Williams portrays in this movie is only one hue of the many facets of Connectors. Frequently, Connectors with a preference for extraversion make their way to the front lines of motivation, while those Connectors with a preference for introversion may choose to support others more behind the scenes. Whatever Connectors decide to do with their lives, it must involve people. They have an inner drive to connect with others as well as to connect with themselves. This style feels a never-ending tug to explore their

own identity and find a sense of who they are from what they do.

The following pages will capture the essence of a Connector's style, values, and motivations. They are simply observations of some common traits shared by many people who have traits of the Connector personality. You or the people you know may have any combination of the several characteristics. The important thing to keep in mind, however, is that the reason for determining which characteristics apply to you or others is to gain understanding and appreciation for the differences in all of us. And, instead of trying to change each other, we will choose to welcome and nurture the differences.

Connector Traits

The following qualities are associated with the Connector personality style. Since all of us are unique individuals, the fundamental Connector traits will manifest themselves a bit differently for each person. However, a general theme or pattern will still exist. Keep in mind that a person can still be considered to be Connector dominant without having all of the characteristics listed.

Craves Connection—Endearingly said, this style likes to connect. Relationships are a top ranking value for them and they enjoy connecting, interacting with, and inspiring others. They also like to connect meaning to actions, events, and their feelings. "When someone does X, it means Y." You will notice this strong drive to connect is woven throughout their lives.

Supportive—Highly empathetic, they are drawn to help others. They enjoy being relied upon as a trusted confidant for a listening ear and compassionate understanding. They have a tendency to overextend themselves, saying "yes" even when their time, energy, and resources are saying "no". But their willingness to go the extra mile and "be there" for others is still overall rewarding and fulfilling to them – often building enduring friendships and strong alliances that last a lifetime.

Kind—Thoughtful and caring, they try their best to be tactful and considerate. They give the benefit of the doubt and make an effort to speak kindly. In fact, if somebody says something they feel is a bit harsh, they'll say something to smooth over what they thought may have been unkind or insensitive.

Positive Attitude—Connectors look on the bright side of life, the cup as half full, and the silver linings in cloudy situations. They tend to smile or nod hello to others, hold doors open or let others in their lane in heavy traffic. "Have a nice day!"

Imaginative—Creative, expressive, and inspired, they may be drawn towards art, music, or drama. Possibly will write and speak with poetic flair or use metaphors. Sees possibility, hope, and future potential.

People Person—Accepting of differences, friendly, and affirming, this style relates well with people. They make an effort to understand, acknowledge, and appreciate others. Most every decision made is determined by how it will affect the people involved. The relationship is more important than being right or always having things their own way.

Collaborative—Encourages team building rather than "may the best person win" attitude. As a group or team participant, they enjoy the friendship and camaraderie of working together on a project or goal. Generally quite eager to cooperate, they believe in consensus decision making, thoughtfully considering everyone's opinion before moving forward.

Mediator—Connectors enjoy harmony and a peaceful atmosphere. Family frictions, coworker conflicts or other demanding disputes can be very

33

distracting for Connectors, even if the conflict does not involve them. They may try to mediate, "You have a good point, and you do too, can't we come to some sort of agreement?" Connectors try to foster collaboration and team spirit whenever possible.

Emotional Athletes—Highly intuitive, Connectors pay attention to emotions and consider feelings as useful information for decision-making. Whether they like it or not, Connectors are born with an emotional range that can be quite impressive. Not only do they experience their own emotions intensely, they seem to have a built-in radar for tuning into and even "taking on" the emotions of others. One of their favorite emotions is romance. For many Connectors, being in love makes them feel more alive and complete.

Helper—Likes to "be there" for others. May volunteer their time to help others, such as serving food for the hungry at Thanksgiving, joining a walkathon to benefit breast cancer, or spending time at the community youth center helping underprivileged kids learn how to read.

Seeks Personal Growth—Connectors believe in the positive potential of people and the possibilities that life has to offer. Not only are they interested in self-development and exploring avenues for their own authentic self-expression, they are often involved in helping others discover their unique talents. They are drawn to programs, books, careers, clubs and other organizations designed to build

self-esteem, improve relationships and, bring out the best in everyone.

Spiritual—This could be in a religious sense or that Connectors ask themselves questions that others might not think about. For instance, "Why am I here? What is my purpose for being on this earth? What am I here to contribute?" Connectors are the most likely of the four personality styles to mesh their work and personal life. They feel that their work is an extension of who they are. They may seek spiritual practices like Tai Chi, yoga, or meditation. They like to be in alignment with their values and know that they are on their path.

Understanding and Appreciating Connectors

Connectors' core values are relationships and self-expression. One of the best ways to understand and appreciate them is to recognize some of their strengths.

Strengths

Accepting
Acting as a catalyst
Communicating
Cooperating
Counseling
Creating
Guiding
Imagination
Intuition
Leading
Listening
Mentoring

Motivating
Optimism
Recruiting
Speaking
Supportiveness
Teaching
Tolerance
Training

There are endless possibilities for how the strengths and preferences of someone operating from the Connector style might be expressed. The following stories are provided to illustrate how just a few of these traits are demonstrated. You may see yourself or people you know in these individuals and circumstances.

The goal in presenting these stories is for you to better understand the motivations behind the person's actions and increase your appreciation for their way of doing things.

Why Am I Doing This?

"This is a scary move," Steve thought to himself, "but I just have to do it. I know it is right; I can feel it."

For the past three years Steve has worked as a sales representative for a nationwide technology development company. He took the job because he could work part-time and get paid quite well. It was a means to an end. He always kept the future in front of him. He was so associated with his future that he felt as though he were already there, living it. That's how he was able to work for the company as long as he did. Working minimal hours and receiving a good salary

made it possible for him to spend time learning more about himself by reading, traveling, and connecting with others. He was able to take many classes in areas that he was drawn toward: mastering emotions, mind/body/spirit, meditation, yoga, Tai Chi, breath work, and hypnosis.

But his present was catching up to his future. Although he was actually an outstanding sales person–top in his field–he just couldn't do it anymore. His heart wasn't in it. He felt like a hypocrite. For this reason, he decided to leave his position to explore other avenues. "I have to be passionate," he confided in his coworker Mindy, "and truly believe in something to sell a product or work for a company. I need to work in an area where I know I am contributing to others on a daily basis, where I can connect and bring out the best in people."

"But you do contribute, Steve," she assured him. "Everyone around here benefits from your compassion and energy. Even those that others find hard to work with, you are able to appreciate. You're everyone's friend."

It was true. Steve was definitely there for the people he worked with. Just this morning he was scheduled to meet with a big client and was heading out of his office when his coworker Shelby appeared. Shelby was involved in a very intense situation and needed a listening ear. Steve thought of his pending appointment, then noticed the look on Shelby's face. He pushed the thought of the appointment to the back of his mind and sat down to give Shelby his full attention. Although Steve heard the words that were coming out of Shelby's mouth, what he was really experiencing was Shelby's emotions, the feelings behind the words. He felt good about being there for Shelby and giving him the opportunity to vent. Helping others was virtually irresistible to Steve. He was aware that he was supposed to be at his appointment, which was important to his own financial well-being, but at the same time he knew this was where he really needed to be. This was more important.

Steve paid attention to Shelby's physiology, tone of voice, and facial expressions. He felt as though he was a conduit for Shelby's emotions. Shelby must have felt it too. After twenty minutes of venting, he was freshly liberated. He stood and shook Steve's hand, obviously relieved to have gotten things off his chest to someone who was so empathetic.

Steve felt exhilarated, taking pleasure that he could be of some help. Yet at the same time he had a sinking feeling inside, knowing he had let down his appointment. At this point he was only fifteen minutes late, but that was late enough. Steve had already made up his mind to be more cooperative in his negotiations with the customer. He felt as though he had to make it up to him

somehow. He quickly ran over options of what he could do. Perhaps he could come down on his price, throw in free shipping, or offer an upgrade. He picked up the phone to apologize. The other person was very understanding and reassured Steve that it was perfectly okay, that he had appreciated the extra time. But this did not allay Steve's guilt. He had made up his mind. The other person would be rewarded for his patience.

Who Am I?

Many Connectors are fascinated by human behavior and relationships. They seek understanding of themselves and how they fit into the world around them. They may be drawn to the self-help and psychology sections of bookstores and are on a constant quest of self-exploration. As they are seeking to find themselves, they are also engaged in understanding how they can connect effectively with those around them. They crave connection on a much deeper level than the other styles typically do. When listening to others, their attention goes beyond the words. They respond to the emotional needs of others. They will try to read for deeper meaning than the question or issue at hand, sometimes uncovering a land mine of untapped feelings. When this happens, Connectors are there to listen compassionately.

Since they have a genuine acceptance for most everyone they come in contact with, they look for the positive attributes in others and usually find them. This is why they are able to get along with and appreciate the approach of individuals that others may find intolerable. Connectors truly feel uplifted when they are able to contribute to others, be it a simple compliment, acknowledgment, or praise for a job well done.

Connectors also enjoy being needed and liked. They aim to please. They have a habit of trying to be everything to everybody. If they are not careful, they can get overwhelmed by spreading themselves too thinly.

The Object of the Game Is to Feel Good

Two second-graders, Justin and Trey, were playing The Phonics Game® called "Silent Partners" with their reading teacher. There were two decks of cards, deck A and deck B. The teacher had started the game with deck A, and each student had won one round. Trey won the first time and was so excited that he jumped up and down. Justin looked almost as excited as Trey as he reached over and patted him on the back, saying, "Good job!" The next round, Justin won and Trey congratulated him.

Deck B was a little harder. Justin won the first round. Trey looked disappointed this time and did not congratulate

Justin as he had previously. During the second round of deck B, Justin had the opportunity to take more than half of Trey's cards, which would assure him a winning game. That would be three games in a row! Justin looked at Trey and his cards. Then he looked at the teacher, who knew from his body language and eyes that he knew exactly what he was doing. Instead of drawing from Trey's pile he drew from the center pile, ending his turn.

On the next hand, Trey won. As a smile burst across Trey's face, a smile shone on Justin's.

Because it is the player's option whether or not to take cards, it is not considered cheating to refrain. The primary objective is to learn phonics, not just to win points. Trey had already gone back to his seat and Justin was helping the teacher put the cards away when she told Justin, "I noticed you didn't choose to take Trey's cards and that's okay. That's your choice."

Justin bubbled, "It's fun, even when Trey wins."

Cooperation and Seeing Others Happy

As depicted in the story about the card game, from the Connector perspective, harmony, happiness, and friendship are valued more highly than personal victory. Connectors derive joy from seeing others happy. When it comes to competition, they seek the pleasure that comes from participating with others. Playing together becomes their objective over winning. If winning will bring joy to other team members, then Connectors will be more motivated to win.

Spreading Smiles

"Wow! That's beautiful," commented a coworker.

Lisa looked up from her work. "Thank you," she beamed as she hastened to finish up the bulletin board she was designing so she could make it to her next meeting on time.

Lisa coordinates the Loss Control Department for her company. She is in charge of employee safety. Each month she tries to pick a safety theme appropriate for the month. Since it was now mid-summer, her theme was fire safety. She had cut flames from red, orange, and yellow paper and had creatively positioned them around some information about preventing fires. One corner of the board was always reserved for announcing birthdays. There she had placed a cut-out picture of a small birthday cake and had arranged around it the names of staff members whose birthdays landed in August.

"Oh no!" she gasped. "It's August 3rd today and Lynn's birthday was yesterday. I didn't get the names up in time for everyone else to know." Lisa felt awful. She tried so hard each month to come up with good themes, make them eye-

catching, and get the board up on time. She rushed to her meeting, thinking about what she could do for Lynn.

Lisa had volunteered to be a member of the Events Committee. Because she spent most of her days working on rules, regulations, and other paperwork, the bulletin board and this particular committee were a welcome break from her heavier responsibilities. The committee had been formed to bring some "fun" to the work environment. Members were involved in activities such as decorating the office for holidays, implementing events for employee recognition, and planning the company picnic. She enjoyed being a part of making the work environment more festive and welcoming. It really brought the employees together and gave them a sense of family and belonging.

Because her laughter can be heard ringing out at any given moment throughout the day, Lisa is often referred to by her coworkers as "Laughing Lisa." She is friendly and positive; a smile seems to be a permanent fixture on her face. People like her the moment that they meet her.

But today Lisa's smile slowly faded from her face. The committee members had strayed from the agenda and were chatting about various situations and people. Lisa was uncomfortable with gossip and never participated in it. She felt sorry for the people they were discussing—after all, they were not there to defend themselves. Her thoughts flitted for a moment to whether these same people also talked about her behind her back. She sat there quietly, not wanting to interrupt their camaraderie but at the same time wishing they would stop.

She was relieved when the committee chair finally called everyone's attention back to the agenda. By the end of the meeting Lisa had volunteered to create a flyer announcing their next event as well as shop for some particular items they would need. A tiny smile returned to her face. The next day Lisa quietly placed a special birthday card on Lynn's desk.

Creativity, Acknowledgment, and Empathy

Naturally creative, Connectors often have an eye for color and aesthetics. They like to have their environment look nice and fashion things so they are pleasant. Since creativity can come in endless forms, Connectors may sometimes be too humble to recognize. It doesn't always come in the shape of creating art and beautiful surroundings, but it is there nonetheless.

Warm and friendly, Connectors will go to great lengths to make sure others feel comfortable around them. Because they are conscientious about the feelings of others, they make sure to give acknowledgment. Connectors enjoy making a person feel recognized and special and can feel horribly guilty if they miss an opportunity. They make it a point

to remember others' special occasions such as birthdays and anniversaries, and other personal details.

Although some Connectors enjoy the social connecting they derive from gossip or "sharing," other Connectors will not participate unless it is of a positive nature. Being empathetic, they can put themselves in the shoes of others and may think, "How would I feel if this were happening to me?" They may keep quiet about their opinion on certain matters if they feel it would hurt the feelings of others, spoil their mood, or create disharmony.

Self-Expression

Nikki remembers when she was eight years old. It was Christmas and she could feel the excitement well up inside of her. She had written a special poem as a gift for her family. It came from a pure place in her heart; it was something she had created. She remembered kneeling on the bedroom floor, writing. "It just came flowing out of me. I felt so mature as I read the words. They sounded so grown up, so unique, so spiritual. I was almost impressed with myself. I couldn't wait to share my gift, to share myself."

But when Nikki read her special Christmas poem to her family she did not get the reaction she had anticipated. "They didn't believe me. 'You didn't write that, you got that out of

39

a book,'" she recalled them saying. "Then they all dispersed! They got up and left, and I was just standing there all alone. I was crushed. They didn't acknowledge my gift; a gift from my heart. It was so painful. I swore right then I would never share again."

Now, years later, Nikki confides, "I didn't see it for all these years. I could have looked at the underlying message–that they thought it was so good they didn't believe an eight year-old could write it. Instead I chose the pain of the illusion that they didn't care about my gift."

Nikki continued to write, but she never shared it with anyone. She kept a journal at night and poured her heart and soul onto the pages. This way she could write freely, without judgment.

One time one of her girlfriends had to write a story for an assignment at school and shared with Nikki that she was at a loss for ideas. Without even thinking, the words popped out of Nikki's mouth, "I'll write it!"

Nikki wrote a story that earned her friend an "A." (Keeping the story tucked away since childhood, she now plans to publish it as a children's book.)

Another joy of Nikki's was singing. "By the time I was twelve, I was belting out Streisand in our family room. I used to hop up on the step in front of the fireplace and give a show, but always in private, where no one could hear me. I was very shy with my voice."

In her mid-twenties she hooked up with musicians and formed a rock band. "It was easy to get out there and sing my lungs out. There was all this loud music, and I was part of a whole so it was more comfortable."

Over time Nikki played with several bands, and she was asked to write songs for them to play. She was up for the challenge. As a group they would brainstorm ideas for her to write about. She said about her writing, "It was always fun but some of it felt contrived. I was writing about something that others wanted me to write about, things that didn't matter to me personally. It didn't feel completely natural. Still, it was rewarding yet scary. It was definitely a stretch for me."

In her thirties she decided to help a friend promote his music and songs. She could no longer hide behind the band and the loud music. It was only her singing and Joe on the acoustic guitar. "It felt good to help a friend, but I still needed to fulfill what was inside of me."

Now Nikki has decided to write and play her own music. "I feel like I am going backwards. I haven't played a guitar in twenty years. I'm taking what I learned in the eighth grade and trying to put it together with my songs. The hardest part is being patient with the process. It's personally challenging. The whole journey has been to get me here to express what is inside of me. It feels more rewarding, more personally fulfilling, and a lot more intimate. Playing my own music is when I feel the most at home, in myself and in the world. I feel connected up with the spirit, the most complete and whole; expressing my deepest sense of purpose."

To Thine Own Self Be True

Connectors shine the brightest and feel the most alive and fulfilled when they are expressing their true selves. Creative and passionate about their interests, they may not share their talents with the rest of the world for fear of rejection.

Nonetheless, they feel a drive or calling to fulfill their purpose to be "at home" with themselves and the rest of the world.

A Skew in View

Connectors have generous natures and a love of people that makes them pleasant company for most anyone. However, sometimes the motivations and actions of this style are misunderstood. The same traits that are viewed as positive by some, especially other Connectors, may actually be irritating to others. It is human nature to evaluate the actions of others. Our values, judgments, and beliefs influence our perception of their actions. It is a matter of perspective. For example, you may observe a person to be "incredibly

sensitive" because they cry at movies.

Another person observing the same behavior would call it "overly-emotional." Which is true? Neither! A behavior is a behavior–period. There are multiple ways to label any given behavior, so why would it be beneficial for us to know how other people may view ours? When we are aware of how our own behavior is affecting others, we can make choices. We may think, "Yes, I do that and it is a part of myself that I cherish." Or, "Gee, I didn't know I did that. Thank you for pointing that out to me so that I can become aware and change it if I wish." For example, have you ever had the opportunity to hear a recording of yourself? If so, did you sound the way you thought you did? Most likely not. Many times when people hear their voices played back, they are surprised at the speed, style, or even accent of their words. Frequently, after individuals hear something in their speech they were not aware of before, they end up making some kind of modifications based on the feedback they received.

Keeping this in mind as you read, think of situations in which the following may apply. Notice whether you are coming across to others in ways other than you intended. Instead of hoping others will change and clearly understand your intentions, pay attention to the contributions you are bringing to the situation. Sometimes just prefacing (or explaining) your behavior for others allows you to still be yourself at the same time acknowledging that you know how it may be perceived by them.

41

Connectors May Be Perceived As

Extremely Sensitive—Others may feel like they need to tip toe around the feelings of this style who can tend to take things very personally. It can be very difficult for some people to give feedback to them for fear that this style will be easily hurt by criticism or critique. Because Connectors read between the lines of communication for a deeper meaning or message, they rarely take things at face value and may misinterpret intentions–getting their feelings hurt by what they believe to be true in their imagination.

Mushy—It can seem as if Connectors get carried away when it comes to romance. When smitten, they are prone to making "puppy dog" eyes, writing poetry, sending love notes, singing songs, giving long hugs and holding hands any chance they get. Their yearning to hear "I love you" and to feel it in their soul can be overwhelming to other styles who do not share this same craving. When it comes to love, Connectors may dive in heart first without checking to see if there is even water in the pool. When looking for love, they may over-romanticize the simplest gesture to mean a sign of "true love".

Drama King/Queen—This style can get accused of creating chaos out of an average circumstance by being overly dramatic. To others, they are perceived as turning something unimportant into a major deal and blowing things way out of proportion.

Woo-Woo—Because Connectors seek out spiritual practices ranging from yoga and meditation to energy work, chanting, crystal healing, or unique diets, they can come across as "new-agey" or irrational. Their belief in these practices can be so rooted that they may prioritize spending money for personal growth seminars over paying the bills.

Unrealistic—Connectors tend to say "yes" to most every request by friends and loved ones (and likely coworkers too). Their optimism and eagerness to help others can back them into situations where they cannot follow through on all their promises. Because they are often intuitive they expect their mate or friends are too.

Naive—Easily swayed by emotions and opinions of others, Connectors may ignore policies or bend rules to accommodate what they believe to be "extenuating circumstances". This gets them labeled as "soft", "too nice", "easily duped" or someone who will let others "walk all over them."

Wishy-Washy—This style has a reputation for not being able to make a clear, solid decision—going back and forth with their opinions. They may avoid giving a direct answer, changing their minds according to what will make people happiest. This strikes others as being overly dependent on external approval.

Codependent— Placing a lower priority on their own needs, this style may end up fostering dependency by not allowing others to do for themselves. They can get so excessively preoccupied with the needs of others that they seem to be living for the other person and not themselves.

Manipulative—Instead of coming straight out and making their desires known, Connectors tend to drop hints— such as "pouting" if others do something they don't agree with. Also called "passive-aggressive", they may mention something in passing, hoping their message gets conveyed—and getting upset if it doesn't.

Excessively Sympathetic—Connectors generally have a soft spot for those they view as underprivileged. Not only do they feel compelled to help, they often believe the general public is obligated to make special accommodations for every person, no matter their predicament. Those with this inclination are also referred to as "bleeding hearts".

Nosey—Having a propensity to ask personal questions, Connectors can come off as "busybodies" who gossip excessively. Their ability to make conversation with just about anyone can earn them the reputation of being prying, snoopy or intrusive.

Clearing Up Misconceptions

It can be quite shocking to this style when others do not view their behaviors in a positive light. The following are the explanations from Connectors as to how they view the very same characteristics from their perspective.

Connectors' Self View:

Caring (Extremely Sensitive)
Of course they take things personally. It's because they care. Warm, compassionate, and considerate. They try their best, so when they are criticized they feel it deeply. Connectors pay attention to the nuances of conversation and have the sensory acuity to notice the message behind the message.

Romantic (Mushy)
Connectors love the excitement of being in love. It awakens the senses. They enjoy all the trappings that come with being in love. Why wouldn't a person want to hug, hold, and be with the one they love? It's fun to notice when someone sends out a signal that they are interested. It's all part of the intrigue and excitement of romance.

Self Expressive (Drama King/Queen)
This style believes that going through life without intense feelings and drama would be meaningless! Emotions and the energy created by them are part of the juice of being alive and keeping them hidden would feel disingenuous and stifling.

Spiritual (Woo-Woo)
Connectors know they have a greater purpose. They would not have been put on this earth to merely exist. They may meditate, pray, or participate in other spiritual practices to get closer in touch with their higher power, themselves and others. They search for the meaning of life and recognize that there are powers beyond what some people might believe. Just because you can't see or touch something does not mean it doesn't exist.

Optimistic (Unrealistic)
When Connectors take on projects, they truly desire to complete them all and truly believe they will find a way (if not several ways). They delight in imagining all the possibilities for positive outcomes. They have faith in people and give them numerous chances to demonstrate their worth. They put relationships as top priority and believe if a person truly loves them, they will "know" their needs and desires, and joyfully want to do what they can to fulfill them.

Nice (Naïve)
Pleasant, cheerful, and accommodating, Connectors want people to be happy. They are generally trusting and give the benefit of the doubt. They believe in the good in others and try to be affirming and encouraging. Knowing that life can throw anyone a curve ball unexpectedly, they see the need for and value of exceptions.

Flexible (Wishy-Washy)
Believing that making a firm stand is not worth jeopardizing a relationship, Connectors will go with the flow. They can put themselves in the shoes of others and can see many sides of an issue.

Caretaker (Codependent)
Sensitive to the needs of others, Connectors try to help in any way they can. This style enjoys being depended upon. They heartily embrace the notion of "a friend in need is a friend indeed" and feel that true friends will reveal themselves as such in times of adversity.

Pleasant, Not Pushy (Manipulative)
As peace-loving individuals, Connectors prefer to make their needs known in a non-confrontational manner. The challenge is that their requests and needs can end up getting buried or lost under their polite approach.

Willing to Work Tirelessly for a Cause (Excessively Sympathetic)
Connectors have the ability to understand and share the feelings of others and "know" when others need help. If they don't lead the crusade, who will?

Genuinely Interested in the Welfare of Others (Nosey)
This style wants to know how people are feeling and what they need and want. If they don't know what's going on, how will they know whether to bake a cake, bring a gift, or offer help? Having a great ability to put anyone at ease and help them feel welcome, important, and recognized, they have an easygoing communication style.

As you can see, depending on which lens you are looking through, what can seem like less than desirable qualities to one can be held as redeeming qualities to another. If you find yourself beginning to make a negative judgment about another person's behavior, stop, and see how you can reframe the behavior to view it in a more positive light. Also, when you are more aware of how your own actions are being perceived by others, it can help you more effectively choose the situations in which you can be most comfortable sharing those aspects of yourself.

Relating to Connectors

First and foremost, Connectors are some of the best friends a person can have. They will be there for you through thick and thin. When others have given up on you, they will keep giving you encouragement. Even though they have their own priorities, they will set them aside to help.

Individuals with Connectors as their top or second style tend to be communicative. They want to interact with others in a warm, caring way. They respond well to kindness and place a high priority on relationships. If you can consider some of their needs important to you, then you will be able to relate to them in such a way that they will naturally be motivated to want to cooperate with you.

Typically, Connectors relate well with other Connectors. They like the predictable style and structure of Planners, the imagination and intellectual discussions of Thinkers, and they take pleasure in the active, entertaining Mover approach.

Maintain a Pleasant Environment

Pay attention to ways in which you can help put a Connector at ease. Connectors look for opportunities to be a source of help in creating a cooperative and harmonious atmosphere. Not only do they want to cooperate and please, they will try to encourage others to do the same. They will usually conform to whatever group, organization, or structure is set up for them, although fitting into that structure is not as important as their desire to feel valued and unique. Acknowledge them for their support and distinctiveness.

WHERE DO YOU WANT TO EAT?
WHERE DO **YOU** WANT TO EAT?
THAT DEPENDS ON WHERE YOU WANT TO EAT.
WHAT SOUNDS GOOD TO YOU?

Point Out How Others Will Benefit

Connectors are naturally drawn to individuals who seem to be having difficulty; social, personal, or otherwise. They often side with the underdog and support various human rights movements. In their element, when they are helping people, Connectors have a knack for cultivating the potential of others. They are self-sacrificing and will forgo the luxuries in life to contribute to others more in need.

This style may be reluctant to get involved in something in which they do not see value. When they realize that their participation really would help others, something transforms inside of them. Simply reframing the situation compels Connectors to want to do the things they may have been trying to avoid just minutes before. Suddenly, they're on a mission.

Understand Their Zest for Vitality Includes Emotions

Connectors like to act out and participate fully in the human dramas of life. They tend to get immersed in the experiences of living such as love, strife, success, sorrow, joy, and so on. A lot of their energy is spent paying attention to how they and those around them feel and what they are going through personally and emotionally. Step into their world to appreciate their enthusiasm. Show care when they are sharing in order to promote a receptive atmosphere for

them to express their feelings. Make sure your body language and facial expressions are congruent with theirs. Support them through strong participation and interaction.

Open Up Opportunities for Personal Growth

Interested in self-awareness and self-improvement, Connectors look for meaning in life. On a never-ending journey to self-discovery, they strive to be authentic, unique, truly themselves. Understand their yearning for their life to have purpose. Allow avenues for self-expression and ways for them to assert their own individual traits. Encourage them to find avenues to present their ideas and be creative. Bolster their ability to share with the world what is unique about them.

Give Individual Attention

Remember that Connectors like to connect. They enjoy forming lasting relationships, having close friends, and feeling loved. Remember their birthday and other personal matters they have shared. Offer a story about yourself. Often the smallest gesture of friendship towards them can go a very long way. They like to enlist and excite others. Provide opportunities for them to train, guide, recruit, and mentor. Operate in the Connector zone for some time with them. Try it on and see how it feels.

Needs

Acceptance
Harmony
Self-expression
Inspiration
Empathy
Affection
To contribute
Love
Relationships
Understanding

Values

Compassion
Friendship
Honesty
Sensitivity
Sharing
Tolerance
Trust
Kindness
Teamwork
Possibility

Desires to Be

Authentic
Self-expressed
Nurturing
Personal
Helpful
Meaningful
Sincere
Accepted
Included
Appreciated

Finds Joy In

Inclusion
Affirmation
Smiles
Seeing others happy
Affection
Love, romance
Mentoring
Teaching,
Conversations
Sharing
Family, friendships, groups
Giving
Making a difference
Being "on purpose"
Creative expression

Bringing Out the Best

To foster an environment for Connectors to flourish, turn to them for actions that bring out the best in themselves and others.

Miranda sat at a table outside her favorite café enjoying lunch in the sunshine. As she dined she took in her surroundings. There was a park nearby with several benches that seemed to be occupied quite frequently with homeless individuals. A glimpse of an elderly gentleman in ragged, dirty clothes approaching her table startled her. She turned towards him, feeling a bit unsettled.

"Got any spare change for a hungry man?" he implored.

"How about some food?" Miranda asked. "Would you like to join me for lunch?"

"I wouldn't want to impose, ma'am", he said apologetically. "But if you have some change that would truly help me out."

"Really," she said with the sweetest, soothing tone, "I would really enjoy your company."

After a bit more encouragement the man took a seat with her. They shared a wonderful lunch together. He talked about aspects of his history as well as his present living conditions. Miranda gave him some money and vowed to him that she would somehow help to make things better. Truly moved by the encounter at lunch, Miranda started thinking about what she could possibly do. "I know," she thought, "I'll call Sharmila. She'll have some ideas."

Sharmila was Miranda's best friend. She was a sociology student and part-time instructor for toddlers at a Montessori school. She, too, had thought about helping out somehow, and the call from Miranda was the impetus she needed to charge ahead. The first thing Sharmila did was to contact organizations that already existed to help feed and shelter the homeless to find out what was being done in their area. Finding out that they were short-staffed and short-funded, the answer was not a surprise; not much could be done with the resources they had available to them at the time.

Miranda and Sharmila decided to dig up some of their own resources. They held fundraisers in front of grocery stores and at the university. They put together a concert of local bands and accepted donations to benefit the hungry. They finally got permission from the city to hold a Saturday afternoon weekly picnic. They gathered volunteers to help them make posters and flyers, contact markets for food donations, and help set up the area at the park. Sharmila and Miranda personally made soup and sandwiches and served them to anyone who showed up with an appetite.

Turn to Connectors for:

Cheering Up—Connectors are optimistic and have a way of helping you feel that everything will be okay. They will aid you in seeing how practically any situation can be used to learn and grow.

Validation—When you need a little praise, acceptance, and understanding, those with this style usually have plenty to offer.

A Confidant—If you need someone to listen empathetically, they will lend an ear. They try hard to not judge others for their actions and have an immense amount of understanding and tolerance.

A Mentor—Because they like to foster growth in others. It feels wonderful for them to be a role model, inspiration, or other positive influence in the lives of others.

Understanding the Impact on People—If you need to know how your project will affect the people involved, ask a Connector. They are connected with people and know their needs and how they might react to changes.

A Friend—Relationships are the number one value to Connectors. They seek out friendships and alliances with others. They can provide encouragement, motivation, and support.

Creative Ideas—Find someone with this style to help you brainstorm ideas. Original, unique, and inspiring, they can help unlock the creativity in those around them. Connectors make great trainers, especially in "people" skills such as customer service, morale, team-building, and communication.

Leading a Human-Needs Cause—When it comes to the charitable organizations they support and believe in, they will lend a hand. This is especially true if they can see their help will benefit others.

Sharing—Most Connectors enjoy hearing a personal anecdote. Especially Connectors with Mover as their second style may utilize "gossip" as a way of staying connected with friends.

Help—When you need a volunteer to pitch in; if you are overwhelmed and need assistance or a favor, turn to someone with this style. If they are not already stretched to the limit, they find pleasure in contributing to others. It makes them feel wanted, included, and needed.

Chapter 6
THE
PLANNER
STYLE

Steadfast, reliable, and conscientious, this style craves a sense of consistency. Responsible by nature, they aim to create a life that is safe and secure. They desire a certain level of predictability, especially in relationships. Once they make a commitment, they like to stick with it and do everything in their power to keep it.

Lyle has been married for thirty-four years. He and his wife, Gloria, have two children, a son and a daughter. Growing up, each child had his or her own chores to complete, including keeping their own rooms clean. They were required to make their beds in the morning before going to school. Lyle had a "policy" that his children should finish what they start. When they were making decisions to join little league or take swimming lessons, for instance, they knew they had to stick with it until the end. No dropping out allowed. Since Lyle and Gloria both worked for schools, and had summers off, they frequently went on camping trips together as a family. Gloria's parents lived close by so they were able to visit them on a regular basis. Every three years they would travel to Minnesota to visit Lyle's family, always the last week in July or the first week in August.

When their son became a cub scout, Lyle became the cub master. When their daughter joined softball, Lyle became the coach. Joining organizations and teams soon turned into an integral part of Lyle's life. Since he worked as the director of transportation for a local school district, Lyle also joined the California Association for School Transportation Officials. The first year as a member he took the position of vice president, the second year he was an active member, and the third year he became president of the chapter. He remained president for five consecutive years, then spent another year as a member before becoming the president again for four more years. Currently he holds the position of past president and is still a very active member. Lyle has also been a member of the American Legion for twenty-eight years, the first year as a member and the next seventeen as commander. He is a good coordinator and finds it easiest to be the head of organizations so that he can designate policies and projects, delegate assignments, and ensure ventures are responsibly brought to completion.

Lyle has many obvious planner qualities. As traditional, rule-abiding citizens, Planners are hard-working and dedicated to their families. Their children are raised to adhere to set rules and are taught a strong sense of what is right and wrong. They are encouraged to be responsible, respectful, conservative, and stable.

Planners have a strong sense of loyalty to their families and have a high regard for membership. They are drawn to service organizations, community action groups, churches, and volunteer associations. Planners derive a sense of great satisfaction from being useful and responsible. Their superb eye for detail and finesse for planning make them excellent coordinators of events and supervisors of projects. Well organized and punctual, Planners thrive on regularity, efficient use of time, and predictability. They derive great pleasure knowing that they can be counted on to follow through.

Planner Traits

Penchant for Planning—This style has a natural knack for determining virtually every step that needs to be taken to reach a goal. Able to realistically determine timelines, Planners are good at linear thinking, and seeing how one thing leads to another. This inclination drives them to make check lists for tasks so they can keep track of the steps and details necessary for goal completion. Even more rewarding than making a list is crossing something off of their list. It is such a satisfying feeling.

Prepared—If Planners had a motto it would be much like the Cub Scouts: "Be Prepared!" They usually have a well-defined picture of what things need to be done in order for successful accomplishment of their goals. Uncomfortable putting things off until the last minute, they can be prone to worrying about things going awry. Therefore, this style thinks ahead to be ready in advance and carries backups "just in case".

Detail Focused—Planners hone in on and identify specifics over generalizations. Not ones to "round up", "round down" or even "guesstimate", they prefer giving and receiving precise information. When asking for instructions, they want step-by-step details including when, where, how and specifically how much. They

want sufficient particulars so they can accomplish their objectives, "the right way."

Punctual—Time conscious and reliable, this style makes every effort to be on time and appreciates it when others are also. More often than not, Planners prefer to give ample time to arrive early for appointments. This way they can be prepared and ready at the appointed time.

Strong Sense of Duty—This style believes in work before play. Filling their schedules with "must-dos" and gotta-get-dones", what should be done next is constantly on their minds. Planners strive to be responsible and reliable. They try to support their family, organization, and community. They can be counted on to implement, execute, and complete their goals.

Protects Policy—Planners understand the need for policies, procedures and rules. They know these guidelines exist to help people know what to do, when and how to do it. They are most comfortable when everyone is following the rules - be it at work, home, or on the highway! In fact, Planners are the most likely of all the personality styles to drive the speed limit or even under it. They respect and follow the established chain of command and will implement, administer, and support protocol.

Values Tradition—Planners are the most likely of all four personality styles to answer the question, "Why are we doing it this way?" with "Because we've always done it that way." This style likes to stick with the tried and true, that way they know what to expect. They enjoy celebrations and rituals. Many times, if they celebrate a certain holiday or occasion in a particular way, they like to celebrate it in a similar manner year after year.

Conscientious—Highly dependable and responsible, this style is reliable. They have a great sense of loyalty and commitment to their family, organizations, and community and take their obligations and roles very seriously. They don't want to waste time, money or resources (like their energy) so they will go to careful measures to ensure efficiency such as setting up recycling stations and making sure folks know which items go in what particular bin.

Craves Consistency—Planners strive to maintain a certain level of predictability in their lives. They will establish daily routines they can rely on to keep them steady, on track and on time. To sustain a sense of security or safety net they will choose to save for a rainy day instead of spending in the moment.

Well-Organized—Those with this style feels the most comfortable within an orderly, stable environment. From knowing the hierarchy or chain of command in an organization, to a nicely arranged pantry with all the cans lined up in neat rows, Planners embrace "A place for everything and everything in its place".

Understanding & Appreciating Planners

The core value of Planners is responsibility. One of the best ways to understand them is to appreciate their strengths.

Strengths:

Accountable
Bringing order to chaos
Clarity
Dependability, follow through
Economical, efficient
Family commitment
Following and enforcing rules
Following directions
Getting the job done
Guarding
Handling details
Organizing
Planning
Preserving customs & tradition
Realistic
Respecting authority, hierarchy
Responsible, concerned
Stable, structured, consistent
Supervising
Time conscious, punctual

Planning Is Golden

Sarah was heading to a conference for work. She registered for the conference three months in advance to take advantage of the reduced rate for early registration. From the moment she registered, she felt an urgency to plan and confirm other arrangements she would also need for the trip.

She began a list:

✓ Reserve hotel room - make sure it is non-smoking

✓ Reserve rental car - search the web for best prices

✓ Get complete driving directions - check whether there is any road construction or detours en route

✓ Where to park - how close to conference site, best prices, safest

✓ Good restaurants in the area

✓ Will there be food available at the conference site - need a meal ticket?

✓ How much cash to carry? Credit?

✓ Is it casual dress? What is the weather in the area?

✓ So much to do, so little time.

Sarah was disappointed that she would not be getting an official agenda of events until she picked up her registration packet at the conference, so she could plan in advance what workshops she would attend. She started another list for the clothes and other items she would need to pack.

✓ Alarm clock in case the hotel one isn't working
✓ Special stain remover wipes

Clothes for the following:

✓ Warm weather
✓ Cool weather
✓ In between weather
✓ Rainy weather
✓ Casual events
✓ Dress up events

Sarah plans when to leave, what stops she will be making along the way, approximate length of each stop, and when she expects to arrive at her hotel. She will depart a day early so she can check out the conference site and know where she will be going. Before she leaves she makes sure the house is clean and all the plants are watered. As a special treat to herself, she likes to put clean sheets on the bed so when she returns she has a fresh bed. Sarah arranges to hold her newspaper delivery for the week and makes sure to give a checklist to the neighbor who will be watching the house.

Planners are most comfortable when they know what to expect.

Planners often anticipate what possibly could go wrong and try to prepare ahead for it. Their joy is feeling "in control." They may worry about events and others, getting stressed if there are too many variables to consider or things don't go as planned.

Respect

When Charlie originally took a position as school principal in 1974, he was troubled by the deteriorating respect he noticed in the students. He further observed that although the teachers and administrators of the district were addressed by their proper names such as Mr. Gonzales or Mrs. Kowalski, the bus drivers, as well as custodians and maintenance personnel, were called by their first names by the children and their coworkers alike. It made it harder for these staff members to enforce the rules and elicit the appropriate respect if they were perceived as buddies instead of authority figures commensurate with their positions. Charlie decided to enact a new policy starting immediately. Because he surmised it was a deeply ingrained habit with the older children, he chose to start with the kindergarten through fourth graders to have them address every employee of the school district with a proper greeting.

It took about five years to establish the new norms, but it eventually brought back the respect they had been losing. Long after the students graduated, even though many are now married with families of their own and it is perfectly

appropriate to use first names, some of them still call their former bus drivers and other school staff by their last name and proper title.

Planners place a high importance on preservation of respect for authority and consideration for the hierarchical procedures of organizations.

Individuals with these Planner characteristics often look to the past for information about how to deal with present challenges. If they feel that a value they regard is deteriorating, they will establish new protocol or help to revive previous standards to restore consistency. They value fairness and strive to treat everyone around them appropriately, paying close attention to the chain of command and specific roles of each individual.

Work-Time, then Play-Time

Charlie is a dedicated and committed worker. But he is not all work and no play, he simply believes in work *before* play. After his work is complete and his responsibilities met . . . he plays! Charlie's number one favorite joy is spending time with his family. He has a camper and loves to travel to the mountains, the coast, and just about anywhere in between. He also enjoys cruises. Charlie even takes the grandkids to Las Vegas a couple of times per year. He can be found karaoke singing at conferences, sharing a good story, and making new friends. His cordial attitude, playful manner, and smile are warm and contagious.

Recreation with family is often a favorite pleasure for Planners. They also enjoy participating in organizational and community events.

Following the Rules

Clyde dropped into the grocery store on the way home from work to pick up a few things that his wife Emily needed to complete dinner. He navigated through the store, picking up the items she had listed in order of the isles in their favorite grocery store. They always shopped at the same market because they knew they would get the quality and service they had come to rely on.

As Clyde approached the check-out stand he counted his items once again to make sure he could use the "Quick Check–Cash Only" line. He counted nine items altogether. "That fit the ten items or less limit most definitely," Clyde confirmed to himself. Just as Clyde maneuvered his basket into the appropriate line, another customer whisked in ahead of him. Since there were already two customers in line before them, Clyde had a while to wait. He could not help but notice that the man who pushed ahead of him in line seemed to have well over the ten item limit. Clyde started to get a bit irritated. First the man cut ahead of him, then to add insult to injury, the man was violating the ten item limit. "I could be wrong," Clyde thought to himself. "I'd better count to make sure." Clyde peered into the man's cart and quickly counted its contents. "Twenty-one items!" Clyde almost yelled out loud. "The man is in the wrong line," Clyde thought to himself. "Perhaps he is not aware of the rules. I would want to know if I were him." Clyde then leaned over and gently tapped the man on the shoulder. "Excuse me, sir, but this is the ten items or less line," he said very politely.

He no sooner got the words out of his mouth when the lady at the checkstand motioned to the man that he was next.

Without responding to Clyde, the man turned his back and started piling his groceries on the belt.

Clyde stood dumbfounded. He didn't know whether he was more embarrassed or mad. The checker was not enforcing the store policy. She acted as if it didn't even matter that he had twenty-one items. Why did the store even have a policy if they weren't going to enforce it? Thoughts ran through his head of not shopping there anymore. If they could not be consistent with their service, what else would they slack on next? He got his answer. The checker let the man write a check!

Clyde quietly fumed. He did not want to be inappropriate and make a scene, but he also did not want to just stand there and say nothing. He decided to wait until his turn. He asked the woman why she let the man continue in line when he had too many items and then write a check. She had no "good" explanation for him, so Clyde asked to speak to the manager. He gathered his groceries (so he would not hold up the line) and stepped aside with the store manager. Clyde voiced his concerns to the manager, who apologetically assured him that it would not happen again. For some reason Clyde found that a little hard to believe. When he got home, Clyde discussed the matter with his wife. They decided they would give the store one more chance—after all, they did apologize. But if it happened again, they would take their business elsewhere.

Not many things will annoy a Planner as much as when people, especially "reputable" organizations, violate their own rules.

This is one reason they may get upset when rules are not enforced. They like to be able to rely upon the stability of knowing the "right" way of behaving in a situation. If everyone followed the rules then everyone would be treated fairly.

"Shoulds" and "Should Nots"

Delores is a strong Planner. She believes there is a right and a wrong way to do things, especially traditional things such as weddings. When her daughter Jasmine was planning her wedding, she shared some creative ideas with Delores. "I think it would be fun to have a potluck and camp overnight," proposed Jasmine. "I know this great campground up in the woods. It's only about a three-hour drive from here." We are not going to bother with a gift registry, we'd rather be surprised.

"What?" gasped Delores. "That's not a wedding, it's a camping trip! You shouldn't make people bring their own food to your wedding. At my wedding we had family members cook for a week to prepare for the guests. People expect to be able to dress up, not wear jeans and sit in the dirt. It would be outright disrespectful to dress so casually. Your friends and relatives will want to choose gifts from a registry so they know it is something you will like and can use. That way they won't waste their time and money. Your father and I had a traditional wedding and people raved about it for years."

Jasmine smiled and hugged her mother. "Thank you for your concern Mom, but this is my wedding. As much as I know you want to help, we are going to do this our way."

Since Planners themselves make an effort to always be appropriate, they imagine that others would want to know when they are not–so that they can adjust their behavior accordingly. Planners may offer considerate advice about what people should or should not do in certain situations.

A Place for Everything

Debbie is an extraverted Planner who expresses her emotions and enthusiasm freely. While shopping with her husband, Debbie spotted an item on sale that she had been looking for for months. She shrieked with excitement as she grabbed it off the shelf. Pulling it close to her chest as if hugging the item, she jumped up and down giggling. "I found one! At last! It's perfect! It's just what I wanted!"

"What is it?" her husband inquired with curiosity.

"A label-maker! A label-maker! And such a great price too! What a find!"

Her husband smiled in anticipation of what projects would be accomplished with this new tool.

It wasn't long before he found out. Debbie left no room unlabeled. In the kitchen she labeled the soap dispensers by

the sink "hand soap" and "dishwashing liquid." She labeled shelves in her cupboard for dishes, pots and pans, food items, and spices. The bathroom medicine cabinet got its share, as well as the drawers and shelves. The children's rooms got stickers with labels on toy boxes, shelves, and in closets. Her boxes of "hand-me-downs" were appropriately labeled with descriptions of size, color, style and designer, as well as date outgrown. Even her suitcase-sized diaper bag got labels for diapers, pacifier, bottles, ointments, etc.

She was in sheer heaven with everything clearly labeled. Now, not only could she spot where everything should be when in its place, but her family and friends could too!

Planners value orderliness.

Planners like to have a place for everything, and everything in its place. This may not always happen, but it is something they strive to accomplish.

A Skew in View

Some of the greatest contributions that Planners make to the world are to organize it and make sure things are "right." This yearning for "rightness" includes, but is not limited to, the right etiquette, choosing the right words when speaking, the right moral values being upheld, things put back in the right place, things done in the right order, and following the right protocol.

In their attempt to get things "right" the first time, they may focus a great deal of time and energy on the details and preparation for an endeavor. They are able to seriously concentrate their efforts and stay on task until completion. When the demands of others threaten to interrupt the well-thought-out plans of a Planner, the Planner may increase efforts even further to meet designated timelines and begin to strongly encourage others to stay on task as well. This intense steadfastness is a gift of our reliable Planners and cherished by employers, families and the communities that depend upon them.

However, while for the most part Planners have very admirable traits that are appreciated and revered, there are times when others may view these same characteristics in a different light. To those who do not possess this drive for responsibility and "rightness," a Planner's actions may appear rigid or controlling.

Planners themselves may get concerned that their efforts to uphold the rules and values of society are going unappreciated and that people misunderstand their intentions. Just because they like to finish their work before playing, does not mean they do not like to play, and some Planners even have a mischievous side that others are surprised to see when revealed. Because their powerful sense of commitment and duty usually directs their decisions toward what would be the most appropriate and responsible, they typically do not totally throw all caution to the wind, and if they happen to, they may feel tremendous guilt afterwards.

Many Planners are aware that they may seem inflexible, boring or even unfriendly to individuals that do not understand their conscientiousness and the drive for responsibility that motivates them. Comparing the descriptions of how others may at times view Planners to the descriptions of how Planners view themselves will help enhance your understanding of the way Planners operate in the world.

Planners May Be Perceived As:

Stubborn—Planners can strike others as being uncompromising. Once a they make a decision they do not like to change their minds. Their attitudes can seem strict, stringent, and unbending.

Restricted—This style can get accused of being "uptight" and resistant to change. They would rather stick with the status quo–doing things as they have always done them. They are not easily convinced that revisions and updates are a good idea. Predictably routine, their conventional way of doing things earns them a reputation for being "stuck in the past".

Boring—Planners can appear as if they do not like to play or have fun. They can give the impression that they lack enthusiasm and spontaneity and won't let go or loosen up. They commonly insist that work is completed before even contemplating the idea of "playing".

Self-Righteous—Planners are characteristically firm in their beliefs and for the most part, view *their* way as the "right" way. This can come across as "acting superior" with pious self-assurance, as if their morals are perfect. Their habit of monitoring behavior (their own as well as others) to make sure it does not deviate from norms, can feel like shaming and criticizing to those folks who do not adhere to the same standards or values.

Neat Freaks—Typically adamant about everything being orderly, not only do Planners like to keep their homes and work areas perpetually clean–they like virtually every other aspect of their lives neat and tidy too. As a result, other people may feel as though they cannot relax around this style, fearing they might make a mess and upset them.

YOU'RE THE ONLY PERSON I KNOW WHO BRINGS A **RULEBOOK** TO PLAY **CHECKERS!**

System-Bound—Planners often have an unalterable adherence to policies, systems and customs. They can get ruffled or even personally insulted if others refuse to honor the hierarchy of an organization or uphold its rules and protocols.

Unimaginative—What is...is. If Planners can't see it, touch it, smell it, they aren't likely to consider it. Those with this style often reject unfamiliar, controversial or esoteric ideas. They may refuse to indulge others in what they view as outrageous, foolish, nonsensical thinking.

Judgmental—Planners appraise actions as "good or bad," "right or wrong," "appropriate or inappropriate." Extremely opinionated, this style may try to coach or inform others of the errors of their ways.

Worry-Wart—Planners seem to worry waaaaay too much! Their concern for safety, security, and appropriateness, can come across as unnecessary fear that holds them back from taking the risks necessary to be successful.

Micro Managers—Spending time around Planners can feel like everyone is put on an agenda and expected to comply with each aspect of a master schedule. This strikes others as demanding excessive attention to minor details.

Clearing Up Misconceptions

It can be perplexing to a Planner when others do not view them in a positive light. Below are the explanations from Planners as to how they view the very same characteristics from their own perspective.

Planners' Self View:

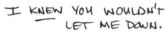

Committed (Stubborn)
Tenacious and persevering, Planners do not like to spend time going back and forth with decisions They take pride in being able to make a sound decision and will take the necessary time to consider the details involved. They like to "plan their work then work their plan" with unwavering persistence. This approach brings regularity to their actions and helps them reinforce that their word is honorable.

Reliable (Restricted)
Wanting others to be able to count on them to always follow through with no surprises, Planners know that sticking with a confirmed plan provides security. If one goes about changing things all the time, it introduces the risk of a time wasting failure. If you stay with what you already know works, it saves you and others from being let down.

Conscientious (Boring)
Planners like to make sure that the work and responsibilities are taken care of before play. Recognizing that there is a time and a place for everything, Planners will typically use discretion in deciding when and where they will "let go" and reveal their often unrecognized playful side. They may share a joke with a close friend or colleague in a social setting that they would never share in a work environment.

Knows What's Best (Self-Righteous)
Planners have a realistic view of what can be accomplished and how. They like to establish procedures, then assist others by articulating the specific steps and methods necessary to stay on track.

Organized (Neat Freaks)
Planners enjoy the satisfaction of a clean house, nicely arranged workspace, and well-thought-out projects with action steps in chronological order for completion. They take the time to test procedures and through trial and error know what works and what doesn't. They

crave order in their environment because order helps them feel in control of their lives. A controlled environment is akin to security for them.

Efficient (System-Bound)
Planners respect authority and recognize that rules and systems are set in place to make things run smoothly for everyone involved. If everyone followed the rules and respected the chain of command, it would save a lot of time, money, and energy.

Realistic (Unimaginative)
Having no illusions and facing reality squarely, Planners view themselves as sensible, practical, and sane. They like to keep their feet on the ground and head out of the clouds. Once they understand a desired result, they make clear decisions and have well defined roles for completion. Their keen eye for details provides powerful foresight for step-by-step planning.

Appropriate (Judgmental)
Planners like to take the guesswork out of decisions. Whether they embrace organized religion, or not, they have strong beliefs about the difference between right and wrong and are not afraid to declare them.

Responsible (Worry-Wart)
Highly accountable, Planners make sure duties and responsibilities are addressed before play. They can get frustrated if others try to put more on their plate than they know is realistically possible, knowing that some tasks likely need to be eliminated in order to add a new one.

Proficient Planners (Micro Managers)
This style does not like to leave things to chance and risk a sub-par outcome, therefore they cover all of their bases to insure success.

Relating to Planners

Planners want to interact with others in a respectful, responsible way. They identify strongly with other Planners who share their need for structure. They also relate well to Connectors who are supportive; Thinkers who are knowledgeable and inventive; and Movers who are optimistic and resourceful.

Count on Them

Planners are some of the most dependable friends or coworkers a person can have. They are reliable and consistent. They want you to place full confidence in them because they are very serious about doing a good job.

When interacting with Planners, remember they enjoy hero stories and anecdotes of honesty, patriotism, and courageous people. They take pleasure in keeping up with current events and receive satisfaction in knowing they are providing support and structure to relationships, organizations, communities, and society as a whole.

Appeal to Their Strong Sense of Right and Wrong

When discussing or introducing ideas, use examples relating to traditional approaches, sense of community, responsibility, and moral values. Planners place a high priority on academic achievement and relate very well to authority, rules, and procedures. Make sure to mention how your goal supports the family, organization, or existing norms.

Be Mindful in Your Use of Resources

Planners enjoy saving time, effort, and money. They like to organize their thoughts and ideas and prepare for their future. There is no excuse for waste in their book. They admire others who are careful to use their resources wisely. Be thoughtful in what you choose to discard and where. Make sure to honor their time and resources. They thrive on being prepared. They put a lot of effort into making sure everything will turn out "right." When their preparations conflict with your spontaneity and desire for options, stop and think before charging ahead with a different agenda. A little notice time before changes goes a long way with a Planner.

Offer Opportunities to Express Traditional Values

Planners are interested in family and moral values. If they will not bend a rule or make an exception to something you find dated or silly, understand their well-meaning intentions in enforcing such rules or traditions. Let them know you would like to pitch in and do your

part, especially if you realize that carrying out the custom or task is beginning to cause them stress, drain their energy, or even make them physically sick. They will continue their efforts at great cost to themselves unless they feel it is appropriate to ask for or accept help from others.

Show How Much You Value Their Efforts

As with most people, Planners especially enjoy knowing their contributions are appreciated. Be specific when giving compliments or praise, and mention their actual accomplishments of fulfilling their responsibilities well. They also welcome recognition in the form of plaques, certificates, and ceremonies.

Needs

Consistency
Reliability
Timelines
Structure
Clear expectations
Responsibility
Respect
Rules & standards
Organization
Closure

Values

Commitment
Security
Professionalism
Etiquette
Duty
Loyalty
Honesty
Membership
Time & resources
Tradition

Desires to Be

Appreciated
Aware of roles
Clear on requirements
Responsible
Respected
Conscientious
A member
Efficient
Realistic
Complete

Finds Joy in

Accomplishment
Organization
Stability
Security
Belonging
Family, home life
A sense of order
Tradition
Timeliness
Doing the "right thing"

Bringing Out the Best

To bring out the best in Planners, rely on them for their responsible nature.

Laura had a knack for arranging events. Her family often counted on her to be the one to plan and organize family get-togethers and vacations. In the early '90s she had the foresight to realize that New Year's 2000 would be a very special occasion, so she set about making plans. She considered places from past events that held special significance.

After careful contemplation she chose the perfect place, a huge inn located right in the heart of a festive island. It had plenty of restaurants and night clubs as well as sightseeing spots within a short distance. People could bring their own cars with them over on the ferry.

With no time to waste, she promptly placed a down payment–ten years in advance! She commenced inviting her friends and family and collecting deposits for their "reservation" in the event. Each year, twice a year, Laura would reconfirm the reservation with the inn, just in case the staffing or policies had changed. She wanted to make sure the reservation would stay firm.

Six months prior to the event she held a "planning party" with the guests that would be attending. They brainstormed what activities they would like to have and how to best make it a memorable experience. Laura asked each couple or group attending to come up with some form of "entertainment" for the night, such as a skit, magic act, or karaoke singing. To make sure that the events were coordinated smoothly and everyone was included, Laura kept a notebook of information for each person attending such as home phone; email; cell phone; make, model, color, and license plate number of the car they would be driving; reservation confirmation; room number; and any medical conditions like allergies, asthma, or diabetes. She also included any other emergency information she might need, such as family and physician phone numbers. Just in case anything happened to this notebook, she kept a back-up copy.

The event went beautifully. It was a grand occasion that was special in the hearts of all those who attended. After the event, Laura thoughtfully created a scrapbook of pictures and stories for each group in attendance for a keepsake.

Turn to a Planner for:

Planning—When arranging an event or project, look for a Planner. They are amazingly gifted at knowing what needs to be done to accomplish a goal. They can think of items and arrangements that need to be addressed and be realistic in setting time lines for completion.

Responsibility—If you have something very important that you need accomplished on time in a quality manner, turn to a Planner. They derive pleasure from taking on duties and doing an excellent job. Because they are very dependable, you can count on them to follow through. They will be respectful, appropriate, and timely. They will keep you apprised of their progress and find a way to complete the task at hand.

Supervision—Planners enjoy taking care of business and others. They easily take on a leadership role when necessary and will direct and motivate others to appropriate action.

Trust—Planners will rarely, if ever, tell a lie, or pass on slander or gossip. They go to great lengths to save face for others they respect and who share the same values. They are conscientious in their endeavors. You can entrust your confidences to them.

Details—If you want directions for doing something or need particulars, refer to a Planner. They have the ability to speculate as to what particulars, articles, or elements are necessary for completion of a task.

The Correct Way to Do Something—If you are wondering what the rules of etiquette might dictate under certain circumstances, of all the styles, a Planner will be your best bet for finding out. They usually know what is the appropriate tradition or norm for behavior in many different circumstances.

The Rules or Policy—If you are unsure of a procedure, policy, or rule, ask a Planner. If they do not know the answer, they certainly know where to find it. They most likely know how to access the information needed to find out what the procedure is for most anything in their organization. If a policy does not exist, they can be instrumental in the implementation of one.

Accuracy—Planners do not slack when it comes to accuracy. They check and double check their work to make sure everything is correct. It is uncommon for them to guess or make something up. When they do not know the answer to a question, they will find out and get back to you. They like to do a good job.

Fairness—Planners are distinguished by their honesty, justice, and freedom from improper influence. They pay careful attention to what would be most equitable in situations. As long as it follows the rules, they try to be reasonable.

Organization—If you are having a hard time locating files you have tucked away, are constantly digging through your clutter to find things, or can't quite figure out how to establish a system for organizing thoughts, words, or things, find a Planner. They have a knack for systemizing and categorizing items for easy access.

Chapter 7

THE
MOVER
STYLE

Playful, bold, and adventurous, this style likes to move! Otherwise known as "Movers and Shakers", they want to be part of the action. They move from subject to subject in conversation, move priorities on a moment's notice and can move mountains with their motivation and delegation skills. They usually move on quickly from setbacks, boldly moving forward to their next endeavor.

Playful, daring, and adventurous, this style likes to have fun! Not wanting to miss out on anything, their favorite time is NOW! Individuals with strong traits of Mover in their personality like to move quickly to seize opportunities when they arise. They need a great amount of freedom and flexibility in relationships, work, and life in general. They are usually very straightforward in their communication. As very physical individuals, they fade fast if they must endure routine or inertia for extended periods. The words to a popular '70s disco song portray a certain attitude of Mover quite succinctly: "I want to go where the action is, I want some action, I want to live!"

The difference between extraverted Movers and introverted Movers can be quite drastic. The storybook character Winnie the Pooh is most likely an introverted Mover—he just sort of goes with the flow. His major concern in life is satisfying his voracious hunger for honey. His attitude is "I'm here, life happens."

Now the character Tigger, in contrast, is a great example of an extraverted Mover. Everyone knows when he is around. He comes bouncing in, full of energy, announcing his presence to all. He prides himself on being the only Tigger in the world and is always ready for the next adventure. Very little stresses him out, except being stuck somewhere.

Mover Traits

Playful—The delightful demeanor of this style brings a fun-filled joy to activities. Even the mundane can seem like an adventure. Goofy, silly, casual or intense, they can be the life of the party. They draw others in with their high spirits and immense energy. They like to banter and joke around, wrestle with others or lead the charge to the dance floor. Interested in the process of reaching a goal as much as achieving it, they like to have fun along the way.

Active—Movers have a high need for mobility and flexibility. Whether it is stretching, fidgeting, pacing or purposeful exercise activity, they like to get physical somehow throughout the day. Commonly drawn to competitive sports and recreational activities, they enjoy skiing, boating, dirt biking, skate-boarding, dancing, rock climbing… you name it.

Negotiator—Charming and persuasive, this style enjoys making a deal. They operate from the assumption that people are just as motivated as they are to accomplish the goal at hand. "No" is often interpreted as "maybe" as they push for an agreement. They will look for options and creative alternatives to suit the needs of both sides of the negotiation.

Desires Change—Restless and spontaneous, they seek variety, newness and trying different things. They resist routine, preferring not to know what's happening next and easily adapting to situational requirements. This adaptability includes many aspects of life such as jobs, relationships, and their environment or life circumstances. They may be involved in one activity, task or conversation and switch gears to another. This makes them natural multitaskers.

Expedient— This style hates to wait. They find planning tedious and can feel as though life is passing them by if they are not in action. They want to "get the

show on the road" as soon as possible. They make decisions and take action quickly. Because they are focused on the current moment, they can exude a sense of urgency that can make their life look like a series of emergencies to those around them. This style's propensity for instant gratification enables them to find the quickest route to getting things done.

Accepts Challenge—Movers derive pleasure in solving problems on the spot. Adept at trouble-shooting and acting in a crisis, when they see a chance to seize an opportunity or tackle a challenge they will dive right in. They thrive with competition and may get involved in situations just to see if they can be more successful than anyone else has ever been in the same situation.

Entertaining—Those with this style can be a bit flamboyant–naturally calling attention to themselves by the way they dress, act, or speak. Quick-witted and humorous, Movers like to bring fun to a situation. They delight in the interest and attention of engaging with others. They may also give extravagant gifts and take pleasure in seeing the reaction of the receiver.

Adrenaline Junkie—Up for adventure, this style seeks active participation with plenty of sensory stimulation. They can get a rush from simple things like taking on ten projects all at once and waiting until the last minute to finish them, driving "a tad" over the speed limit, or arriving at an appointment at the very last minute. Natural risk-takers, they

71

enjoy surprises, crave excitement and may live a bit "on the edge" by pushing the boundaries of physical, social, relationship, work and community convention.

Spontaneous—Movers find planning tedious and like to leave options open so that they have the freedom to choose as opportunities arise. They can easily get distracted from the task at hand if interruptions aren't kept to a minimum. Because they like to live in the moment; they may arrange their life to include making on-the-spot decisions. As quick decision makers, they have a tendency to also change their minds as instantly as they made them up.

Appreciates Immediate Feedback—Delayed feedback is almost meaningless to Movers. They prefer giving, as well as receiving, straight responses in the moment. This style sums up the situation, brushes off set-backs and moves on without spending a great amount of time meticulously analyzing decisions or wallowing in regret.

Likes Leeway—Etiquette and hierarchy can be challenging and cumbersome to Movers who seek the freedom to make decisions in the moment. They can get bogged down by red tape and are adept at finding loopholes in the system. Rules can be interpreted more like suggestions or guidelines so they may bend them if necessary to accomplish their goals.

Self-Confident—Not content to sit on the sidelines, Movers want to be involved. They may jump in and take over a leadership role if others are perceived as ineffective or hesitant. They can be skillful at delegation and motivating others, seeing what needs to be done without delay and recognizing who is the most willing to do it. They can radiate a distinctive magnetism that gets attention and action.

Understanding and Appreciating Movers

The core value of the Mover style is freedom. One of the best ways to understand them is to recognize some of their strengths.

Strengths:

Assertive
Dealing with chaos
Decisive
Determination
Direct communicator
Doing many things at once
Eclectic, diverse, changing
Expedient
Free spirited
Going with the situation
Hands-on
Master of tools
Negotiating
Open to opportunities
Proficient, capable
Resilient, bounces back easily
Risk-taking
Welcomes change & new ideas
Trouble-shooting
Welcomes adventure

These strengths may show up in a variety of ways. The following stories illustrate many of the characteristics, strengths, and preferred ways of operating for Movers. You may ask yourself, "How would I act in the same situation?" Your answer to this question will help you determine the level of Mover traits you possess or already appreciate in others. By paying close attention to the underlying force behind the actions of the characters in the stories, you will gain further insights into the motivations and values of Movers.

Living Moment to Moment

Rachel, in her mid-fifties, is quite a head-turner. She has blonde hair cut in a classy, yet playful, style. She usually wears her trademark red lip-stick with matching nail polish and dresses quite fashionably. She also drives a white Corvette.

This car will come in handy today. She will be leaving in a few hours for a business trip she booked last month. She will be gone for an entire week, and she really needs the break.

Rachel scrambled to tie up some last-minute projects at the office before stopping at home to pack on her way to the airport. She quickly stuffed everything she would need into one roller suitcase so she would not have to wait in line at the baggage claim later. The contents of the case were mostly shoes and a minimal amount of mix-and-match clothes made of low-maintenance, wrinkle-free fabrics. She had to push the speed limit just a bit to make it to the airport, but she had

the right car to do it. On the way to the airport she started thinking of a few other arrangements she needed to make such as rent a car, get a hotel, and figure out the conference location. She hoped she had packed the information about where the conference was being held. If not, she could always call the office when her plane landed.

Arriving at the gate moments before the plane was to take off, she sprinted to the check-in counter. They had just made the final announcement for boarding. Good thing she didn't have any luggage to check. As she climbed aboard the plane, the flight attendant closed the door behind her and the engines were started. Noticing an empty seat in first class, she asked the flight attendant if she could have it. The attendant agreed, and Rachel settled back in her seat. "Ahhh," she sighed, "I made it just in time."

Style, Convenience and Time Management

Many Movers have a certain eye for style and may dress with flair, flamboyance, or flirt. The way in which they dress can send a message (blatant or subtle) that says "look at me," "notice me," "I am fun." Even the cars they drive and "toys" they own imply a more playful approach over practical priority.

Especially when traveling, convenience counts. They don't want to be bogged down with too much stuff or too many "inconveniences." If it does not add to their fun, they don't want it along. Their aim is mobility and freedom. Some

Movers may pack ahead and even use a list, but for many Movers, planning or packing ahead of time is simply not a priority. More often than not, Movers get in the habit of putting things off until the last minute. Sometimes they want to leave their options open or their schedule is jam-packed with other "priorities," but many times it's just for the fun of it. Many Movers enjoy the challenge of trying to beat the clock and push the "limits."

The Rush of Feeling Alive

Manuel loves to play a variety of sports and get involved in recreational activities. "Whether I'm playing football, soccer or baseball," he declares, "it's the same for everything. You've got to go full out. It's a competition with myself and others."

His latest love is motocross dirt biking. "It's pretty intense," he describes. "The whole thing is to try not to get hurt, but to go fast enough to know that you could. I like being in control of the direction of the machine. It's such freedom. It's like being on top of a car going 60 miles per-hour—you're not in it, you're on it, and you could fall off at any time. It's exciting. I'm not really thinking— I'm totally present in the moment. I'm looking for lines and pointing the bike where it is supposed to go. I'm trying to avoid rocks. You run on pure instinct, reactions, and reflex. If they don't work, you're in trouble."

"When you're in the air," he continues, "fighting for your life to stay on that bike, that's 100% what it's all about. Getting

dirty, feeling the rush of the wind on my face and body, the smell of the gasoline, the sound of the motor and the vibration, it's exhilarating. It lets you know you are alive."

"I have the most fun being on the edge of out-of-control."

What Manuel describes is how many Movers feel about life.

This style enjoys their senses. Whether it is dirt and mud on their skin or the rush of the wind, they like to experience the sensations of smell, touch, taste, hearing, and sight. Often, they aim to feel a certain "edge" or "rush." There are many ways to get this "rush"; it doesn't have to be partaking in high-risk activities or contact sports. It can be things like negotiating their way into or out of a situation, performing on stage, or having ten contracts to close on the same day. One thing for sure is this "rush" or "edge" is what makes them feel alive. If they don't have it in certain areas of their life, they will seek to find or create it in other aspects: work, relationships, or added activities. It is perhaps one of the main reasons they are driven to push their physical limits, relationship margins, or societal boundaries.

Show and Tell

Crystal was a very excited volunteer. She had joined the Overdose Aid Program through the YMCA. This was a program in which volunteers were trained in what to do for victims of drug overdose. When rock concerts came to town, the volunteers would don a green arm band with a white cross on it and were allowed in the concert for free in exchange for patrolling the crowds for drug over-dosing concert-goers and taking care of them as needed. They would meet in the Overdose Aid (ODA) room, designated for taking care of the more serious victims.

At the concerts, Crystal always had a flamboyant story to tell her director, Jeanette. Crystal would explode into the ODA room, shouting to anyone within earshot, "You should have seen this guy, he was barfing bright pink! He had fallen down the stairs and . . ."

Jeanette, interpreting Crystal's tone of voice as panic and her explicit accounts as a cry for help, would practically come unglued. She would think to herself, "Crystal is trained in this. Why can't she handle it?" Usually overwhelmed with her own emergencies, Jeanette would offer some quick advice: "What are you doing in here? Go help him up! Find someone to help you if you need it. Get the vomit off the floor so no one else slips in it!"

Crystal would usually pause for just a second, looking confused, and then say, "Oh, I already got Maurice to clean it up. The guy was fine. I walked him back out to the concert. He was nice; his name was Billy. I gave him my phone number."

Several times throughout the evening Crystal would have to be reminded of her purpose for being at the concert. She could be found up in the first rows of seats sitting on some guy's shoulders, bouncing to the music. Often, when Crystal brought "victims" to the ODA

room, she was assisted by other male concert-goers she had recruited to help her.

One night, Jeanette had a revelation. After about five outrageously descriptive "crisis stories" from Crystal describing various rescues involving convulsions, vomiting, and hallucinations, Jeanette exclaimed, "I've got it, Crystal! I've finally figured it out! You are not complaining, you're bragging!"

Getting Excited

Movers like circumstances that are larger than life. They enjoy trouble-shooting and creatively emerging triumphant from a situation. They also have a knack for eliciting the help of others and having fun along the way. If they can squeeze just an ounce of juice from a situation to liven things up a bit and add some fun, they will.

Recognizing and Seizing Opportunities

Brad and Shirley wanted to cement in a portion of their side yard as a patio. Shirley repeatedly asked her husband, Brad, when he was going to put the patio in. He kept getting distracted with other jobs that cropped up at the moment and spent the money Shirley had budgeted for the patio on those jobs instead.

One cloudy night at about 3 a.m., Brad drove up to the corner gas station to buy some cigarettes.

"Looks like rain," the clerk behind the counter was commenting when a loud screeching of tires interrupted their conversation. He and Brad both looked out of the windows of the store front in time to see a truck skidding around a corner to catch the entrance ramp of the highway. As the truck barely made the curve, several bags of something came flying off the back of the truck. They watched as the truck sped off into the distance.

The clerk and Brad looked at each other. "Well, whatever it is will be worthless when it gets rained on," the clerk offered. "Why don't you check it out?"

Brad was game. He ran across the street to investigate. As he approached the corner he could not believe his eyes. There were about 100 sacks of cement strewn off the side of the road!

The clerk made his way to the door of the store. He lit up a cigarette and, taking a big drag, shouted, "Hey, what is it?"

"Cement," yelled Brad.

"What a waste," the clerk said, shaking his head. "The rain's gonna soak it."

Brad lit his cigarette. There was a moment of silence. The night air was crisp. The wind was blowing as the cloud-filled sky loomed overhead. It appeared by now that the driver was not returning. The clerk could tell Brad was thinking over his options.

"Wish I could help you," he said to Brad as he tossed his cigarette to the ground and stepped on it, grinding it into the dirt. "Good luck!" he hollered as he turned and went back in the store.

Brad quickly snuffed out his cigarette and went to work. He drove his van over to the piles of cement and started loading them up. Brad labored diligently, working up a sweat. As the van filled, it became lowered with the extra weight. A misty moisture started to drizzle ever so slightly from the sky. Brad's adrenaline surged as he drove his first cargo home to unload. His back and arms ached as he lifted bag after bag. His heart beat faster and he worked harder. "All that cement will go to waste if I don't hurry back," he thought to himself. Picking up his pace even more, he hurled the sacks of cement into his garage, then sped back to retrieve the rest.

Brad's body was beginning to hit the edges of fatigue. He fought to push past his pains to salvage what he could of the remaining cement. Trembling and exhausted, Brad finally decided enough would have to be enough.

He had salvaged about 80 bags of the cement before the sky started to pour rain. His body ached all over from fatigue. "Wow!" he thought, "What a night!"

By the time he got home, Shirley was up having an early morning cup of coffee. Excitedly sharing his triumph, Brad announced, "Honey Bunny, we've got our patio!"

Urges, Opportunities, and Action

Movers may not keep customary hours or predictable schedules. In fact, some Movers are predictably unpredictable. They may think nothing of heading to the store at 3 a.m. if an urge hits them. They may even say they will be "right back" and get distracted by another priority that just "came up." When circumstances present themselves to a Mover, they are quick to grab ahold of the moment if they are motivated to do so.

For example, have you ever noticed that while some people are still mulling over options, others have already dived into action? This is typical for Movers. They are quick decision makers (and can be equally quick at changing their minds too) and will seize an opportunity when it arises. They may ignore physical discomfort to accomplish their goal. Triumph over this discomfort may even add to the fun and the challenge.

Dancing Fools

I was at a conference that had nearly 6,000 attendees. I had given a personality workshop in the morning for about 150 people. The evening entertainment happened to be a live band and dancing. I, myself, look for any opportunity to

dance, so of course I went. When I arrived, I headed straight to the dance floor and was pleased to find a group of individuals gathered already dancing in a group.

I recognized them as participants from the earlier workshop who had determined that they had a predominance of Mover and Connector characteristics in their personality line-up. An intriguing phenomena seems to happen after individuals find out what their personality line up is: they start to shine much brighter, especially around others who also know their styles. The Movers in particular were no exception this night. They were dancing wildly and playfully, skipping around the floor—some with arms out-stretched as if in flight. They started rumba lines and dance trains, diving between other dancers on the floor, laughing and giggling and having a great time.

By the time the band took their first break, the Movers were just getting revved up. As a group they decided to stay on the floor during the intermission DJ music. They continued to smile, laugh, and act goofy—providing plenty of entertainment for those people who chose to take a recess from dancing.

I had to rip myself away from the dance floor to get a drink of water and use the restroom. While in the closed confines of a restroom stall, I could hear a couple of women chatting while they washed their hands.

"Did you check out that crazy group on the dance floor? They remind me of the acid-droppers of the '60s, skipping around and pretending to fly."

"I know, they're probably all high or drunk or both!"

At that moment, I thought about how misunderstood Movers are sometimes. Their playful, carefree style can be mistaken for a drug-induced high to those who do not allow themselves to experience the exhilaration of being fully in the moment. Yes, of course, some individuals may use drugs or alcohol, but a great many others are accused wrongly because others just do not understand their motivation.

A Skew in View

As you know by now, Movers (especially the extraverts) are usually fairly easy to spot. They are most likely fast-paced and where the action is. If they are interested, they are involved. They may act in a dramatic or flamboyant manner. Whether they are the center of attention or otherwise helping to stir up a little excitement, you know it when they are around. You'll see plenty of active body movement and vivid facial expressions. They appear excited and may even fidget. Many will speak in a loud, fast-paced, or direct manner. They have an air of confidence about them and yet are playful.

Often, people who don't have large amounts of Mover characteristics themselves have a tendency to view

those who do as acting in unacceptable ways. People in general may label any characteristics as being less than appealing if they would never act that way. As is true with all the personality styles to a certain extent, Movers in particular have a different style that can be greatly misunderstood by others.

When the motivation behind someone's actions is not understood, it can be interpreted in very unfavorable ways. What one might perceive as a negative quality is oftentimes an exaggeration of a good quality. Movers can be very intimidating to those who don't appreciate their flamboyant tendencies. Sometimes Movers are confused as to why someone would view them that way; other Movers are not surprised at all.

One or more of the characteristics of this style described on the following pages may be true for you or the people in your life. As you read them, keep in mind that although you may not fully understand certain actions and may find these traits unfavorable or perhaps even inexcusable, Movers pride themselves on their abilities and gifts. These "gifts," of course, vary from person to person. However, taking a more objective point of view will enable you to discover that even the traits that may seem unfavorable at first glance have merit in the right context.

Movers May Be Perceived As:

Rude—The mannerisms of this style can feel abrupt or blunt to those with a milder constitution, coming across as pushy, loud and boisterous. It can seem like Movers do not stop to notice how their gestures, behaviors, or communication are affecting the people around them–especially when they are talking loud and attracting lots of attention. In addition, if they boldly talk about "inappropriate" subjects in public places or use foul language, it can cause others to cringe and want to shush them or hide in embarrassment.

Irresponsible—Movers are known to fly by the seat of their pants, not thinking ahead to consider the long term consequences of their actions. This earns them the reputation of being flaky, unreliable, or lacking commitment. They can appear to have a blatant disregard for time lines by constantly running late or changing their minds at the last minute.

Not Serious—It can seem like some Movers makes a joke out of everything, putting more effort into fun than into work. They can give the impression that they do not grasp the importance of completing certain tasks or undertaking specific responsibilities. When it comes to comprehending the depth of consequences that can result from the failure to give the situation their full attention and concern, their casual attitude can strike others as lackadaisical and thoughtless.

Ignoring the Rules—This style can give the impression that rules were made to be broken. They may act like rules don't apply to them and if they are able to get around certain regulations they are proud of themselves for "beating the system."

Self-Centered—Movers can appear to be extremely self-serving, focusing on what would bring them the most pleasure in the moment. They may agree to an arrangement or appointment but by the time it arrives for them to show up or follow through, they go for what would benefit or please them the most, *here and now*, not taking into account what others want and need. If others protest, they may try to turn things around and accuse them of being the selfish ones.

Manipulative—Wanting to have things their way, this style will go to great lengths to sway others or the situation in their favor. They may lie, cheat, exaggerate, or minimize to accomplish their goals.

Impatient—Because Movers do not like to wait, they can appear constantly rushed or in a hurry. They can come across as demanding, hasty, or edgy when made to slow down. So they can forge ahead without delay, they may cut ahead of others in line, circumvent protocol, bypass the chain of command or skip getting permission.

Easily Distracted—This style is often thought of as being scatterbrained or unable to stay on track. They often work on other things when people are trying to talk to them. Their workspace and home can be cluttered with unfinished projects.

Unprepared—Movers are known to push things to the last minute, "winging it" instead of planning ahead. They will go into a situation without doing prior research or formulating proposals for solutions. This habit can create stress for others who feel they must make up for a Mover's lack of preparation.

Taking Advantage—This style can get a reputation for being dishonest, disrespectful, and untrustworthy–using others for personal gain without reciprocation.

OOPS! DIDN'T I TELL YOU I WAS FLYING TO TAHITI THIS WEEKEND?

Clearing Up Misconceptions

It can be amusing to a Mover when others do not view them in a positive light. Below are the explanations from Movers as to how they view the very same characteristics from their own perspective.

Movers Self View:

I'LL GIVE YOU $2000 TAKE IT OR LEAVE IT.

USED CARS

Straightforward (Rude)
Mover's like to be direct in their communication. They are being open and honest with their message by not putting on pretenses. Many Movers would rather "tell it like it is" than beat around the bush or "candy coat" something. Not all Movers use foul language and those who do, feel it expresses their intensity for a subject matter or helps emphasize a point.

Easy-Going (Irresponsible)
Preferring to leave options open and go with the flow, many Movers use the term "plan" quite loosely. For the most part they like the thrill of being surprised at what comes up next and the challenge of being able to rise to the occasion. At the moment they make a commitment, they feel it's a good idea. But as the date approaches, new options may have appeared or the previous commitment now doesn't sound so fun or interesting. Many Movers are most comfortable making commitments with the option to change their mind.

Enjoying the Process (Not Serious)
Very serious about producing desired results, Movers believe in having fun along the way. In general, this style feels that social etiquette restricts their freedom to be themselves. They'd rather relax and have a little fun. Many Movers imagine themselves to be incredibly entertaining and like to think others welcome and enjoy a little amusement as well.

Productive Freedom (Ignoring the Rules) Movers typically get things done in any way they can. If they need to push a few limits, so be it. They do not like to be bogged down by too many restrictions that can block their ability to take quick action.

Now-Oriented (Self-Centered)
Movers believe in living life to the fullest in every moment. Why compromise their immediate needs when tomorrow may never come? They expect you to flex with them as circumstances unfold or at least understand their need for spontaneity.

Gift for Fiction (Manipulative)
This style truly has a talent for resourceful improvisation. Movers don't consider themselves "liars" if they stretch the truth a bit to paint a better picture. They feel they are creatively helping others open their minds to possibilities. Their optimistic motivation pushes them to find a way to enlist others in their quest.

Mover and Shaker (Impatient)
Eager, enthusiastic and efficient, Movers don't believe in wasting time. They want to make things happen, not merely watch things happen—or worse, sit around discussing it. They like to take the most direct route, even if it means navigating around hierarchy or protocol.

Multitasker (Easily Distracted)
Stimulated by variety and change, Movers enjoy working on several things at once. They can achieve a significant amount of work in a short period of time by switching gears quickly and keeping themselves in motion.

Spontaneous (Unprepared)
Movers purposely do not make plans because they are energized by crisis or chaos and like to troubleshoot on the spot. They enjoy not having everything planned out and are confident they can take anything that comes their way.

Succeeding (Taking Advantage)
Movers feel that others don't always understand the road to success so they pave it for them. They believe the end justifies the means and they have the ability to do what it takes to accomplish the goal at hand.

Relating to Movers

Movers want to engage others in a mutual, fun-loving way. You can relate to them most effectively when you are active and in the moment. They are naturally drawn to the energy and flexibility of other Movers. They get along well with Connectors who are friendly and patient, enjoy the knowledge and great ideas of Thinkers, and appreciate Planners who are productive and goal-oriented.

If you want Movers to go along with your ideas then make sure they are in on the decision-making process.

Movers hate feeling stuck. Let them know your preferences and then encourage them to come up with some other options for accomplishing the goal. Determine which ones you would be willing to accept if it came down to it. Just knowing they have choices puts a Mover at ease. They won't necessarily take advantage of the other options, but somehow just knowing they could if they wanted to, allows them to feel content going along with yours.

Expect Some Spice

Remember Movers are instinctive troubleshooters. There is something about rising to the moment that entices them to take action. They welcome change and new ideas and are rarely set back by defeats because they take them as being only temporary, a new challenge to face and conquer. They believe that if you spend too much time looking backwards you'll miss out on what's coming next.

This style can deal with chaos and are apt to create some if there isn't enough in their lives. Don't panic! They like to test the limits. They might just be stirring up some chaos so that they can figure a way out of it. It is a fun contest to them.

Don't take it personally if Movers don't always make their relationship with you their number one priority. You may be highly important to them, whether it seems that way or not. Frequently, Movers enjoy the comfort of knowing you are in their lives and may turn their attention to other avenues for the moment. It does not mean that you are not valued by them. It simply means that their concentration is temporarily directed elsewhere.

Understand Their Impulse to Live in the Moment

When left to their natural expression, Movers are carefree, playful, and spontaneous. Their craving for action, variety, and excitement may pull their attention elsewhere in an instant. It can be surprising how well things seem to work out for them with so little forethought. Because they are most comfortable in environments that are unstructured, it can be a challenge to get them to adhere to a fixed schedule or plan. If you know the Mover in your life has a tendency to forget or "blow off" appointments for something that has come up at the moment, a gentle reminder or double check on your part may help save you from disappointment.

Allow Them to Show Off Their skills

As natural performers, Movers need the freedom to express themselves. Their lighthearted charm, wit, and fun can be irresistible. You may find yourself being motivated by the charisma and style of a Mover. They are good negotiators and can be incredibly persuasive. As natural fun-seekers, they like to recruit others to play along with them. For the most part, whether they admit it or not, they enjoy being the center of attention. They often feel there isn't anything that they cannot do. They love any opportunity to show their skillfulness, cleverness, agility, and precision.

They are proficient, capable, hands-on people. They have a love of tools and are masterful with them. They can perform miracles with a paper clip, a piece of string and chewing gum. Whatever they find in their vicinity can be used skillfully as a tool to remedy a problem at hand. Give them immediate feedback and praise for the clever way they handled a situation.

Avoid Slowing Them Down

Movers like immediate results and therefore complete tasks quickly. Because they consider waiting and routine as emotional death, they may take shortcuts to accomplish their goals. Once they set their minds to something they want to jump in and seize the opportunity. If things take too long or remain static, they are apt to get frustrated and are prone to taking off for somewhere else to follow the "action." As excellent multitaskers, they are capable of, as well as rather enjoy, doing a variety of things at once. For best results, don't insist that they drop what they are doing and give you their full attention. Instead, figure out what you can do to help them finish their projects or otherwise fit into their world.

Needs

Action and activity
Freedom
Flexibility
Make an impact
Attention
Adrenaline rush
Variety
Physical contact
Fun & play
Competition

Values

Adventure
Forthrightness
Options
Flair
Spontaneity
Productivity
Opportunity
Winning
Expediency
Boldness

Desire to Be

Noticed
Active
Involved
Physical
Expedient
Tangible

Spontaneous
Appreciated
Doing
Resourceful

Finds Joy in

Being the best
Excitement
Moving their body
Performing
Action
Taking risks
Troubleshooting
Saving the day
Freedom
Attention

Bringing Out the Best

To draw out the greatest from Movers, call upon their innate preference for action.

At 12:30 in the afternoon, Trudy (Mover-Connector) got a call from her sister Rose (Planner-Connector). Their brother George (Thinker-Connector) was in a tight spot and needed some help. The health club he managed was supposed to have a CPR training that afternoon and the instructor had just called in sick. They had set this date aside for months and meticulously coordinated schedules with their other three clubs.

Both Rose and Trudy were certified instructors of CPR. George had called Rose at noon to see if there was any possibility that she or her sister or both could teach the class at 2:00 that afternoon.

Before Rose called her sister Trudy, she spent a half-hour going over the requirements for teaching a class that size. There are many regulations that must be met in order to teach a CPR class. They would have to get all of the necessary equipment and books. The instructor that called in sick was not willing to lend his equipment. It was Saturday and the local Red Cross' switchboard was closed to the public except for disaster emergencies, which obviously this was not. Rose could not call to reserve equipment, which should be reserved two weeks prior anyway. The stock room was closed on Saturdays, and equipment must be picked up on weekdays. To top it off, she did not have the videotapes that were used to instruct the class. All the brainstorming and decision-making had already taken up a half-hour of the two hours they originally had, leaving her only an hour and a half to find the equipment, acquire a video, get to the gym (which was a forty-five minute drive in itself) and get set up for the class, which usually takes a minimum of thirty minutes. The way she figured it–NO WAY! But with a bit of urging from George, she called Trudy to see if she had any ideas or resources.

Open to Options

Trudy had a different response to George's request. Although she had a full day of obligations and projects she had promised to address, Trudy could not pass up an urgent challenge. When she heard the situation, her mind started spinning. "I have a friend who owns equipment;

maybe I can talk her into lending it to me. If I can't get ahold of her, maybe we could use stuffed toys or dolls, or some other props they have at the gym as mannequins. We really don't need the video: I can ad lib," she thought, running over the possibilities in her mind.

Going for It, Finding a Way

Trudy tried to call her friend who owned the equipment but was only able to leave a message on her machine. Trudy wouldn't give up that easily. Her mind raced, searching for solutions. Although Rose thought it would be better to give a firm "no" than to leave someone

hanging until the last minute, Trudy called her brother and said, "If we can pull something together in the next hour we'll be there. Otherwise, we can't do it."

The class did happen. They were able to get all of the required equipment and videos for the training. Trudy and Rose spent nine hours of their Saturday, on a moment's notice, contributing to others. Although Rose would have preferred to plan further ahead and follow the customary protocol, she gave her full support to help. Trudy admitted she would not have wanted to do it at all if it hadn't been a "full-out, fun emergency."

You may have noticed the tendencies of the Movers in your life and already know where some of their skills are best utilized. Sometimes we don't recognize the potential or usefulness of a Mover's energy, panache, and drive. For example, some teachers and parents may suspect their child has Attention Deficit Hyperactivity Disorder (ADHD), when in reality it could be that the child has strong Mover tendencies. Understanding and appreciating the Mover personality can open your mind to finding useful ways to channel their energy by providing avenues for them to move and play while learning.

Turn to a Mover for:

Leadership—If you need someone to take charge of a situation with confidence, ask a Mover. Movers are able to take over and manage a situation with flair, even when they have little experience with the circumstances at hand.

Trouble-Shooting—Movers are quick decision makers. When faced with a challenge, they find it almost irresistible. Their minds go straight to work figuring out a way to make things happen. They are flexible, innovative, and not afraid of trying something new.

Tasks Requiring Risk and Chance—Many "daredevils" are Movers. Race car drivers, bungee jumpers, and firefighters tend to be Movers. If you need someone to go first in an activity or try something uncertain, chances are a Mover will volunteer before you even get the opportunity to ask. They enjoy a good adrenaline rush.

Fun Ideas—When brainstorming for events, from family reunions to conferences, Movers can contribute a plethora of suggestions for outrageously fun activities.

Action—If you want something done now, ask a Mover. They have the ability to easily stop what they are doing midstream and change direction. They are ready for action and aren't hesitant to do what it takes to accomplish their immediate goal. They realize that quickness is important and usually are aware of all the shortcuts.

Proficiency with Tools—Skillfulness, agility, and precision can be quite natural to Movers. Frequently, they are able to build or make something with ease and accuracy. Talents they take for granted may be difficult for others.

Variety—When you want a change of pace, find a Mover. They arrange their world to ensure variety and are even known to create a crisis or two just to stir things up. If you want a new or different way of doing something, you need only observe a Mover in action.

Negotiation—If you run up against a "no" from someone and need a "yes," enlist the help of a Mover. They have a charming way of gaining cooperation from others. They are full of options and choices and won't usually let up until they get their way, or a close compromise.

Entertainment—Movers relish the art of telling a great story, adventure, or even some juicy gossip. They can describe situations in larger-than-life representations. They are expressive and energetic. They are involved in a virtual kaleidoscope of pursuits.

A Good Laugh—Practical jokes, cartoons, and other forms of humor are part of the nature of Movers. They can reframe the most mundane or even unfortunate circumstances into something to jest about. They love to laugh and to make others laugh, as well.

Straight Answers—Movers will "tell it like it is." While others are being careful to be politically correct, Movers like to give it uncensored. Often, they will speak their mind on a subject even if no one else agrees or is even listening. If you want to cut to the chase and get some frank, forthright responses, ask a Mover.

87

Chapter 8

THE
THINKER
STYLE

Objective, observant, and curious, this style is often mentally active–absorbed in their thoughts and ideas. They enjoy pondering and deciphering life's mysteries and are known to contemplate for hours. They derive great pleasure from exploring the complexities of human nature, science, technology and the processes of thinking, learning, and evolving. They like having time to think and process before reaching a conclusion.

Is Something Wrong with Him?

Joyce went to see her doctor about her son. She thought he might be depressed and was gravely concerned. "He's a loner," she explained. "He really doesn't like to play with other children. He spends hours alone, reading, playing on the computer, or taking things apart like the telephone or vacuum cleaner, then putting them back together again. If I make him go out and play with other kids, I notice that instead of playing he's looking at an ant hill or exploring something by himself. When I ask him why he isn't playing with the other kids, he just shrugs his shoulders and says, 'don't want to.' What am I doing wrong? I don't want him growing up a misfit!"

After asking the usual questions about eating, sleeping, and other patterns, the doctor, an avid user of the Personality Lingo® system, smiled and told Joyce he would be right back. He returned to the room with a sheet of paper with a brief explanation of a "Thinker." Joyce got wide-eyed as she read the description.

"This is my son," she said, looking up. "This is him all the way!" she emphasized, pointing at the paper. She didn't know whether to be relieved or worried.

The doctor explained that far from being abnormal, her son was quite "normal," yet had a personality type that happened to be different from hers. "In fact," he continued, "most Thinkers are quite intelligent and many grow up to be doctors!"

The following are characteristics that many Thinkers have in common. As with all of the styles, some Thinkers have more of the traits than others, and some traits may also be stronger and more obvious. In addition, there can be quite noticeable differences between introverted and extraverted Thinkers.

For example, let's compare and contrast Bill Gates, the founder of Microsoft and the late Steve Jobs, founder of Apple Computer. Both have exhibited many Thinker traits. Both were pioneers in the computer industry–visionaries, constantly innovating, pondering how to improve–pushing beyond ordinary thinking to discover and create different uses for the personal computer. However, even with all of those traits in common, they communicated and interacted with others in very different ways. Bill Gates has a reserved demeanor. He holds his composure, speaks in a modulated manner and appears to pause and think before responding.

Steve Jobs on the other extreme was notoriously outspoken and intense. He tended to share his opinions on the spot without much reservation or tempering for tone. He exhibited flamboyant body language of large gestures and obvious facial expressions.

Keep in mind that just like the other personality styles, Thinkers can display a wide range of characteristics. There are many aspects to a Thinker's personality, and how you decide that you or someone else is Thinker depends on the combination of the characteristics below. Use your imagination to explore the possible ways these traits might describe the Thinkers in your life.

Thinker Traits

Innovative—Those with this style diligently work to devise elegant solutions and proficient systems for accomplishing their goals. They have a tremendous amount of tenacity for figuring out solutions and enjoy the challenge of doing so. They can get especially motivated when someone tells them that the problem cannot be solved. They'll stick with it and figure it out when others would have dropped it and moved on.

Asks "Why"—Inquisitive and curious by nature, this style asks "why" questions. Not ones to blindly follow the herd, they want to know the logic or theory behind things. "Why do we have to do it this way? Why are we using this formula, how was it derived? Where is the proof that this is valid? Responding with "Because we've always done it that way" is not acceptable and can be rather irritating to them. Their curiosity often extends far beyond questioning everyday occurrences,

reaching to interests in technological, metaphysical, philosophical, the cosmos, and beyond!

Complex—Abstract, speculative, and conceptual this style has a natural ability to connect concepts, cause and effect, and imagine "if, then" scenarios. They think globally, looking at the big picture first before examining the details. Why accept the "simple" solution when you can have the most precise solution? They use systematic approaches to situations or activities, including personal relationships.

Visionary—Filled with ideas, and insightfulness, their vision and tenacity to improve upon the status quo brings top notch advances and never-ending development. Often inventors, technicians, scientists, and engineers, they establish new protocols and systems, especially for technological progresses that may influence society as a whole. They are the Einsteins and Edisons of the world.

Maintains Composure—Wanting to be rational and level-headed, Thinkers typically keep their self-control in situations where others may become outwardly emotional. They consider the expression of feelings (such as crying) as getting in the way of relationships instead of enhancing them. They often look at the principles involved in a situation and can consequently work without harmony. Decidedly objective, many times the outward facial expressions (or lack there of) are not a reflection of what is going on inside their heads.

91

Craves Knowledge—Thinkers have a voracious appetite for information that never gets fully satiated. They enjoy investigating matters further. Once they learn about something, they want to know the information behind the information. Many Thinkers have a rather expansive vocabulary–know a tremendous number of "big words" and how to pronounce and use them.

Guardedly Social—Thinkers tend to guard their energy socially–not wanting to "waste time" on idle chit-chat. The exception is when they are interacting with someone sharing similar interests. In that case they can become quite verbose in discussing the minutia of distinctions they know about a topic. As children they are often misunderstood because of their inclination towards solo or cerebral activities. They may spend a great deal of time lost in their thoughts and ideas and can derive an immense amount of pleasure from doing so.

Independent—This style seeks autonomy. They generally like to keep their personal life separate from their work life. If you work with Thinkers, you may not know anything about their personal lives and they like it that way. Because they see the big picture and don't want to have to depend on several people for parts and pieces of the whole, they prefer working independently as opposed to participating on panels or teams. They

work best without constant direction or coaching and like to try new ways of doing things outside the norm.

Driven by Competence—Proficient and capable, those with this style will go to great lengths to make sure they have researched required data, tested their conjectures from several angles, and thought about extenuating circumstances that may influence the outcome in order to draw a sound conclusion and make a logical decision. If they are presenting their findings they won't usually ad lib,

WHILE YOU WERE LOOKING FOR THE IDEAL PLACE TO PARK, THE MOVIE STARTED FIVE MINUTES AGO!

but want to be well practiced–especially to field any questions that may arise so they can competently respond. Thinkers feel rewarded when the job is done well. They strive for expertise in their field or areas of interest. Achieving measurable success is motivating.

Analytical—Naturally investigative they are able to find flaws and imperfections. They have an uncanny ability to spot a mistake and find it hard to move past an error unless it's flagged for correction. As diagnostic, critical thinkers they are good at asking questions that get to the root causes and inner workings of things.

Logical Approach to Relationships— Thinkers take an objective approach to personal interaction rather than emotional (head over heart). They may seek "formulas" for having successful relationships, "If I do this, I will get this result." They can find it cumbersome to keep up with social expectations.

Perpetual Learner—They enjoy discovering the information behind the information and may know a little bit (or a great deal) about just about everything! Once they "know" something, they will debate it to confirm they know their position.

Understanding and Appreciating Thinkers

The core value of the Thinker style is competency. They are good at what they do and take pride in doing it well. Following are some of their strengths.

Strengths:
Analyzing
Conceptualizing
Curiosity
Designing
Determination
Developing
Diagnosing

Inquisitive
Intellectualizing
Inventive
Mapping out
Non-conformist
Problem solving
Rational thinking
Reasoning
Researching
Skeptical consideration
Tenacity
Technical know-how
Theoretical

Thinkers have vision and creativity; they take their pursuits seriously. Their interests and quests may be drastically different from the general population. What is fun to them may seem like work to others. They may spend hours on what others may dub as "hair-brained" ideas or invent systems for things they think are important. While others may not consider it, Thinkers will ponder the "why" of the world. For the most part, they like to keep their feelings on the inside so they can get on with other things. When it's time to analyze their feelings they will do so, but they don't make it a habit to share them with whoever they encounter.

Mr. Fix It

Lydia wanted to watch a television program so she picked up the master remote control to their new entertainment center with a large screen HDTV and clicked the power button. The TV instantly came on–but all she got was a solid blue screen. Then she

93

remembered she was supposed to click <main> first, then the power button so she clicked the entire system off to start over. She carefully clicked <main> then the power button. This time she got a blue screen with a line across the bottom along with some other icons. Not knowing what they meant she stared at the remote. "Maybe I need to press the <menu> button at this point, or was it <guide> or <info>?" She tried pushing all kinds of buttons–but was getting nowhere except frustrated. Just then her husband, Larry, walked into the room to get something out of a desk drawer.

Glancing at the TV, he said to Lydia, "Having trouble?"

"Yes!" she responded. "I tried everything! I pushed just about   every button on this darned thing and I can't get it to work."

"Everything?" he questioned, walking towards her. He took the remote out of her hand and pushed a couple of buttons to get to the program she wanted.

"Here ya go," he said, handing the remote back to her. He then resumed his search for whatever he was looking for in the desk drawer.

"You would think I could just pick up the remote and press 'on' and it would work," she mumbled under her breath as she finally sat down to watch her show.

Larry stopped and looked up. "You're right, you should be able to," he said walking up to the TV

he paused for a moment. "Hmm... he murmured.

"Leave it alone, Larry," Lydia insisted, anticipating what would come next. "You can figure it out later, after my program is finished."

"I'll bet I can reconfigure it so it will work that way. This will only take a minute," Larry said, as he started exploring all angles of the TV to gather data for his plan of action.

"I am fine Larry, it can wait," urged Lydia.

But her words seemed to fall on deaf ears. He was in his own little world. As if hypnotized, he slowly turned the TV turned around to reveal a tangle of cables. Connections to and from the cable box, receiver, DVD, play station, and

computer. Mesmerized, he stared at the tangled mess the installation team had left. Lydia knew that look all too well. It was too late to shake him out of it. His curiosity was already piqued. There was no tearing him away at this point. Lydia surrendered and trudged upstairs to finish watching her program on their iPad.

Meanwhile, Larry worked diligently. He picked up each cable and mapped out its path – drawing the cable system schematically on a piece of paper. He thought, "If I just added this one connection…it should work". He took a trip to the hardware store to get a new HDMI cable. He was back lickety-split just to find it was a couple inches too short. But that wasn't a problem because upon further scrutiny, he realized he needed a cable splitter anyway—so back to the store he went for more supplies. Returning home, he became so completely engrossed in his projects that he hadn't even noticed that a couple of hours had passed. Lydia was finished with her program and already had dinner on the table.

"Honey, come and eat," she called to him from the kitchen.

"Almost there," was his response.

After about fifteen minutes or so Lydia came into the living room. There stood Larry triumphantly. "Well, what do you think?" he asked, handing her the remote control. "Try it," he encouraged.

She clicked the power button…

"Amazing!" said Lydia, duly impressed. The picture came on immediately to her favorite station. She clicked it on and off again several times just to make sure. Her program was over hours ago, but he had saved her tons of time and frustration for the future.

Finding a Way

Solving a problem is nearly irresistible to a Thinker. Their strong drive to have things work "right" can compel them to spend a tremendous amount of time trying to fix things or find solutions to conditions that others might not concern themselves with or may have given up on. A Thinker's innate talent for figuring out how things work can be uncanny. Unraveling mysteries and working out puzzles fascinates them. They see it as a game, an intrigue, a challenge.

The Perfect Gift

Troy was deliberating about what to get his girlfriend, Helen, for her birthday. He knew a gift would mean a lot to her. He had picked up on her hint that she wanted flowers—the first time she alluded to it. "I just don't see the logic in buying something so useless," he thought to himself. "Thirty-five dollars on something that is just going to die in a week and have to be thrown out seems so ridiculous." Troy remembered that Helen had also mentioned several times how much she loved chocolate. "But she's always complaining about her weight. I don't want to make matters worse by buying her some chocolate so that every time she eats it she feels guilty," he pondered helpfully. "I know what I would want—a gift certificate. That way I would have options to buy whatever I wanted."

He smiled, content with his choice, as he set off to pick up a gift certificate.

After purchasing the certificate Troy stopped by a store to get Helen a birthday card. Taking nearly a half-hour to sift through the selection, he found one that made him laugh out loud. "Perfect," Troy grinned. Reading it once again for pleasure, he recited the words on the front of the card, "On your birthday remember, you're not getting older, you're getting…" He opened it to reveal the punch line, "Well, I guess you are getting older! Happy Birthday anyway!" He chuckled all the way up to the cashier.

The look on Helen's face when she read the card and examined the gift certificate was not one of joy and amusement as he had expected. Instead she barked, "You call this a gift? How much thought went into this? Where is the 'I love you?' You don't love me, you just like making fun of me!"

Bewildered, Troy defended himself. "Of course I do sweetheart." It seemed obvious to him by all the thought and time he put into buying the gift certificate and picking out the card that it was an indication of his love for her. Why wasn't it obvious to Helen? He wouldn't do that for just anyone.

"See you can't even say those words to me now?" Helen prodded.

"I love you," stated Troy firmly and clearly.

Helen sighed audibly, "But I want you to want to say it, not just say it because I want to hear it!

"What's the difference? If you want to hear it, I will say it!" Troy felt like he just couldn't win. If she would just tell him what she needed from him in order for her to be happy, he would do it and they would both be happy.

Practical Love

Thinkers like to establish a personal relationship and then leave it to maintain itself while they pursue more intellectual accomplishments. For this reason, some Thinkers may not want to direct a lot of attention to making sure their relationship stays alive. They assume it will. Why wouldn't it?

Other Thinkers may try to devise a strategy for keeping their partner satisfied. For instance, if they know their partner wants to hear "I love you," they will try to make a conscious effort to say it, but it can be quite an effort. They prefer not to be so redundant. Many Thinkers believe that once they have stated something it should stand until they say otherwise.

When it comes to gift giving and receiving, Thinkers enjoy the different possibilities of choosing for themselves. Therefore, many Thinkers assume that others do also. A gift certificate is a great gift for a Thinker to receive because it does just that—gives them options. Often, they put many hours and a lot of thought into picking out the "perfect" gift for their mate. The only trouble is that it might just be perfect for them. It may be hard for Thinkers to override their deeply embedded value system and sense of logic to purchase something they view as frivolous.

A Quest for Information

Kirk and Sophie had been going out for four years now. Kirk was always amazed by the tremendous amount of trivia Sophie had at her fingertips. It came in very handy at social gatherings, where she always seemed to know something about every topic discussed. Be it politics, science, wine, or gardening–it seemed that Sophie had a never-ending fund of knowledge. Yet at other times, it was frustrating–not because of the information she possessed, but because of the lengths that she went to to acquire it. Kirk related one of those times.

"We were at a dance and they were playing a song that was just awesome. I leaned over to Sophie and let her know how much I liked it, and within seconds she was shuffling around in her purse for her phone. She took it out and held it up for a bit, looked at it, smiled then returned it to her purse without saying a word. It happened so fast I forgot about it until later that night. I thought we had both gone to sleep but I awoke to find her viewing something on her laptop.

"Sophie, what are you doing? I asked. "It's two o'clock in the morning!" She looked over at me with kind of blurry "doe eyes" and said, "I'm reading all about that song you liked." She went on to explain that she had a phone app that could recognize the music playing and identify it. She told me that she had found the song on a search engine that led to a site about the band. The site described the story of how the band got started, what other albums they had put out, what additional artists the band had recruited for backup drums, as well as the symbolism behind the artwork on the cover. She was even able to play samples of the song right off the Internet. Agghh! It was too much for me at two o'clock in the morning. I felt kind of bad when I couldn't match her enthusiasm. I was just so tired that I turned over and went back to sleep.

In the morning I found my MP3 on the seat of the car when I went to leave for work. It was cued up to that very song. She had taken the time to download it from the internet, upload it to my MP3 and cue it up so all I had to do was press the power button and listen. I can still remember the first time I listened to it on my way to work that day. Knowing all that information about the band that Sophie had told me really did make listening to the music more enjoyable.

I was still humming the tune as I walked into work. Someone from Sales overheard me and said, "I love that song!" Immediately engaged, I found myself sharing about where the band had come from, who the band members were, what the artwork on the cover symbolized...."

Hmmm... That's Interesting!

Thinkers enjoy gathering interesting details about various subjects. Before watching a sporting event they may look up the history and statistics on the players, as well as particulars about the event itself. Before making a decision, like a purchase, Thinkers want to gather all of the facts, and then some! They want to make sure they have all of the information possible so they can make a sound decision. Sometimes even after a decision has been made, they will continue to gather data to back up the fact that they made the best decision.

The Excitement of Learning

"San Francisco Amateur Astronomers Club—Mount Tamalpais Astronomy Program," Ceni read out loud from a flyer posted on a bulletin board in the hallway of the Student Services building at her college. "A popular series of lectures, slide presentations, and night sky viewing," she continued. "Presenters are from the NASA/AMES research center, the SETI Institute, the Morrison Planetarium, and nearby universities. Dr. John Miles from Lockheed will be discussing Extraterrestrial Planet Finders. Telescopes will be available after the lecture for night viewing."

Grabbing a mechanical pencil from her backpack, she copied down the contact information. "Wow! That sounds like fun," she thought. "If I went this weekend, I could get a head start on my Astronomy class. It would be great to be familiar with some of the information before I get into the classroom. I would love to get a membership so I could get the newsletter and stay informed on the latest discoveries on a continual basis." Her thoughts reeled, thinking of possibilities. Then, suddenly realizing that she had stood there thinking longer than she meant to, Ceni snapped her attention back to the present moment. She hurried down the hall to the tutoring center where she worked as a calculus tutor.

Just last week she had brainstormed ideas with the instructor about how to take the program to a new level. They wanted to improve the old instructors' manual (that the tutors used) to incorporate methods for teaching to the various learning styles of the students. With this new tool, the tutors could ascertain various techniques to help the students learn faster, increase their comprehension, and retain the information longer. Once the manual was written, they could test its effectiveness and determine if it were a valid instrument. After they proved its validity they could publish it, so that other universities across the state and possibly the nation could incorporate it into their own programs. Ceni had already purchased a few carefully selected manuals and checked out several books from the library to study the various theories. She wanted to do a good job of integrating the learning styles material into the existing tutoring curriculum. She was confident she could assist the trainer in putting together a usable manual for the program.

Besides having a knack for incorporating information, she also seemed to have an intuitive eye for being able to display the information in a usable format. Just last year, she was a teacher's assistant for her chemistry lab. The students were confused as to how to arrange their lab notebooks and the instructor turned to her for help. He asked her if she could put something together as an example for them to review. Ceni knew she could not just show them her notebook because it would have all the answers to the lab problems, so she made up one with mock data points and calculations. It was fantastic. The students were delighted to have an example of how to organize their manuals, and the chemistry instructor enjoyed receiving well-organized notebooks from the students all year.

Ceni decided this year, instead of assisting in the chemistry lab itself, she would take a position as a teacher's assistant for correcting homework and test papers. She figured that correcting papers would help her reinforce the concepts inside and out. This would prepare her more thoroughly for her next chemistry class. This position was not a paid one like the classroom tutoring. She thought of a quotation she had heard earlier that day and felt it summed up her philosophy quite well: "Symbolic Analysts

are people who manipulate symbols. Their jobs are something they would do even if they were not getting paid for it."

"Yep, that's me!" she reconfirmed, as she scurried off to her next class.

New and Improved! Better than Before!

Thinkers are on a never-ending quest for improvement of the status quo. They enjoy developing concepts and are intrigued by advances in progress, especially those of an intellectual or scientific nature. Complex individuals, not only do they think about how an issue impacts them, they think of how it produces change in the world and even beyond! For them, "work" is play, as long as they have an interest in what they are doing. They will sometimes spend a great amount of time on projects that others may perceive as "work," such as reading, attending lectures, and studying. Embarking on ventures that require them to investigate data, figure things out, or test theories is exciting and can be spellbinding. Many Thinkers take pride in the display of information they have gathered. They derive gratification from a well-designed spreadsheet, charts, graphs, or reports. Mastering their subjects is a great source of pleasure to Thinkers, and they will seek avenues for enhancement of their competence.

Books, Books, Books

Dwayne, a self-professed "Pure Thinker," shared his philosophy on owning books. Because he believes in

99

recycling and sharing the knowledge contained in the pages of books, he limits himself to owning only approximately 200 books at any given time.

Although he never went on to college after high school because he did not like "conforming to the rigid structure of our educational institutions and being stifled in my thinking," he continues to read and study on his own. Some of his interests include math, from algebra through calculus, non-linear dynamics, fractal and chaos theory, magic, biology, psychology, and philosophy. He enjoys religion and has read the Bahagavad Gita, Koran, Bible, Book of Mormon, and Cabala, just to name a few.

He has also read The Lord of the Rings trilogy and a variety of books about astrology, yoga, and human anatomy. He likes to keep a 50 percent "roll over." In other words, he reads at least 50 percent of his books before purchasing a new one. Dwayne keeps a book in his car, at work, and at home to read during increments of time when there is nothing else he can do. He always has three or four going at a time.

Thinkers' abstract reasoning makes it easier to understand highly theoretical material.

Other people can read the same book as a Thinker and have no idea what the author is talking about because the words and concepts are not familiar to them.

A Skew in View

Thinkers are perhaps the most misunderstood of the personality styles. Their ability to make objective decisions with a high degree of independence leads others to misread them as cold and uncaring. Because Thinkers are constantly thinking, their minds are sometimes not in the same room or even plane of existence as the people they are with. Oftentimes they are internally focused on creating an idea or working on a problem instead of externally connecting. Their gift for critique compels them to seek perfection and may alienate those that don't understand or share a similar drive.

The following are ways that people sometimes interpret Thinkers. If you are Thinker dominant in your personality, you have probably been accused of having one or more of these attributes.

Thinkers May Be Perceived As:

Intellectual Snobs—Thinkers can come across as acting superior to others–getting irritated with "mere mortals" who don't grasp their vast knowledge, and refusing to interact with people who do not have their intellectual prowess. They may use "big words" to show off their own extensive vocabulary or use a tone of voice that conveys, "anyone should know that."

Know-It-Alls—Related to the previous, this style can seem to obnoxiously purport an expansive comprehension of all topics. They may override the opinions and ideas of others by offering unwanted advice or information. Questions such as, "Did you know?" often pepper the vocabulary of many Thinkers, followed by "data dumping" or "spewing of specifics" upon unsuspecting others. They may miss cues that others have ceased to listen and are now getting irritated.

Condescending—Thinkers are accused of sending subtle messages that devalue or discourage others. Their routinely expressionless demeanor can be interrupted with sighs or rolling of their eyes–seemingly in exasperation. This is often perceived as them judging others as "stupid".

Uncaring—This style can appear to be cold hearted–ignoring or getting annoyed by those who try to express their emotions or share personal feelings. Because Thinkers may devalue subjective pleas and pay keen attention to the facts, they give the impression that they can fire someone or eliminate them from their life or interactions without mercy or giving a second chance.

Odd Sense of Humor—Thinkers are known for their sarcasm and quirky humor that is not fully appreciated by some. Their deadpan approach to wordplay, puns, and jokes involving incongruity and discordance with norms, delivered matter-of-factly, gets lost on some folks and may be interpreted by others as "mean".

Demanding—Thinkers can get suspicious when others are "too complimentary" towards them, so they themselves can be stingy with praise. They usually expect others to adhere to rather high standards of performance without feeling the necessity to show appreciation for the effort involved. Thinkers commonly insist that things are done correctly and logically. They can get extremely annoyed with incompetence and anticipate that others should know more than they do.

Nerd or Geek—Thinkers can strike others as having strange ideas and opinions or behaving out of the ordinary. They can spend what appears to others as an inordinate amount of time investigating, and participating in, rather uncommon hobbies, games, or pursuits. They can get so eagerly engrossed in their projects that they seem obsessed. They may also be socially awkward and not at all fashion conscious.

Anti-Social—Thinkers can seem unwilling or unable to associate in a "normal" friendly way with other people. They are not generally attracted to social activities and may avoid interacting with others. They do not typically express an interest in getting to know others and may in fact work with someone for years without knowing anything about them on a personal level.

Unapproachable—Thinkers do not typically wear a constant smile on their faces nor do they offer a profusion of customary nods when engaged in conversation. They normally do not pause what they are doing to acknowledge others. This comes across as unfriendly or even hostile to people who can feel overlooked, ignored, or discounted by this lack of interaction.

Critical—Thinkers quite naturally look for errors and mistakes, pointing out flaws and exceptions. Instead of focusing on the positive aspects of what has been accomplished or the effort involved, they tend to hone in on what is lacking or imperfect. Typically they cannot endure listening to others who mispronounce or misuse words. This can be perceived as nit-picking or fault-finding, as if Thinkers are expressing disapproving comments or judgments.

Clearing Up Misconceptions

Of all the styles, Thinkers are usually aware that others do not always view them in a positive light. They are used to others not understanding what they are trying to convey and can actually be surprised when someone "gets them". Below are the explanations from Thinkers as to how they view the very same characteristics from their own perspective.

Thinkers Self View:

WHAT SOME SEE AS **PEDANTIC**, I SEE AS **FELICITOUS**, TO QUOTE **SOCRATES**...

Knowledgeable (Intellectual Snobs) Because Thinkers typically seek out and

enjoy complex information, it can be hard for them to find intellectually stimulating people to socialize with. Having no one to discuss their interests and theories with can be very isolating. They regularly use accurate words for precision, not to "one-up" others or demonstrate superiority. Some Thinkers will try to alter their speech and topics of conversations so others will comprehend or stay attentive, but this is tiring and unfulfilling.

Well-Informed (Know-it-Alls) Thinkers commonly have varied interests and spend time researching their curiosities, so they may in fact, know more than the average person about many subjects. They can be excited to share this wealth of knowledge with others and met with bored stares or feigned curiosity—or worse, irritation from those who mistakenly think this style is just trying to show off.

Fact Focused (Condescending) Thinkers are usually so focused on figuring out the facts that they are unaware of their body language (or lack thereof). They may roll their eyes or respond without monitoring their voices for tone or tact, using their brain cells for what they consider to be the most important—solving the problem, figuring out a solution, or comprehending what the speaker is attempting to convey.

Objective (Uncaring) Thinkers gather information and facts relevant to the "case' to make a rational decision. They find it frustrating when others make subjective decisions based on feelings. Generally more task-focused than people-focused at work or when engaged in a project, Thinkers consider themselves eminently reasonable. They do care deeply about certain people and prefer to share intense emotions only in close relationships.

Witty (Odd Sense of Humor) Off-beat and unique, Thinkers often have the kind of ambivalent humor where they'll say something and it lands so that the other person isn't quite sure whether the comment was meant to be serious or a joke. This produces an uncomfortable questioning in the mind of the receiver that Thinkers typically find amusing. Some people might refer to this as

sarcasm, but it can be a bit different in that it is often more subtle than the typical blatant mockery aimed at making their target seem foolish. The humor lies in the ambivalence of the unknown, not the "sting" of the remark.

Visionary (Demanding)
This style likes to think everyone is working to the very best of their ability and that, in itself, is reward enough. They believe receiving praise for accomplishment of trivial tasks is equivalent to an insult. Thinkers recognize possibility, relevance, and usefulness in areas that may be incomprehensible to others. They see the need and value for technology and change. They are able to calculate and anticipate the future consequences of actions and inventions so they hope that others can too.

Intellectual Leaders (Nerd or Geek) Creative, original, and often very smart, Thinkers have the ingenuity and resourcefulness to take ideas to fruition when others would have given up. They would rather spend time on worthwhile endeavors than to fritter it away on common pursuits. To them, work is play. Known for spending a lot of time and energy in certain areas (like studying chess) or learning specific technical skills (such as computer programming), they can be more interested in their minds than their outward appearance.

I KNOW THIS GIRL YOU WOULD **LOVE**, SHE'S JUST LIKE YOU.

BALD? WITH A MUSTACHE AND HAIRY LEGS?

Independent (Anti-Social)
Able to work alone proficiently, Thinkers have plenty of interests and prefers to connect with others of similar propensity, for a specific purpose, other than social ritual merely for the sake of partaking in a custom or expected convention.

Deep Thinkers (Unapproachable) Those with this style are often concentrating on their rich internal world, pondering and working on solutions. They can get so engrossed in their thoughts that they are unaware of others. In fact, interrupting Thinkers when they are deep in thought can disrupt their work so tremendously, it can sometimes take them hours to gain their momentum back.

Able to Find Flaws (Critical)
Typically, Thinkers believe they are being helpful by pointing out discrepancies and imperfections so that others can improve. They honestly just want to share their thoughts for improvement and most often they are not trying to imply that others are incompetent. Their favorite way to offer feedback is in an unfiltered manner, which to the uninitiated can be misinterpreted as cruel. Also, when a word is mispronounced or misused, their minds get distracted with searching for the correct term instead of paying attention to the speaker. They enjoy being able to find and use the precise word for different situations and automatically assume others would want to know the correct word or way to use it as well.

Relating to Thinkers

Thinkers seek to express themselves through their ability to be competent in everything they do.

The secret to relating to Thinkers lies in stimulating them to use their minds in an atmosphere of rationality and freedom. They have the ability to acquire the skills and knowledge required to perfect any product or system on which they choose to focus, from computers to world peace. Their ability to conceptualize is a gift that they contribute, given the opportunity to do so. They relate well to creative Connectors, helpful Planners, and resourceful Movers.

Honor Their Need for Privacy

Thinkers are most comfortable in an environment that allows for creativity, privacy and discovery. Their loved ones, friends, and coworkers must understand their need for independence and solo time. They like to sit by themselves and think without noise or intrusion. Don't insist they share without first allowing them time to gather their thoughts. Once they have collected their thoughts, they are more ready to interact with others. Insisting that they sit and listen to you share about your day before allowing them this solo period could prove to be rather futile, as well as frustrating.

Understand Their Propensity to Question

Extremely curious, Thinkers have a drive to learn and comprehend. Not ones to take things at face value, they want the reasons and logic behind a decision. Instead of interpreting their questions as a test of your competency (and getting personally insulted), learn to appreciate their determination to find the facts and insure sound rationality. Although they very well may be challenging your competency, when you find objective ways of expressing yourself you will gain more cooperation than if you resist their inquiries. You can keep them engaged and motivated by asking for their opinions and fascinating facts about a topic.

Realize They Have Feelings

Because many Thinkers don't show their emotions readily, they can appear rather stoic and unfeeling. Especially introverted Thinkers may be more reserved in demeanor or seem difficult to approach. Although they feel their emotions deeply, they usually do not show many of their feelings about situations, people, or stress.

When discussing problems with Thinkers, remember they enjoy playing on words and demonstrating their large vocabulary, but have little tolerance for redundancy or stating the obvious. Their sense of humor can throw non-Thinker styles off guard. Keep in mind that their wit is usually for amusement, not to hurt.

Thinkers generally pay little attention to verbal cues and have often become accustomed to others failing to grasp what they are saying or thinking. Therefore, to focus their attention on problems concerning them, be logical and objective. In private, explain the logic behind a rule or protocol. Stick to the issue, avoid sarcasm, and allow them the opportunity to help fix or improve the situation.

Recognize Their Drive for Competency

Thinkers pride themselves on their intellectual ability to investigate, analyze, and understand new ideas and concepts. Realize they need validation for their own ideas. They take mistakes very seriously, so don't take it personally when they focus their attention on problem solving instead of relationship building. You can encourage and reward achievements by commenting on their creativity, competence, and ability to gather, understand, and explain information. To elicit the best, involve them in situations and activities where they have a chance to show their competency.

Appreciate Their Varied Interests

Thinkers often notice and are intrigued by things that some people simply don't even think about. They may be concerned with developing models, admiring intelligence, being a perfectionist, utilizing precise language, exploring ideas, striving for competency, storing wisdom and knowledge, handling complexity, and understanding human systems and the environment. They are interested in analytical processes and abstract thinking. They know how to work, or even invent, equipment to meet their needs. They are also good at figuring out a way to get things to work. Often, they take initiative on things that are important to them, even if others are not in agreement. They act with confidence and a sense of urgency to solve such problems.

Don't be mad at them because they don't embrace your interests. It can be equally frustrating for them when you lack interest in their ideas and conversations. Instead, encourage them in their endeavors and provide avenues for exploration and contribution.

Needs

Intellectual stimulation
Autonomy
Challenge
To question
Time to ponder
Information
Competence
Privacy
Innovation
Objectivity

Values

Expertise
Intellectual achievement
Wisdom
Logic
Technology
Accuracy
Ingenuity
Strategy
Self-sufficiency
Improvement

Desires to Be

Competent
Well-informed
Emotionally composed
Recognized for their ideas
Innovative
Analytical
Logical
Continually learning
Rational
Precise

Finds Joy in

Exploring new ideas
High achievement
Meeting challenges

107

Gaining knowledge
Figuring things out
Doing what "can't be done"
Creative freedom
Humor and irony
Elegant solutions
Laws of nature

Bringing Out the Best

To bring out the best in Thinkers
ask them for additional insights and
observations.

"Somebody has got to do something about the smell around here. This is getting ridiculous!" Amy was talking to her coworker Matthew, both coaches for a gymnastics studio. You can imagine that after hundreds of children have tumbled around on the mats hour after hour working up a sweat, it would leave some effect on the air.

"I know," said Matthew. "By the end of an eight-hour day my sinuses are clogged. The problem is we're trying to cover up the odors instead of eliminating them. I've always been a bit concerned about the perfume air fresheners we have. They emit chemicals that can't be the best for us to be breathing. The other day I put a new garbage bag in a trash can and sprayed it with the citrus extract we have. The next day I noticed the can was moldy. There are so many harmful effects this could have on our health."

Amy was pleased that Matthew had taken a vested interest in her complaint. He promised her he would personally take it upon himself to get rid of the odor

and mold problem once and for all.

Matthew was aware that negative ions help freshen the air and can even enhance the moods of people. So he went to his employers and told them he wanted to invest in a system. He anticipated some resistance and was prepared to talk them into it. To his surprise, they had already tried an air purification system in another location without success. They said the units "didn't work" the way they wanted them to so they weren't using them anymore. Matthew suggested they give the units a try at his location.

"When I picked up the units, I was disappointed to discover that they only had analog controls. And they had settings for both ion production and ozone production. Although ions help eliminate airborne particles, they are not completely effective against eliminating odors. I knew that ozone was an antigerm and antiviral agent. However, I also knew that breathing ozone in high amounts over long periods of time can lead to respiratory problems. I wanted to have the healthy beneficial ions in the air during the daytime while people were in the gym. I needed the ozone to be produced only at night when no one was there to be subjected to them.

In spite of the assurances on the label on the machines that they didn't produce ozone in high enough amounts to be harmful, I did not want to take the risk of exposing anyone to the potentially harmful effects. With only analog controls, I was faced with the dilemma of inconveniencing myself or someone else to climb up a ladder morning and night in order to readjust the settings.

At last I came up with another solution. Although the machines themselves did not have digital timers or the ability to change settings, I realized that I had two machines and could use them alternately. All I had to do was add my own timers. So I purchased two timers and set one machine on only ions, to be turned on during the daytime, and the other machine on only ozone, to be turned on after closing and turned off in time for the ozone to dissipate before anyone arrived in the morning."

The representative who sold the units to Matthew's employer was so impressed that he referred his other clients to Matthew. In addition, another vendor called and asked Matthew if his company could refer their clients to him to learn how he was using the units. They had never seen such sophisticated and effective use of their product.

Turn to a Thinker for:

Ideas—Thinkers are talented, tenacious innovators and problem solvers. If you want to get the big picture on an idea, or concepts for improvement, Thinkers have a knack for creating masterpieces from mud.

Information—When you need a logical explanation or data, Thinkers most likely already have what you need or know where it can be found. They pride themselves on being a wealth of information on a variety of subjects.

Competence—Thinkers strive for brilliance. They want to be proficient and

expert in their endeavors. If you need someone who knows what they are doing, ask a Thinker.

Tenacity—Although Thinkers have a tendency to brainstorm plenty of ideas for projects and can be content to let others finish them, if they are interested in the challenge at hand, they will not stop until they have the problem solved. Once the challenge is gone, they will move on.

Firmness—Since Thinkers are very objective, they are able to hold their ground without feeling threatened. If you need someone who will not be easily manipulated or duped to deliver a message, send a Thinker to do the job.

Objective Decision Making—Thinkers use their logic to examine the pros and cons of a decision. They explore issues from many angles and have the ability to see black, white, or countless shades of gray.

The Right Word—If you are looking for accuracy in language, turn to a Thinker who can often provide correct usage, meaning, or even spelling.

Technology—The most likely personality style to have an intense interest in or passion for technology is a Thinker. They know how to use a variety of equipment and systems that may be foreign to the average person.

Critique—Thinkers can easily spot what can be improved in situations, people, and theories. They welcome an opportunity to share their insights on what they think is good and what could be modified to be more effective. Ask for their feedback.

To Learn—Thinkers are usually quite eager to enlighten others on various topics. Their main concern is whether the person they are educating has enough of a background in the subject to comprehend the information they are receiving. If you have a genuine interest in a subject that deals with ideas, systems, theories, religion, etc., ask a Thinker.

To Get Something Fixed—Thinkers have the uncanny ability to know how to fix things or create more efficient ways of using things to progress forward.

To Invent or Create—Got a problem and don't know where to go from here? A Thinker's innovative mind is always creating new possibilities for solving challenges.

Chapter 9
STYLE
COMBINATIONS

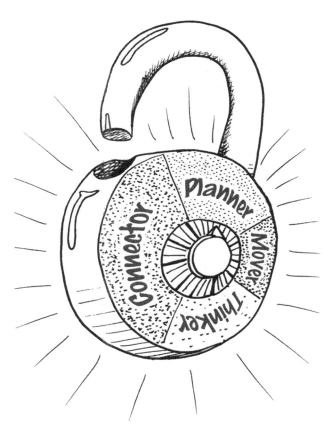

The previous chapters laid the foundation for understanding by providing examples of the traits that are the strongest for each style. Some individuals find that they operate a majority of the time by expressing traits from their most dominant style. However, each of us has a blend of traits from all four styles whether we use them regularly or not. Although we may primarily access traits from our top style, traits from the other styles are often part of our personality as well. So, even though a person may be Planner dominant, traits from their Connector, Mover, and Thinker can also be expressed.

Many people find that their first and second styles are equally strong and interchangeable. They are so closely intertwined that they almost merge together. It may be hard to discern whether one is really more dominant or preferred than the other. Since our most dominant styles are considerably easy to access and naturally called upon, we often refer to the top two styles in a person's personality instead of just the top one. For instance, we might say someone is a "Thinker-Planner" Although these individuals still have traits from their third and fourth styles, for simplicity, we refer to only their first two styles.

For some folks, their second style influences their first in a strong way. For others, their second style may have only a slight impact. Other people are somewhere in between. It's simple to understand how certain style combinations easily go together and how they naturally influence each other. You may recognize some of the following style combinations in yourself or people you know. The following are examples of how combinations of style might show up.

Common Combinations

Mover-Connector

It's quite obvious that the wit, charm, and spontaneity of the Mover characteristics would positively enhance the enthusiasm, empathy, and genuine love for people of the Connector. When the Mover traits are more dominant than the Connector traits, the need for freedom and flexibility can often take precedence over the need to connect with others. When Connector characteristics are predominant, relationships will be placed ahead of the powerful tug to switch attention to whatever captures it at the moment. Those whose Connector comes first will have a stronger tendency to check with the other people involved before diving into another endeavor. Those who have Mover as their top style might not.

Connector-Planner

The strong desire to influence others, the need to contribute, and the caring of the Connector go well with the loyalty, dependability, and preparedness of the Planners. When Connector is the top style and Planner is second, organization, tradition, and procedures may give way to extenuating circumstances of family members, friends, or coworkers. When Planner is first, obligation, responsibility, and duty will be prioritized along with the people involved. In either case, this is a friendly, dedicated combination.

Planner-Thinker

A Planner's thoroughness, sensibility, and punctuality blend nicely with the objectivity, proficiency, and tenacity of the Thinkers. When Planner is foremost, attention and efforts will be focused first on the completion of tasks, maintaining an organized and structured environment, and following procedures. The Thinker traits become a logical backup for objective decision making and analysis of data. Both Thinkers and Planners, of course, prefer to think before making a decision. When Thinker traits are more abundant than Planner, innovation and independence can lead to the creation of new rules and standards. This combination is great with data, details, and being forthright and firm-minded in their decisions. High expectations are usually placed upon themselves and those around them. They are competent, capable, and dependable.

Thinker-Mover

The visionary, nonconformist, problem solving of the Thinker combines readily with the natural trouble-shooter, resourcefulness, and boldness of a Mover. Those with Thinker dominance will strive for competence and to create a better, more advanced world than before. Their Mover provides a "charge-ahead" attitude that can propel these individuals toward high goals and expansive endeavors. Mover-Thinker unifications may try new challenges before they've gathered all the data or gained the high level of skill generally required by most Thinkers before they feel comfortable taking action. They are naturally eager to boldly dive in and "Go for it!" Their competitive, troubleshooting, risk-taking nature compels them to continuously take on new challenges. And if things don't work out, they can easily switch gears to a new undertaking. These endeavors may have a tendency to take precedence over attention to personal relationships. Their Thinker traits provide them with the big picture insights, along with the vision and ingenuity to keep trying. The nonconformist nature of this combination allows them to live by their own standards. Variety and change are familiar friends to them.

Seeing Opposites?

The previous combinations might seem to unite with each other rather naturally. However, there are some combinations that might seem to be contrary to each other. For instance, Connectors often make decisions based on how they feel or how the outcome will affect the relationships and people involved, yet Thinkers decide according to facts and logic. So, how can they both be dominant in a person? Further, Movers seem to thrive on pushing boundaries, while Planners like to enforce the rules. Aren't these direct opposites? One might think so, at first.

113

Connector-Thinker

Individuals with a Connector-Thinker combination, with Connector being the most dominant, will put the feelings and needs of others ahead of their own, in most situations. They may try to guess what the other person wants and act accordingly to accommodate them. They are caring, considerate, and kind. However, having Thinker as a second style may cause an internal conflict because although they love people, they will have a strong need for independence and private time. Their pursuit of information, perfectionism, and mastery for using systems may override their attention to relationships. Since intellectual competence is important to them, they will excel in their chosen field and use their broad base of knowledge to help others.

Thinker-Connector

Although one may think a Connector-Thinker and a Thinker-Connector would be quite similar, there are some definite differences. Individuals with Thinker as their top personality style and Connector as their second are probably the most misunderstood of the combinations. Their ambition for perfectionism, the high standards they set for themselves and others, as well as their drive for accuracy may alienate people. They put proficiency and competency first. They may not want to be bogged down with having to say "good morning" to people or remember their birthdays. They may choose to

avoid certain social functions, instead preferring to read a good book or invent a new system for doing something. But because their second style is Connector, they may not understand why some people perceive them as cool, aloof, and unsocial. The Connector in them will take things personally and may feel hurt for long periods. Others may never know they have hurt this person because they are most likely not going to open up and share. Although others may find them unapproachable, Thinker-Connectors may feel they are open-minded and communicative. They want people to like and understand them without having to spell it out for them.

What Thinkers and Connectors have most in common is their ability to see endless possibilities. They usually look at the big picture before the small details. Both are very creative, imaginative, and idealistic.

Mover-Planner

These are the fun-loving, spontaneous individuals that fancy a challenge. They derive great joy from experiencing the here and now. They have an attitude that "tomorrow may never come" so they seize the moment, often without thinking of consequences for the future. This is where their second style (Planner) can haunt them with guilt. Because it is in a Planner's nature to plan ahead, the Mover-Planner has a tendency to act now, regret later. They may browbeat themselves for being irresponsible and make sure that everyone else around them is abiding by the rules. They may have the world around them super-organized so that they can take advantage of opportunities when they arise without upsetting the balance of their lives. Planning ahead and keeping organized makes it possible for them to act with more freedom and speed than if they had to wade through things to find opportunities. This way they are unencumbered and free to act on a moment's notice. They are prepared to take on any challenge that comes their way.

Planner-Mover

The Planner-Mover actually has quite the opposite challenges of the Mover-Planner. These individuals have a drive to be responsible at all costs. In order for them to play, their duties must be met first. They may want to be spontaneous and stay overnight when the time gets late, but their sense of responsibility won't allow them. They may have internal arguments with themselves about what is right and wrong. Both the Planner-Mover and Mover-Planner combinations can be powerful unifications. The self-confident, practical, take-charge traits of the Mover combine well with the plan-ahead, dependable, consistent follow-through of the Planner.

Opposites Work Together

So, what may seem like such opposite characteristics may actually combine into a synergistic alliance. Acknowledging that every trait is one worth having and developing will help us better understand how to channel our natural tendencies and bring out the best in everyone.

Same Style Combinations Different Personalities

Just because you have the exact same personality style order as someone else, does not mean you have the exact same personality.

Rick, Terry, and Aaron are good friends. It's not unusual for friends to have similar characteristics and interests. Often that's what ignites a friendship in the first place; having something in common, such as working at the same company, taking a class together in college, or owning the same kind of pet.

These three friends have quite a bit in common. First, they all happen to have the same personality style line-up: Mover-Connector-Thinker-Planner. They are all very physical and like to lift weights.

Their conversations with each other are loud and open. A topic that seems to permeate their dialogues is sex. They talk and joke about it freely and often. All three love to dance-dance-dance! They are very playful, easy-going, and friendly. They like the adrenaline rush of an unpredictable situation and are constantly negotiating. It is amusing to watch any one of them at a restaurant trying to coax the server into adding some free food onto the order, or at a store, trying to get an extra discount. None of them seems to be able to drive the speed limit. In fact that's where they all met—in traffic school!

So Similar and Yet Different

When people with similar style combinations get together it can bring out their style traits even more. Planners are very comfortable around other Planners. Connectors seem to feel freer to express themselves around other Connectors. Thinkers articulate more with other Thinkers who have similar interests. And Movers can relax and let it all hang out with other Movers. However, when you take a look at the individual characteristics that make up someone's personality you will notice that the same traits can be expressed in very different ways.

Terry

Terry is a motivational speaker. He thrives on standing before a large crowd and sharing passionately about how to live life to the fullest. He enjoys the challenge of hearing an audience member share an issue and being able to think "on-the-spot" of a solution or options for resolving it.

He practices what he preaches and spends his time ardently achieving his goals. Although he has moved thirty-two times in the past ten years, he maintains a long-distance relationship with a woman he has been seeing for the past five years. Though they have a child together, they have not seriously discussed any marriage plans. When Terry is not on the road, their relationship is like a whirlwind romance. They squeeze every bit of juice out of the time they spend together. Terry is occasionally late, putting things off until the last minute and rushing to meet deadlines.

Aaron

Aaron is a Ph.D. student. He is married to a designer who is busy building her own career. He loves the freedom that a committed relationship affords him. He appreciates being able to come home and share his day with his wife, equally enjoying hearing about her tribulations and triumphs. Aaron and his wife participate in many activities together such as marathons, exercising, and even taking classes. He has a part-time job as a counselor at a middle school. He enjoys the one-on-one with the students and the feeling he gets when he knows he has affected their lives in a positive way. Figuring out what to do for each unique situation that arises is a fun challenge for him. He is virtually never on time for anything. You can almost count on him being late. Of course when he arrives, he is so charming and friendly, one cannot stay mad at him for long.

Rick

Rick is a mechanical engineer. His job is to troubleshoot what needs to be done in situations to make machinery work. He is good at jumping in and saving the day with his ingenuity, knowledge,

and skill with tools. But the adrenaline rush does not end at work. If someone happens to cut him off in traffic on the way home or takes his parking spot when he stops at the bank, he'll jump out of his truck and pound his fists on the hood of the other car, loudly daring the driver to get out and fight. Rick seems to be the center of attention in most places he goes, usually because he is stirring up some kind of trouble. He has been in and out of several relationships. He loves the excitement of meeting a new woman. The flirt, the chase, the catch. But that is usually when things start heading downhill – after the catch. He begins to get a bit bored and finds himself more and more restless. It is not long before he

117

is distracted by new prospects. Strangely enough, Rick is always on time or even early for appointments and events.

We may have the same characteristic in common with someone else, yet manifest it in different ways.

Isn't it interesting to note the general commonalities in the three friends while noticing how different they are in their specific behaviors and lifestyle choices? For instance, all three of the friends enjoy problem solving and troubleshooting on-the-spot. Because their circumstances are different, they get this need met in different ways. Rick troubleshoots to make machinery work, Terry finds solutions to his workshop participants' questions, and Aaron figures out how to help young students with their problems.

Our upbringing, culture, age, location in which we reside, and numerous other circumstances all contribute to our behaviors. Therefore, we may act specifically different than someone else with the same trait combination, yet in general, very similarly. It is important to keep this in mind when you are trying to discern your personality style or the style of others. Some people have a tendency to think that if they do not have the same interests or lifestyle they cannot possibly have the same personality traits. Think again! It is the motivations behind the behaviors, not the behaviors themselves that are the signposts that point us in the direction of our true nature.

Part III
COMMUNICATING
ACROSS THE STYLES

No matter what you wish to accomplish during your day, chances are you will need to communicate to accomplish your goal. Learning these principles will enhance your interactions and allow you to communicate more easily, effectively, and eloquently with nearly everyone you encounter.

Do You Understand What I Am Asking?

Susan was interested in joining a health club and asked her mother, Roberta, to come with her to look at a few places. Roberta belonged to a fitness club that allowed her to go to any of their clubs in California. One of these clubs happened to be close to Susan's apartment, so they decided to explore this one first. On the way to the club, Susan explained that she wanted to check out the atmosphere. She was looking for nice, helpful workers-people who would acknowledge her and greet her with a smile when she came in. She wanted a place that was not too crowded, other members that were friendly and patient if it did get

crowded, and clean locker rooms, as well as clean, functioning equipment.

When they walked in the door they asked the receptionist behind the front desk if they could look around the club. The receptionist handed them both clipboards, told them to have a seat and fill out the forms, and someone would be right with them. Roberta asked her if it was really necessary to fill out the forms. All they wanted to do was look around and get a feel for the place. The receptionist told them that if they were not members, then "for liability reasons" they were required to fill out the forms. Roberta got out her membership card and showed it to the receptionist, letting her know she was already a member. The receptionist barely glanced at the card and said "make sure to note that on the form," then abruptly went back to what she was doing.

Susan and Roberta were already getting "bad vibes" and thinking about leaving without even seeing the place when a trainer came walking out, grinning heartily.

He motioned for them to give him their clipboards, which they did. Grabbing the clipboards, he continued to walk right past them without a word. The smile dropped from his face as he scanned the forms and talked to the receptionist behind the desk. As he turned to approach Susan and her mother, the smile suddenly reappeared.

"How are we doing today?" he

HELLO.

WELCOME!!

STAFF

asked, reaching out to shake Roberta's hand. She explained again that they just wanted to look around and see what the club had to offer. Seeming uninterested in their requests, he asked if they received their mail at the same address.

Susan and Roberta looked at each other puzzled. "Yes, we do," they said in unison.

"What does that have to do with a tour?" Roberta asked.

"Well, I see you are already a member, and in order for your daughter to be eligible to join you must receive your mail at the same address," he replied.

Suspecting he might be referring to some sort of family membership, Roberta was just about to clarify that her daughter would be joining on her own when Susan answered his question with "we do receive our mail at the same address!"

The conversation went even further awry as he fired off more questions.

"Do you live in a house or apartment?" he asked.

"A house—"

"An apartment—"

Roberta and Susan spoke at almost the same time.

"Which is it?" he said, frowning as if they were trying to pull a fast one on him.

"I live in a house; she lives in an apartment," Roberta responded.

"I thought you said you get your mail at the same address!"

"We do! We use a PO box," they both said.

"Well that won't work unless you have some kind of utility bill with your names on it," he said with a scowl on his face.

"We both get our utility bills there, and of course they have our names on them!" Roberta said.

The man scowled at them just before he looked down to jot down some notes on his clipboard. During the momentary pause, Susan and Roberta looked at each other. Their eyes widened in mutual agreement as Susan quickly and almost indiscernibly nodded her head towards the door. Feeling interrogated and utterly flabbergasted they stood up without saying a word and practically ran out of the place.

121

The next health club they explored was a bit further from Susan's apartment. When they walked in, the receptionist behind the counter greeted them with a big smile and said, "Hello!"

Susan said, "We are interested in looking at your facilities."

"Terrific!" responded the receptionist. "Would you like me to give you a tour or would you like to look around on your own?"

After the experience at the last gym it was no surprise when Susan said, "We'll look on our own, thanks!" Susan walked around the place. It felt cozy and friendly. Even the people exercising smiled as she walked by. It took her an entire five minutes to decide to join.

Communicate to Motivate

It's easy to notice that there was better communication in the few sentences spoken at the second club than in all the words spoken and forms filled out at the first club. Why? What was the difference? If you said something like "they listened" or "they paid attention" at the second club, you're right!

If the trainer at the first club had been fortunate enough to have been familiar with the personality concepts, he would have recognized the Connector needs of Susan right away and could have tapped into her motivational values and addressed them accordingly. The girl at the second gym might have met Susan's Connector needs coincidentally because she happened to be a Connector as well. When interacting with others, especially as a salesperson, it is best not to leave rapport to happenstance.

When people do not understand the personality style and needs of others, a lot of words can be exchanged without any intended communication taking place.

The following chapters provide valuable ways for enhancing communication with the different personality styles. Discern how the information applies to the particular people in your life. Some suggestions will be more relevant than others, and some may need to be modified or combined to accommodate the differences in second style combinations.

Chapter 10
UNDERSTANDING
CONNECTOR
COMMUNICATION

Martin came bounding in the door, an ear-to-ear smile on his face and a twinkle in his eye.

"So how was your vacation?" he bubbled, as he reached out to give his co-worker, DeAnn, a big hug. "We missed you around here."

Gladly returning his friendly, welcoming embrace, DeAnn said, "I'm surprised you even noticed I was gone. It was only three days."

"Are you kidding?" said Martin, beaming with warmhearted cheerfulness. "The place just isn't the same without you. So tell me, what did you do with your time off?"

"Actually," DeAnn answered, "I just relaxed around the house and caught up on a few things."

"How wonderful. Isn't it great to be able to do that? It always helps me get more centered."

123

"How was your weekend?" inquired DeAnn.

"Oh it was great! Besides soccer practice, a T-ball game, and gymnastics lessons, we took our little guys to the zoo. They have a new monkey exhibit. We had a whole group of little ones with us, most of the children on our block. It is so fun to watch the kids giggle and see the looks of fascination and wonder they get."

"Mayra and I are 'Zoo Parents,'" Martin continued. "We have a lifetime membership to the zoo. We thought we would give the other parents in the neighborhood a break for the day and take the kids on a safari adventure. Before we left we all made animal headdresses from scraps of fur, cardboard, and paint. You should have seen them. Little Oscar made up a 'zee-la-ger.' It's a combination of a zebra, elephant, and tiger! The children were so proud of their artwork. When we paraded them in the front gates of the zoo there were plenty of smiles and comments from admirers."

"Wow, sounds like you had an action-packed weekend," DeAnn said.

"Well, I think it is so important for children to be able to be creative and self-expressive. It was a remarkable experience," beamed Martin. "Tonight I was hoping to check out a class on dream interpretation and journal writing, but it's our turn to cook so I may not be able to make it."

"Your turn to cook?" DeAnn asked.

"Yeah. There are four other couples on our block that Mayra and I swap-cook with. Each couple takes a turn cooking one night a week. We just make more

of what we're cooking, divide it up, and place the meal on each other's porches. It's wonderful to come home and find a surprise waiting on the porch!"

"What a system you have worked out," said DeAnn. "It sounds wonderful."

"Relationships are so important," explained Martin. "That's what life is all about. What's on your agenda for today? Anything I can help you with?"

How Connectors Communicate

A Connector's world revolves around people, relationships, and fostering growth in themselves and others. When speaking, they focus their attention first on establishing or reestablishing the relationship. The information they wish to convey is woven into this relationship-building endeavor. Their communication style can be described as:

Friendly—Generally very approachable and neighborly, Connectors make it a point to acknowledge others. They also enjoy being acknowledged and will attempt to seek a connection with a handshake, smile, hug, comment, compliment, question, or conversation. Their tone of voice may vary from mellow, soothing, and polite to animated, enthusiastic, and excited.

Helpful—Connectors like to help. They will offer their assistance to friends, family and even strangers. They often volunteer for committees and events they think are worthwhile. Sometimes this style can get so caught up in a cause, or feel so compelled to pitch in, that they may offer their help before realizing just how much they already have on their own plate. Then they may experience stress trying to follow through on their commitments.

Takes Time to Relate—Before they begin an interaction, Connectors will pause to establish good eye contact and give their full attention. They may ask a few questions about how someone's day is going and comment on things they remember from past conversations. They seem to be capable of talking to just about anyone and listening endlessly, especially to those in need.

Expresses Emotions—Connectors speak with feeling in their voices. From tears to laughter, they feel and display the dramas of life. Their facial expressions and body language will usually reveal their moods, and their language may include expressive words and adjectives.

Optimistic—Those with this style typically have so much faith in peoples' good nature that they continue to give individuals the benefit of the doubt or

another chance, even when others would have already given up. They frequently have a kind word to say and can find specific examples of positive qualities in others. At times they may be so enthusiastic that others misinterpret their eagerness, generosity, or gratefulness as insincerity.

Fosters Harmony—Because Connectors want people to get along and be happy, they will go to great lengths to circumvent conflict, often capitulating their own needs for the happiness of others. They avoid or minimize conversations that feel too negative or critical, especially if the topic seems harsh toward others.

Empathetic—Connectors can sense the emotions of others and imagine what they must be thinking or feeling. It is as if they are able to enter another's world and experience it from that person's point of view. Connectors avoid imposing their own beliefs and have a tendency to change their minds or make decisions based on others' opinions or desires.

Indirect—Connectors may interpret straight talk as rude, especially when communicated loudly at a brisk pace. They prefer warming up first, before getting to the point. In fact, their

125

conversations may seem wandering and difficult to follow. They may tell stories, or create a metaphor to enhance understanding. They are known to avoid telling "harsh truths." Instead they may sugarcoat things a bit so they won't hurt the other person's feelings.

Annabel was a freelance writer who was having a difficult time collecting her payments from a company who was now a full year overdue. Month after month when Annabel inquired, she would get their latest excuse.

Not wanting to sound "mean", Annabel would start her conversations or emails with an empathetic opening, "I hope all is working out with the new bookkeeper. Sorry to hear she has been sick. Hopefully you have been able to figure out the new software program. It can be very frustrating to learn a new system."

Then Annabel would lead into her overdue payments.

"I wanted to let you know that it has been twelve months now since I received a payment for my work. I just finished the latest project for you and am hoping you will be able to distribute a check soon. I am excited to start the new writing project next week."

In response, she would get more excuses along with a request to "hang in there."

Annabel really believed in this company and wanted to continue working with them, but she was getting extremely anxious and feeling personally offended by their repeated non-payment. She tried to give the benefit of the doubt.

Eventually, one year became three. None of her kind pleas or empathetic efforts to collect the money had worked. Finally she contacted an attorney who asked to see the correspondence exchanged throughout the years. After perusing the emails, Annabel's attorney told her that although she had let them know her payments were overdue, she did not directly request her payments. Annabel was in utter disbelief. In her mind it was obvious that she had been begging and pleading for her payments! She combed through the years of emails looking for supporting proof. But alas, the meaning of her message was indeed buried under her abundance of kindness and indirect communication. After a key letter composed by her attorney was sent by certified mail to the company, her back payments were paid in full.

Polite— Related to previous, Connectors are very kind in communication and often use softeners, such as "I don't want to be any trouble" or "would it be okay if..." They rarely use what they deem as "strong language" unless they feel extremely frustrated, betrayed or endangered. Their focus is on relationships, harmony, and comfort. They may apologize if they notice the other person is feeling uncomfortable or disregarded.

Creative— Highly imaginative, Connectors enjoy discussing ideas, insights, and concepts as they pertain to people, the human condition, and possibilities for a brighter future.

They may embellish points during conversations and make use of many-sided examples. They enjoy artistic expressions of poetry or pros and may try to convey meaning through the use of vivid verbal imagery.

Reads Between the Lines—Connectors do not usually take things at face value. Instead, they try to look behind actions and words for intention and deeper meaning, paying attention and giving credence to hunches, speculation, and intuition.

Personal—Connectors often enjoy sharing stories about many aspects of their life and thus can be fairly easy to get to know. Some of their subjects may seem very intimate to others.

How Connectors Listen

During conversation, Connectors are focusing on more than just the words. They are attending to the meaning behind the message. They evaluate what they see, hear, and feel is being communicated, first about the speaker, then the message. They listen for the suggested values and assess whether theirs are in alignment or not. If they are not, then Connectors consider whether the values should be accepted or rejected. This is one way of determining how they feel about the speaker. They get a sense of the extenuating circumstances around the speaker and will give the benefit of the doubt if they feel the person is sincere and cares about others.

Once they have determined that it is okay to relate to the speaker, then they discern how they feel about the message. The message will not get through fully if the relationship is not first established.

Tips for Communicating with Connectors

Start by Connecting—First and foremost acknowledge the Connector as a person before diving into your agenda. Find out what is going on in their world. Ask how they are doing and be prepared to hear more than just "fine." They like to let you know how they are doing, not just at work but personally as well. They can get frustrated if they are asked how they are doing merely as part of a ritual, when the person asking is not really interested and does not pause long enough to hear the answer. Some Connectors, if asked a question without being acknowledged first, will stop their questioner and say, "Good morning!" to remind them to pause and recognize them as a human being.

However, for them it is better to be acknowledged as part of a ritual than not at all. If you say "hi" to everyone else in the department and they are in the corner cubicle where you might not see them, they will take it personally if you do not make the effort to say "hi" to them also.

Let Them Know They Matter—Show them you care about them as a person. Discover how they are unique, notice their contributions and let them know that you appreciate them. To truly understand what Connectors are trying to communicate, listen with both your ears and your heart.

Mandy was in charge of a meeting and had ordered sandwiches from a new establishment. She asked one of the women on the committee, Elizabeth (a Mover), how she liked the sandwich from the new place. Innocently enough, Elizabeth thought Mandy really wanted to know how she liked the sandwich so a decision could be made as to whether or not to order from the place again. So Elizabeth responded with, "Actually, it was kind of yucky; the bread was doughy and soggy. I really prefer the other place."

It was obvious to those observing that Mandy was offended by the comment. Noticing Mandy's facial expression and body language, Elizabeth tried backpedaling by saying, "Oh Mandy, thank you for ordering them and trying out a new place. We really appreciate all your effort."

Plainly still flustered, Mandy forced a smile and left the room. Later that afternoon, Elizabeth ran into Mandy. Elizabeth inquired, "Was I a little too blunt at lunch when you asked me about the sandwiches?"

Mandy paused and held her body in a stiff, defensive posture. Her face flushed as she quipped, "Actually, when you said that you didn't like them, I thought to myself, 'Well then, you can get them for yourself next time!'"

Although your top priority and concern may be the project at hand or getting your information conveyed, remember that a Connector's first concern is the relationship. Acknowledge them as a person, confirm the relationship, and recognize their efforts first when communicating. If you aren't already a natural at this, the following can help:

Include Them—Connectors can feel hurt when left out or singled out. Encourage them to be involved. Ask for their opinion and consider it in your decision making. Connectors thrive on making a contribution and can wither if they feel they or their opinion are unimportant. They want to know how alternatives will affect the people involved.

Pay Attention to Congruency—
Connectors are good at noticing the body language of others and are likely to assume that everyone else has the same ability. They can tell if someone is overwhelmed or upset and will try to wait until the "right" moment to approach them, if at all. Often, if Connectors are "able" to take on a responsibility, they feel "obligated" to come through for others.

Notice when a Connector is really trying to say "no," and let them know that they will not be jeopardizing the relationship if they do. Their attempt to say "no" may not be very obvious to some. For instance, you might ask if they have time to finish a project, and they may say, "I'm really swamped, but if you are desperate I'll do it." Now, to some individuals that may sound like "Yes, I'll do it!" But check again if you suspect they are just saying "yes" to keep you happy or not let you down. You may end up getting disappointed when they are unable to finish the project because of overload and over commitment. Their intentions are terrific, yet they can underestimate the amount of time and energy it will take to complete something and then get backed into a corner of not wanting to let anyone down. Although some people do not appreciate this double-checking, many Connectors actually welcome it. They have every intention of finishing what they promise. However, sometimes their ability to see the details and estimate the time involved can get blurred by their aim to assist and please.

Have Patience—Connectors have a tendency to read between the lines of communication. For some, this is a welcome sign of empathy. For those who have not gained the confidence of a Connector yet, it can be frustrating. However, once you have established enough rapport, Connectors often shift suspicion to perception and can tell what you genuinely want to communicate without you having to say it. Continue to foster the relationship, and they will increasingly accept your messages at face value.

Listen for Feelings—When you try to communicate with a Connector, listen to the feelings behind their words. If they are upset, it is better to talk with them privately and allow them to vent emotionally before you

SURE, I'D BE HAPPY TO DO IT.

IN   OUT

try to have an objective conversation with them. Practice patience when helping or counseling a Connector to overcome certain feelings, stress, or behaviors. Don't be condescending. It helps to share a similar experience.

Let Them Share What They Know—
Allow Connectors to express their feelings and emotions. Listen to their concerns. They enjoy talking about opinions, ideas, and dreams. Connectors will often bring up a subject just because they want to talk things through. For best results, don't hurry the discussion. Unless they specifically ask for advice, don't try to solve their problems. Be patient about their need to process.

Use Gestures of Friendship—
Connectors are usually comfortable with a handshake, hug, or when appropriate, a hand on the shoulder. They love smiles, cards, gifts, and compliments.

Say hello when you see them. Call them by name. Notice when they have been gone for a while and acknowledge their return. You may even want to ask them about their trip. If you do ask, take the time to listen! Show empathy for sad situations.

Remembering their birthday would be quite endearing to them. To go the extra mile and show you have been paying attention, make mental notes of other things on the personal side so you can bring them up in conversation. For example, if you know they own

a dog named "Frankie" that they love dearly, or that they write music, inquiries about Frankie or their music would be appropriate and endearing to them.

Although Connectors are usually quite comfortable with affection, do not assume it is okay to invade their personal space if they or their body language tells you otherwise. Don't make the mistake of interpreting Connectors' friendliness as sexual attraction.

Hear Them Out—Connectors can feel anything from crushed to furious because someone did not at least listen to what they had to say. If you don't listen, they feel that you don't care. Even if you have already made up your mind, if you just let Connectors finish their sentence or story, they will feel more validated. It also helps for the listener to share with the their

understanding of what was said. Focus on what you agree upon. For example:

"I understand that you feel silly handing out pencils at a health fair because you think it is a waste of your skills. I get a sense that you think I don't value your skills. Actually it is because I do value your skills with people and your knowledge of the department that I think you are the best person for the job."

I used to get frustrated with my mother because I felt she took too long on the telephone telling me stories instead of getting to the point and getting off the phone. Sometimes when I would call I would give her a time limit. She finally told me that if I did not have at least half an hour to talk then I shouldn't call at all because having any less time made her feel rushed and cut off. She, in turn, allows my Mover needs to be met. She doesn't mind if I multitask while on the phone. I wear my headset around so I can fold laundry, clean the house, or work on other projects while we talk. She gets her half-hour and I get to move!

Be Tactful When Offering Feedback— Pay attention to the amount of "constructive" criticism you offer to Connectors. You may think you're helping, or being accurate, but Connectors may perceive that they are being constantly corrected. If you need to discuss a behavior or misunderstanding, don't shame or embarrass them in front of others. Speak in a soft, modulated manner. Indicate you are meeting with

them because you care. List the things they did well first and validate them for their contributions before sharing the challenges you are having. Ask them for their feelings about the situation and what they believe can be done about it.

Connectors are sensitive to teasing and sarcasm, so do not poke fun at the unique way they do something or about their generosity. Although Thinkers may not mind and actually enjoy this kind of ribbing from their peers, most Connectors find it uncomfortable and even mean-spirited.

Finish any discussion of problems by focusing once again on their strengths and positive contributions.

If You are a Connector

Because it is quite natural for you as a Connector to have the ability to adapt to the styles of others, you will enjoy reading through the following suggestions. You most likely are already aware of your own communication habits and the effect they have on others.

Your willingness to be flexible and learn new skills will come in handy when practicing these suggestions. The benefit is the enhancement of your interactions with others.

Practice Objectivity—Recognize when you are reading too much in between the lines of communication. In the example with the sandwiches, Elizabeth was just commenting truthfully as to whether she liked the sandwiches or not. She was not trying to hurt Mandy, nor was she being unappreciative of her efforts.

If you notice yourself starting to take a comment personally, pause. Note your immediate reaction and ask yourself, "What meaning have I linked to this and why?" You may need to clarify that what you heard is really what they said or meant to convey. Make sure that

your definitions match. Notice if there was something in the delivery of the message that could have caused you to second-guess the words. Let go of any preconceived notions, grudges, or overly suspicious thinking. And give the benefit

of the doubt. (Really pay attention to discern the difference between intuition and old, habitual thinking patterns.) Next, ask yourself "How can I use this at face value?" And finally, even if it isn't packaged the way you'd like to hear it, be open to the gift of feedback. Be resourceful with what you learn.

Speak Up—Say something before you are pushed to your limits. It's okay to be more direct. Most people value feedback they can clearly understand.

Gloria was making omelets for herself and her boyfriend, Adam. She had just finished cracking her last egg and turned to the counter where she noticed a small carton of egg substitutes.

"Where did this come from?" she asked Adam curiously.

"I put them there," he said.

"Did you want me to use them?" Gloria asked.

"I was hoping you would—I like them better than regular eggs," he responded.

"Then why didn't you just say so?" she asked. "Why did you just put them on the counter?"

"I didn't want to tell you how to cook. This way, if you noticed them and chose to use them then great, if not, then that would be okay too," he said.

"What about your needs?" Gloria questioned. "If you like them better, I would have liked to have known."

"This is exactly what I wanted to avoid," responded Adam, "an argument over eggs!"

We all have needs. Don't make people guess at them. People will appreciate your frankness more than if you hide your feelings so you won't hurt theirs.

Add "No" to Your Vocabulary— It's okay to disagree or say "no" to a request you don't have the time, energy, or desire to do. Be more realistic about time and how much you can accomplish. It's one thing to be optimistic; it's another to be overwhelmed. People can do things for themselves or find someone else to help them. And some things don't have to be done at all. To get some practice saying "no", ask a coworker, friend or relative to support you by asking you for favors they know you are not willing or capable of doing. Of course prepare them ahead of time that you are practicing your "no". You might start off with a weak or even silly "no" response and even get the urge to follow up with an excuse. Then take your practice to the next level by role playing more resolute "no" responses that are kind *and* firm.

It's also okay to *hear* "no." Don't take offense when others make their preferences and boundaries known. It

doesn't mean you were wrong for asking.

To reduce feelings of rejection and judgment, practice asking questions for which you expect to receive a "no" answer. For instance, the next time you visit a restaurant ask your server if you can have a free salad bar with your meal. Ask in the most polite, sincere way so they take you seriously.

Think of other creative questions to ask people. Get outrageous. The more you hear "no," the easier it is to understand that it is not a judgment or rejection of you personally. It is just a response.

Let It Be— Owning up to a blunder is admirable. When you make a mistake you may feel bad, guilty, even horrible. You may crave some reassurance that you have the other person's forgiveness, but repeatedly apologizing is like picking

a scab. It does not allow the wound to heal. Continually telling the other person how bad you feel about it keeps it on their radar. In order to smooth scars and promote healing, definitely apologize, even twice if you feel like it–then *let it be*. Allow them time to process and heal at their pace. Some people need to forgive and forget–but it is difficult to forget if you are bringing it up all of the time. Let them heal and move on.

Recognize the Difference Between Politeness and

Interest—Notice if others are actually interested in your story or are only listening to be polite. You've probably been in a similar situation yourself when you've stuck around to listen to someone just to be courteous. Because Connectors can get so enthusiastic about their subject, they sometimes assume others

THEN WE SAW THE CUTEST LITTLE ...

share the same fascination. Discern when to conclude your anecdote, explanation, or comments by watching for cues of body language or listening for exit remarks such as, "Okay then, I've got to go." Ask yourself, "Am I rambling?" Know when to get to the point or get off the subject.

Seek Other Avenues—If you find that your need to express yourself is going unmet by significant others or certain coworkers, don't make them feel that they are wrong. Don't try to get them to change or "punish" them for it either. Instead, seek out others that enjoy sharing like you do. Find friends to share with. Enroll in workshops or classes in subjects that interest you. Avoid participating in things that you really don't enjoy just to hang out with others.

Chapter 11
UNDERSTANDING
PLANNER
COMMUNICATION

Two insurance agents were sitting at a table, eating lunch together. Mike complained that a client had the nerve to turn in a claim for thirty-seven dollars, a year and a half later.

Susan asked from across the table, "What is the policy on that?"

Mike said, "I checked into it, and there isn't one that applies."

"Well, if there's not a rule that says not to pay it unless it is turned in by a specific time, and it is a legitimate claim, then we should pay it," said Susan.

"But we shouldn't have to pay it. People should submit things in a timely manner. They shouldn't wait a year and a half to turn in a claim and expect us to pay it—it's just not right," Mike insisted.

135

"I agree that people should be responsible enough to turn things in on time," said Susan. "We should have a policy, something in writing so they know what is expected of them."

Mike replied, "I think so, too. We are having an executive meeting next week, and I made sure that the issue got on the agenda so a policy can be made and guidelines set for its enforcement."

"Terrific, that's the responsible thing to do," agreed Susan. "Way to stay on top of things. I will support you 100%."

How Planners Communicate

In general, Planners have a tendency to come across in a businesslike manner. They speak of structure, responsibility, and the "shoulds" and "should nots" of life. Of course, depending on the situation and what their second style is, they can appear friendly and approachable, yet still cautious. They are usually conservative and firm-minded in their views. Following are some patterns that appear to be common for those communicating in a Planner manner.

In Writing—Planners like to be accurate and responsible. Recording information enables them to have all the details for future reference. This way they don't have to rely on their memory. Instead, they have a sort of physical check list they can look back on to make sure they fulfilled their obligations in the manner they promised. They also have precise

documentation in case there is a question about the conversation, timelines or responsibilities.

Purposeful—Unless the situation is a special one, or they are on a break from their regular schedule, Planners will usually state the reason for their conversation up front or early on in their communication. They experience an urgency to stay on their timelines, especially at work, and get frustrated if they feel they are wasting time chatting instead of doing.

Appropriate—Planners try to use proper language, avoiding slang or politically incorrect wording. They also pay careful attention to their timing to make sure it is the right instance to communicate as well as the correct mode. They will pause to find out whether they should be talking to the individual directly, or going through a chain of command. They will also determine whether they should communicate in writing or fill out a form verses making a phone call or communicating in person.

Very respectful, they would not fool around in a serious situation by telling an off-color joke. Especially in business, they frown upon others that use inappropriate language or raunchy humor. They may further try to guide or correct those that are not following the proper norms for the situation. However, they are apt to be a bit less formal with their joking and receptive to the humor of others amongst friends or in a social situation where that kind of thing is accepted and maybe even expected.

Task Focused—Once the purpose of the conversation has been established, Planners like to stay on topic. It is very frustrating, and often interpreted as rude by Planners when others disrupt the conversation by interjecting comments or changing subjects. Planners may center their conversations around accomplishing the goal at hand. And if the goal at hand is to have a conversation, they like to give their undivided attention to the interaction, making good eye contact and avoiding multitasking as much as possible.

When extenuating circumstances, people issues, or interruptions arise, they may refuse to spend much time talking about them or figuring out alternative solutions. Instead they may try to redirect the dialogue back to the original goal or plan.

Loyal—During conversation, you will notice that Planners speak in ways that support the organizations for which they work or volunteer, their spouse, families, and their communities. As dedicated citizens they may mention policies, rules and customs and how they uphold them as well as share how many years they have been working for a company, been married, been a member, positions they have held, or projects they have worked on. They usually feel it would be inappropriate to publicly criticize but may do so if someone has been disloyal or broken too many rules.

Predictable—Comfortable with consistency, Planners like to speak and respond in anticipated manners. Rarely will they pull a fast one and spill a surprise request on their listener. Unless they are under a tremendous amount of stress, you can count on them to be consistently reliable in their communication.

I UNDERSTAND THE BUILDING'S ON FIRE, THE SOONER WE FINISH HERE, THE SOONER WE CAN EVACUATE.

Traditional—Because tradition is something Planners value highly, they will proudly follow customs that have been passed on to them through generations.

A man had been married just a few weeks when he invited his parents over for a holiday dinner. His wife was preparing a festive dinner of ham with all the trimmings. She had just started to put the ham into a baking pan when her husband stopped her.

"Wait," he counseled, "you must first cut the ends off the ham before putting it in the pan!"

Puzzled at the urgency of his request, his wife questioned, "Why do the ends need to be cut off the ham?"

"My mother always cut the ends off the ham. It turns out delicious that way," he informed her.

"But it seems as though that would be wasteful," she declared. "It is perfectly good ham."

"That's the way we've always had our ham," he insisted. "Just try it, you'll see."

Wanting to please him and her new in-laws, the woman cut the ends off the ham before baking it.

When dinner was ready and she began to serve the ham, she turned to her mother-in-law with burning curiosity.

"Why is it," she asked, "that you cut the ends off your ham before baking it?"

Her mother-in-law replied matter-of-factly, "So it would fit in the pan!"

In the speech patterns of Planners you will notice references to the way things have been done in the past and a tendency to want to stick with what they know and can rely on.

Chronological—One communication method that keeps Planners on track and helps them remember details is to speak of events in order, from the past to the most recent. When asked to explain one aspect of a problem, they will start at the beginning and explain the entire linear process. During conversation, if a step is missing or a Planner gets interrupted before completing the sequence, they may begin their communication over again from the beginning to make sure everything has been included.

Planners don't like to start "in the middle". When a conversation is first initiated, they like to establish a purpose for the communication up front. They may ask for the history or background so they can get their bearings on a situation or project. It helps them to listen.

Detail Oriented—Rarely do Planners like to talk in generalities or interpretations. They like more concrete details and logistics. For instance, if you are traveling and ask for directions from a Planner, instead of simply saying, "Take Highway 5 north, exit Watt Avenue south, turn left on Keifer," they will give more details. Their directions will be more like: "Take Highway 5 north about 10 miles, when you see the exits for Howe Avenue and Florin Road, you will know your exit is coming up. Take the Watt

Avenue Exit south, when you get to the top of the ramp turn right. Five lights down make a left on Keifer Boulevard. Go about three miles down, you'll go through about three stop signs. As soon as you pass the Albertson's Shopping Center on your right, start looking for the post office. The driveway comes up quick."

Closure—Planners desire completion. They like to be able to finish their sentence or thought. If you are on a phone conversation with a Planner, and you hang up the phone before they are absolutely complete with the interaction, say to take another call or because of a time constraint, they may phone you back to "bring closure" or "close up" the conversation. They do not like to be left guessing about what is expected or where

MR. JOHNSON? DID WE HAVE ANYTHING ELSE TO GO OVER AFTER YOU TOLD ME I WAS FIRED?

to go from here. Planners can get quite uncomfortable with too many options left open and may insist that a choice be made. Their discussions from that point on, center around fulfilling the requirements to satisfy the choice that has been made, accepting no excuses for quitting early.

Status Quo—Because consistency is such a high ranking value for Planners, they often speak of "The way we have always done it." They like to look at the past for reference of how things should be done now. When others suggest a different approach, a Planner's first response is usually to defend the current approach. They like to get used to things and are not likely to jump into something without it having a proven track record. When someone starts talking about a "new way," Planners just may change the discussion to, the "old way."

Judgments—Before responding to another individual, Planners will first judge whether what the person is saying or doing is right or wrong. Once they have decided, Planners will give their views on the matter, often peppering their conversations with words like, "should" and "should not." They may come across very authoritarian, "That is wrong, what should be done is..." They may also speak in comparatives, "What will the neighbors think? What would George Washington do in this circumstance?"

It is usually very clear to a Planner what the correct action is in a situation. If it is unclear, they like to make it clear by establishing a rule or finding facts to back up their thinking. Once they institute a standard, locate confirming information, or decide upon a certain value, their communication leaves no room for interpretation. They make sure the listener knows exactly what they are talking about and what action is expected as a result of the communication.

Accountable—Concerned with law, equal justice, and general standards of order, Planners help us realize that our actions are an integral part of a system and can affect it positively or negatively. They will caution us if we are straying from the principles and use them for their own guidance as well in their decision-making. These general standards of order create a common ground for everyone in the system, be it an organization, family, or community, and establish certain rights and expectations. Planners will inform others of these rights and expectations, not to support their own personal opinions, but rather to help others know what to expect from one another, especially when nothing else seems certain.

Planners may put aside their own immediate interests for the sake of their principles and can lose sight of their own personal needs and priorities. Committed to a specific code of conduct, they are not comfortable with exceptions to the general rule and will communicate this in their interactions.

How Planners Listen

Planners listen for details, in order. They can lose their train of thought if the conversation is interrupted or a person speaks off target. They do not want to fill in the blanks. Planners listen for responsibility. They listen for the purpose of gathering information and understanding their part. They pay attention and ask themselves, "What is my duty? What should I do with the information?"

Planners are concerned with whether something is right or wrong. They are listening to decide the correctness of the speaker's intentions as well as their status within the given context. The more they are able to determine the appropriateness of an interaction or response, the more comfortable they are in conversing.

Tips for Communicating with Planners

Be Specific—Fill them in on the details they need to know. Don't overwhelm a Planner with too many abstract ideas or generalizations. When making a request, let them know what specifically needs to be accomplished, by when, and they will get it completed.

Outline Priorities—Be very clear about expectations and order of importance. Planners are most comfortable knowing they are on track and meeting the requirements. Planners generally enjoy working together with others to successfully complete tasks, projects and events. Ask for their suggestions on how to prioritize and plan. Make sure to mention how your plan upholds the organization, family, or community.

Save Surprises and Novelty— Planners thrive on predictability, regularity, and efficient use of time and resources. When outlining a plan, mention what has worked in the past. Be practical and financially sound in your appeals. The words "new" and "improved" are less interesting to Planners than "established" or "quality you can count on." Don't switch methods or plans on them without warning and/or a good, solid reason.

Christine is an engineer for a military contract firm. Holding top

> OH BY THE WAY... WE ARE HAVING TEN GUESTS OVER FOR DINNER TOMORROW NIGHT DEAR.

security clearance, she had been away on a business trip for over a week and was looking forward to getting home. Her week had a grueling agenda of meetings, measurements, calculations, double-checks of requirements, and problem-solving. Not only had she been in a different time zone, but a different

climate, interacting with unfamiliar personnel and dealing with a drastic change in her regular schedule. That's a whole lot of variety for a Planner who prefers consistency. When her husband Jon picked her up from the airport, he suggested they stop at a hardware store on the way home to pick up some items for some cabinets he was installing at home. Christine was exhausted, "Can we please just go home? I am hungry. I was looking forward to a warm meal and sleeping in my own bed."

Jon smiled and said, "It will just be a quick stop."

"Please," Christine insisted. "I need to eat or I am going to faint. Let's just go home."

Jon reached over and squeezed her hand in his. "Oh sweetheart, I was trying to surprise you. I made reservations at your favorite restaurant. We weren't really going to stop at the hardware store."

Filled with appreciation and relief, Christine leaned over and hugged her husband. "That's so sweet of you Honey, but I really don't like surprises. If you had told me you made reservations, I could have been excited instead of anxious."

Pausing for a moment to think, Christine continued. "I know you like surprises. So how about we agree that I try to surprise you and you don't surprise me? That way we will both be happy!"

Don't Interrupt!—When beginning a conversation with Planners, wait until they have finished what they are doing and acknowledge you. Planners find interruptions rude as well as irritating. They like to complete their sentences, thoughts, and tasks before turning their attention elsewhere. Be polite and greet them before diving into your agenda. Don't bombard them by having two or more people speaking at once. They prefer to listen to one person at a time. Trying to listen to several people talking at once from different directions can cause them stress.

Plan Ahead—Knowing what you are going to say before you say it is helpful when conversing with Planners. They like it when you are prepared. If you intend to brainstorm with them, let them know that is what you want ahead of time.

Stay on Target—They can get irritated if you don't complete one concept before skipping to another. It helps maintain their attention when you present concepts in chronological order and in a step-by-step manner.

Apologize When Appropriate—Planners are pleased and validated when you take responsibility for your actions. Own up to it when you "blow it" and let them know you are sorry. Trying to cover up your mistakes can make matters worse.

Appeal to Their Strong Sense of Right and Wrong—Make sure your idea or plan supports the appropriate rules or practices. Let them know that you were conscientious in following procedures. Keep in mind they are usually honest, trustworthy and concerned.

Acknowledge Their Hard Work—Remember to notice and comment on the effort Planners put forth in various areas. Comment on their work, family, church or community involvement.

Maintain Composure—Planners appreciate it when you are poised. Loudness as well as exaggerated gestures can be interpreted as boisterous or rude.

Be Consistent—Treat everyone fairly. They get rather irritated when they believe "special" treatment is given to some and not others. Don't arbitrarily make exceptions to rules. If a rule is constantly being bent or broken, make one that is enforceable.

If You Are A Planner

Planners are generally respectful and responsible in most areas of their lives. This is also frequently true when it comes to communication. If Planner is your most dominant style, you'll most likely size up a situation for what would be most appropriate before responding. However, as you are well aware, not everyone shares your same ideals for what is appropriate. Therefore, conflicts can arise. One of the best ways to show consideration for yourself and others is to appreciate each individual's unique style. Instead of trying to convince others that your way is the right way, use the following suggestions to enhance communication and promote alliances.

Have Patience—When people talk in different directions, do ten things at once, and don't stick to the agenda, be open minded about their communication style especially if you are a listener or the one that has approached them with something you need.

Praveen approached Liz and Carrie for some information he needed to complete a project. He first addressed Carrie with his question. Carrie was only three words into her response when Liz excitedly piped in with an idea. Irritated at the eruption, Praveen asked Liz to hold her thoughts so Carrie could finish her sentence. Carrie, waved her hand back and forth quickly in the air as if to erase his request, saying, "That's okay, let's hear what she has to say." Reluctantly, Praveen listened to Liz's idea. Just as he started becoming intrigued with her suggestions, Carrie added in a few more ideas to elaborate on Liz's. Praveen glared at Carrie trying to send her the signal that interrupting Liz was inappropriate, but neither Liz nor Carrie seemed to notice as they continued their brainstorming. No sooner would Carrie start a sentence when Liz would interrupt it or finish it for her and vice versa. In frustration, Praveen tried harder to regulate who was speaking by requesting that only one person speak at a time. Carrie and Liz seemed to completely ignore his requests as the energy of their discussion escalated.

In exasperation, as well as self-preservation, Praveen finally said, "Why don't you two just discuss this, jot down your ideas and get back to me."

Carrie and Liz looked at him momentarily puzzled. Shrugging their shoulders they said, "Okay," then eagerly returned to their conversation.

Praveen's frustration actually lead to a great idea. If it is too uncomfortable for you to adapt to a communication style that is extremely tangential, you may want to make your request for information, then ask that they respond to you when they have gathered their thoughts. Of course if you are the "boss" you have the right to expect that others

143

adapt to your style of communication. You could provide an outline of the format in which you would like the information submitted to you. However in either case you risk stifling the creativity of others.

Consider Other Options—Planners have a tendency to judge very quickly whether a person's actions are "right" or "wrong" on the onset of a conversation. Pay attention to whether or not you are missing the whole point of the discussion because you got stuck on something that you decided was "wrong" in the beginning of the interaction.

Practice Peripheral Listening— Instead of honing right in on the details, practice discerning the concept, big picture or overall question.

Some time ago, a fellow speaker shared a story about how he had rushed to the airport and forgotten to print his flight itinerary (he was definitely not a Planner). In a hurry, he approached the nearest airline counter and asked the customer service agent if the 9 a.m. flight to New York was on time. Honing in on his specific request, she checked her computer and informed him there was no 9 a.m. flight to New York.

Horrified that perhaps his flight had been cancelled, he asked her to check to see what happened to the 9 a.m. flight. He waited as she clicked away on her keyboard searching for the answer to his specific question. After several minutes she looked up, shook her head and said, "I am sorry Sir, there *is not* and *never was*

a 9 a.m. flight scheduled to New York for this morning. Perhaps you are flying on a different airline or a different day?

"Can you look me up by name?" he asked, quickly rattling it off without waiting for her response. His panic was increasing as he watched the minutes tick by.

"One letter at a time Sir," she requested trying to get him to slow down and articulate so she could get the correct spelling of his last name.

He took a deep breath and gave her each letter of his name "M...e...".'

Again her fingers tapped methodically at her keyboard. Finally she looked up. "Here you are Sir, you are scheduled on flight number 1868. Departure is at 9:07 a.m. out of gate 11-C," she said with a smile.

Planners naturally sort for specifics. The airline agent took this man's precise request at face value and looked for a 9 a.m. flight instead of searching for departures *around* 9 a.m. It can be frustrating to both parties in communication when you can't seem to get someone to give you the details you need to help them. Practice pausing to widen your view of the big picture. Once you have a general idea of the request, take a deep breath and gather your wits as you patiently help others get more specific.

Accept Others—Even if you are in a position to supervise others and it is your job to correct their actions, when their values are not in line with yours, it may prove be fruitless and irritating try to change them. Know that others have different skills and values than you, and different does not mean wrong.

Give It a Break—Remember... you are not the general manager of the Universe. Be aware of how hard you are driving yourself and others. Take the weight of the world off your shoulders. Relax a little and realize there are just some things that don't have to be perfect. Sometimes "good enough" is good enough.

Chapter 12
UNDERSTANDING
MOVER
COMMUNICATION

Michelle had hitchhiked across three states to see her sister Karen and arrived quite exhausted a little past midnight. Karen insisted they both get a good night's sleep because she had arranged a hiking trip for the next morning as a fun way to introduce Michelle to her fiancée Glen.

The next day Michelle awoke refreshed. As she sipped her morning cup of coffee, she began to share some adventures of her trip. Karen listened for only a few minutes before reminding Michelle that Glen would be waiting promptly at 10:00 a.m. to meet them for their planned hike.

"Oh, he can just take a chill pill—we're getting there!" Michelle joked, giving no indication that she was willing to move any faster. It had been a long trip and she wanted to relax a little before getting in a car again to ride with Karen to meet Glen. Karen finished packing a picnic lunch for the day and informed Michelle that it was fast approaching 10:00. She once again encouraged Michelle to hurry along and told her that Glen would not understand their tardiness.

By the time they arrived at the meeting point, Glen was fuming. "You're ten minutes late! Where's your integrity? You made a commitment to be here. I was here on time and you kept me waiting!"

Without hesitation, Michelle looked Glen straight in the eye and said, "You're a jerk! I'd rather hike without you." With that, she turned and tromped up the trail, leaving Glen dumfounded where he stood.

How Movers Communicate

Of course, as with any personality style, there are varying ranges of the ways Movers communicate. When Movers are extraverted, they will demonstrate a great many of the communication patterns described in the following list.

Introverted Movers have several of the same tendencies but usually display less intensity and volume in their manner of speech.

Confident—Whether they know what they are talking about or not, Movers will come across as if they do. They speak with certainty, sureness, and decisiveness. This style likes to take control of the situation and be in the spotlight.

Loud—Because they don't mind the attention, they may turn up the volume to be heard. Some people find this abrasive, but other Movers find it refreshing! They can be boisterous, intense, and enthusiastically expressive.

Casual—Friendly, playful, and inviting. Movers may use slang, "street talk," or even profanity to emphasize a point. They tend to use first names of prominent individuals instead of using their titles.

Desire to Speak in the Moment—Generally, Movers will want to share their opinion the minute it hits their mind. They may make comments or promises so quickly that they don't remember they did so, or aren't prepared to back them up.

"Now" Oriented—Because Movers like to live for the moment, they may interrupt others. They like to act now, and "now" doesn't include waiting until you finish your sentence!

Quick—Movers appreciate immediate feedback and will swiftly give it, sometimes switching subjects before the listener is ready. They also hate to wait for an answer. They want to know immediately so they can act "now." They may even assume a "yes" response if the person seems indecisive.

Brief—This style doesn't usually spend a lot of time leading up to their point, or pausing to connect and ask how your day is going. Wanting to get the greatest amount of information into the shortest breath, they may not pause to compose a perfect sentence, or worry too much about their grammar or syntax. They say it and move on.

Straightforward—Movers like to give it pure and simple without trying to soften their delivery. They can be very blunt and explicit. In their world, they would rather not fog frankness with tact.

In Motion—Movers crave mobility and are likely to fidget or work on something else while you are talking to them. Wanting to be "productive" during a conversation they may even conduct business while exercising or recreating. They often embellish their stories with large body movements–pointing their fingers, waving their arms and sometimes even jumping up and down to act out the scenario they are describing.

Flexible—Although they are usually quick in making a decision initially, they reserve the right to change their mind midstream, and often do.

Varied—Their attention span for things in which they are not directly involved can be minimal. They seek opportunities, options, and choices, switching gears often. Most decisions are not final. Many times they just want to keep things moving along, so they choose whatever option seems the best at the moment.

Involved—Movers are generally playful, like to laugh, and will joke around. They delight in spontaneity and action, and may argue just for fun.

How Movers Listen

Movers listen for entertainment, impact, relevance and usefulness. Unless you are incredibly engaging or reveal immediately how the information you are conveying is useful to a Mover, they may lose interest, especially if your communication is lengthy. If you fail to stimulate or keep their interest, they will do it themselves, making connections to what you are saying so they can in turn tell you a colorful story of something that happened to them. Their minds can whirl a mile a minute as they playfully hop from subject to subject.

They also try to figure out the motive of the person speaking, what do they want, need or expect from me? They do this almost simultaneously as they look for opportunities for themselves. They want to be able to take action with what is said, be it to share a quick joke, seize a challenge, or perform some feat. They listen in the present and process contextually, usually not linking so much to the past or distant future, but instead figuring out what they can do with the information in the moment.

Tips for Communicating with Movers

When Movers are interested in being expedient and clear with their communication they can be very straightforward. Some people may perceive this as brash, inconsiderate, or even aggressive. Planners may interpret Movers' communication style as rude, Connectors may feel it is mean or pushy, and Thinkers may find it too dramatic or flamboyant. Movers who have a high amount of Connector as their second style are often perplexed by people's reaction to or perception of them.

For example, many Movers report that oftentimes servers in restaurants are caught off guard by their directness. A Mover ordering lunch may sound something like this: The server asks, "May I take your order?"

"Yes, this grilled chicken sandwich… is the bread grilled or the chicken grilled or both? Because if the bread is grilled, I don't want it; it's too greasy. I'll be sick half the day."

"The bread is not grilled, only the chicken."

"Good. I'll have that then, and can you leave off the mayonnaise? I'll just have mustard on it, and toast the bread. I'd like to substitute the green salad for the potato salad, unless of course it's gloppy. Is it real gloppy?"

"I'm not sure what you mean by 'gloppy.'"

"Well, never mind then, I'll just take the green salad, but put the dressing on the side. And can I have a side order of mashed potatoes and gravy?"

"I'm sorry, we only serve mashed potatoes and gravy for dinner. We do have French fries."

"French fries are too greasy. See if you can ask the cook about the mashed potatoes and gravy. And, I'll take an ice water . . . thank you."

The server acts offended, and the Mover is perplexed as to why. In the Mover's mind he or she has only asked for something specific and tried to make it clear so that the server would not get the order wrong and have to go through the trouble of taking the food back and starting over again. Of course, some Movers that read this might say to themselves, "Hey, I'm not that picky. I'll eat anything that's put in front of me." But the ones that like their food in a particular way can relate.

The following general guidelines are meant to assist you in communicating to win the motivation and cooperation of a Mover. Note the particular behavior of the Movers in your life. You will then be able to know which methods to use with which person for the most success.

Be Prepared to Hear It Straight—Keep in mind Movers are not trying to be rude when they "tell it like it is" without warming up to a topic. They are trying to accomplish a goal. Think twice before attempting to slow them down by requesting they stop to acknowledge or greet you. Is it really wise to slow down their momentum for etiquette reasons or because you prefer a milder approach? This can derail them in an entirely different direction. It might not be worth it. Let them do their thing and be on their way.

Lighten Up—See how much you can enjoy their playful behavior. Keep in mind that even though their approach may be lighthearted, they are serious about accomplishing their goals. "Casual" does not equal "disrespectful" or "unprofessional".

Use Sound Bites—Movers get distracted and bored easily, be direct and to the point. Remember they are multitaskers and thus like to work on several things at a time. This includes having a discussion. If you want to meet them in their world, instead of trying to get them to set everything down or stop their activity for a long discussion, encapsulate your information into small, concise bites, like commercials. Use thirty-second elevator speeches. If you had to tell them something and had only an elevator ride to do it in, what would you say?

Match Their Speed—If you speak too slowly, they will have a tendency to fill in your words for you or move on to another subject.

Appreciate Their Flare—Movers speak with confidence and flamboyance. They may embellish their stories for impact: "I was on hold for 10 minutes!" (When actually it was more like 5 minutes). In communicating with Movers that you know have a tendency to exaggerate, take their overstatements with a grain of salt. Instead of arguing with them over the accuracy of their statements, look underneath for the intention. If you really need to know precise specifics, ask in a curious or playful tone (instead of an accusatory, *I don't believe you* tone). Otherwise, why bother? Be amused.

Move with Them—You will accomplish a lot by having a conversation with them while they walk or do some other physical activity. If they are already on the phone, they usually don't mind being interrupted for a quick question. Check to be sure. Go with the flow.

Give Them an Audience—Movers have a need to share their excitement. Allow them to tell you an adventure or blow off some steam without

trying to give them advice or to channel their energy into problem solving just yet. Oftentimes, they just need to get things off their chest. If they are particularly extraverted, they probably won't even want a comment of any kind. They'll supply the entire conversation. Otherwise, to avoid irritating or insulting them, make sure they really want help before offering any.

Offer Options—Give them choices. Movers need the freedom to choose or they will feel too limited. Ask for their suggestions.

Make It a Challenge—"I'll bet you can't guess what I need you to bring with you!" Invent a game.

If You Are A Mover

We all want validation for our own unique style of doing things. Wouldn't it be great if everyone we interacted with had an understanding of personality styles? When those around you become more aware of your mode of operation and intentions, they recognize the benefit of allowing you room to "be yourself". However, most folks we encounter have not been through a workshop or explored the personality concepts. The following suggestions will help open lines of communication with those that seem to be stopped by your approach. If it is important for you to get along with them, use these tips for modifying your own behaviors to build bridges for communication. Once the bridges are established, you will have more freedom to express yourself in your preferred style.

Be Aware of How You Are Coming Across—You may want to "tell it like it is," but some people need to have it wrapped in a nice package. While you might not care about certain things, others do. If it is important to you to be heard, modify your speech to fit the patterns used by your listener.

Wait for a Response Before Proceeding—A pause does not equal a "yes." Give people time to think. Your mind may run a mile a minute, but others may prefer to plan before taking action. Pay attention to whether the listener is still thinking or wants more information or not. Be prepared to take an extra minute to chill while they form their opinions and have a chance to respond.

Identify Others' Requirements—Some people simply cannot listen until you connect with them first. If that's the case, pause to say a quick "hello, how are you?" Try to pace their tempo a bit before blasting full throttle. Even though you may like to keep busy and take advantage of every second of the day, when you involve yourself with tasks or activities during conversation it can be distracting to some who like more eye contact. Instead of insisting they keep up with you, or stopping reluctantly and grudgingly giving them the "okay now I am paying attention" look (staring directly in their eyes for emphasis), let them know when would be the best time for you to sit still and for how long. If you want to build rapport and gain their confidence; pause. A small investment of your attention can pay off big time.

Notice When You Are Exaggerating—If you embellish too much, too often, people will not believe you anymore and try to second-guess you. It can be fun to add some color to your conversations but be aware of the response of others. You might want to save your best stories for those that you know will appreciate them.

When Listening to Others, Keep Your Mind Focused—Remember, not everyone can switch gears as quickly as you can, or even wants to. Your enthusiasm can be exciting to experience and those interacting with you can benefit from understanding your tendency to

153

interrupt in the moment. However, this zeal can become exhausting if the other person doesn't ever get the chance to finish their thoughts. Although you may not mean to dismiss what the other person is saying, it can come across that way if you don't take a couple of breaths and listen once in a while. If you just can't seem to hold your thoughts and are afraid you are going to forget what you are thinking if you don't get it out immediately, jot down a quick note so it is out of your head and you can pay attention to the speaker. When they have completed, seize the opportunity to share your thought.

Pause Before Making a Commitment—Before you hit the "send" button on that email, or sign on the dotted line of that "irresistible offer", ask yourself if this decision can wait 24 hours (some decisions can wait–others need to be made in the moment–come on, you know the difference!). During that period, gather more info, double-check with friends or colleagues, do an ego check. It is amazing how different our thinking can be when the adrenaline rush has passed.

Recognize Others—Other people need praise too. Find out how they like to receive it and give it to them their way.

Use Softeners—When making requests or giving directions, using "please" and "thank you" goes a

long way with the population. Think of how the other person might like to hear something phrased.

Make a Decision and Stick to It—Leaving your options open may be freeing for you, but it can make others nervous. Think past the moment to check and see if you can really follow through. Set up ways to remember the promises you made yesterday.

Find Other Movers—Some people may take offense to the "straight up" way you communicate and interpret a "harmless," playful comment as being "mean," "harsh," or "judgmental." Find other Movers so you can "let it all hang out." This will give you a channel for your energy.

Chapter 13
UNDERSTANDING
THINKER
COMMUNICATION

Randall, a custodian for several office complexes, came over to his friend Carson's house to borrow a special tool he needed for a project. While Carson ran upstairs to see if he could find the

tool, his wife Shala offered Randall a cup of coffee. They sat at the kitchen table, and Shala shared with Randall that she was thinking about getting laser surgery on her eyes, but her regular eye doctor thought her pupils might be too big. "He says that the laser can only cut so wide on my eyes," she explained. "At night the lights would catch on the edge of the surgery when my eyes dilate. I don't quite understand why they just can't make the laser a little wider so my pupils won't hit the edges."

"Well actually," Randall clarified, "the cornea only extends barely to the perimeter of the iris before it amalgamates with the sclera. Expanding the circumference of the laser beam could compromise the integrity of the eye."

Noticing the blank look on Shala's face, Randall lifted his hands, making a fist with one and covering it with the other. "Say my fist is the eye and this hand is the cornea," he began. "No wait," he said. "May I?" He gestured toward a couple of plastic eggs that had strayed from the kids' Easter baskets and happened to be in a bowl in the middle of the table.

Shala nodded her head and said, "Yes, please do."

He lifted the toy eggs and split them apart. Stacking the sides on top of each other creating several layers, he began to explain. "Laser in Situ Keratomileusis, or LASIK, corrects vision by reshaping the corneal tissue beneath the surface of the eye. An instrument called a microkeratome makes a protective flap from the epithelium that covers the cornea."

He continued his explanation until he got confirmation from Shala that she understood the procedure, as well as the anatomy of the eye. By now, Carson had appeared in the room, triumphant in finding the tool he was looking for. "Speaking of lasers," he said, "did you hear that they recently disproved Einstein's theory about the speed of light?"

Randall perked up in his chair. "I heard that!" he said excitedly. "That corroborates my own personal theory that the speed of light represents the ability to get information in our lives. The limit of the speed of light as being the fastest anything can travel simply denotes our ability to measure movement. We assumed it was the limit of which things could move, movement itself."

"Yes!" Carson said. "It makes me think about instantaneous information transfer. Take what we experience as gravity. I believe that we are going to discover that gravity is an instantaneous effect produced by the proximity of matter or energy. Once we learn to reproduce gravity waves and transform them, we'll be able to send and receive information instantaneously, regardless of the distance."

"I'll bet we discover that our subconscious mind already does this," said Randall, starting down yet another avenue.

Shala wanted so much to participate in the conversation but she could find nothing to contribute. She sat there looking back and forth at the two speakers as if watching a tennis match. After several minutes she got up from the table and drifted out of the room.

"Furthermore, we will have to rewrite our current public paradigm," she heard her husband say.

How Thinkers Communicate

Thinkers, for the most part, communicate for the purpose of gaining or sharing information. They automatically have rapport with those who understand their communication style and are excited to share ideas and concepts. They usually have a wide variety of interests and may know quite a bit of information about many things. During a conversation, their attention is usually focused on the subject at hand. It is not generally aimed at establishing or strengthening the relationship with the other person with whom they are communicating. Yet, as you no doubt have noticed by now, some people like to chat a bit first before actually getting to the topic. When two people have different agendas for a conversation (as in the following story) the message can get lost.

Char had been working on a project for the past week. This morning she had already been at it for almost two hours. The statistics and figures were coming together nicely. She had worked at it much like a puzzle, strategizing where to fit what piece and figuring out what was the best method to present the information in a logical, precise way. All she needed to complete the project were the statistics from her coworker, Kelly.

Char checked her e-mail. She had sent a message to Kelly two days ago, and again this morning, but hadn't received a response yet. Char tried reaching Kelly on the phone but the line was busy. She really needed that last bit of information so she walked over to Kelly's cubicle. Kelly was just hanging up the phone.

"Kelly," began Char, "do you have those figures for the K-7 project?"

"Good morning, Char," Kelly said.

"Good morning," Char responded. "Do you have the statistics for the K-7 project? I need them to finish up."

"How are you this morning?" inquired Kelly, not responding to Char's question.

"Fine," Char replied.

"Did you get your haircut?" asked Kelly. "It looks great."

"As a matter of fact, I got them all cut," answered Char. "About those K-7 statistics, are they ready?"

"You know, my son missed the bus this morning and my computer crashed twice already. What a morning!" sighed Kelly.

"So is that a 'no'?" asked Char.

"I'm sorry," said Kelly, seeming to just now join Char. "What is it that you need?"

"The K-7 statistics," Char repeated.

"Oh," said Kelly with a bewildered smile. "Why didn't you say so?"

The following will help you gain further insights into the values, motivations, and intentions behind the communication style of Thinkers. See if you don't notice some of the attributes below in your next interaction with a Thinker.

Purposeful—Most Thinkers avoid "small talk", feeling as though it is a waste of time and brain cells. They are not drawn to "brainstorming" because they do not like to share ill-formed or incomplete thoughts. They want to make an impact, not just noise. The more extraverted a Thinker is, the more likely they will push to get to the pertinent information more quickly. You may find yourself deep in the middle of a discourse, just to have a Thinker interject, "And your point is...?"

Private—Especially in public or at work, this style prefers to talk more about ideas, information, and strategies than relationships issues or personal matters. However, just because Thinkers are private, does not mean they are quiet. They can be very opinionated and candid about certain topics. They just don't like to share intimate details of their personal lives.

Logical—Thinkers like to approach conversations in a logical manner, using analysis to reach conclusions. They try to stay level-headed and objective during interactions, so more often than not, their voice and demeanor are modulated and they appear quite stoic. They do not usually respond positively to emotional input and may tune out during discussions that with highly charged overtones.

Think Before They Speak—Those with this style like to pause and reflect before communicating. Sometimes they do not feel the need to speak at all. They may sit back and allow others to fully explore and discuss issues. They prefer to observe and process the information they've gathered in their minds, working out a solution –

or several different responses. They will take in the necessary data and consider timing, appropriateness and accuracy. Once they have everyone's input, then and only then, do they open their mouths to share a well-formed purposeful response.

Irritated at "Stupid Questions"—Thinkers can get bothered when people don't stop to think, look, or try to figure something out before asking a question.

Avoids Redundancy—If a person over explains something, particularly if Thinkers know more about the subject than the person doing the explaining, they may get irritated or mentally leave the conversation.

Theoretical—Hypothetical and abstract, Thinkers peak of new ideas and future plans. They may incorporate hand movements or models to explain certain concepts. They avoid "tried and true" methods, seeking freshness and improvement instead.

Like the Big Picture—Thinkers go for the main idea or concept before honing in on the details and like others to do so as well.

Explores Ideas—Thinkers enjoy exchanging thoughts and having discussions with people that understand what they are talking about. They usually try to determine the credibility of speaker before they invest time listening to them. Once legitimacy is established, Thinkers will banter, embellish or upgrade concepts scrutinized in the course of the conversation. Thinkers seek to discover new connections, new possibilities, and new uses for the information discussed. Elements that seem inconsequential and not worthy of deliberating to some people, may fascinate a Thinker and turn out to be important keys to new discoveries.

Asks Questions—Constantly looking for opportunities to learn more, Thinkers have an insatiable curiosity. During conversations, they like to challenge beliefs and ideas about how things work.

WILL THE DESCRIPTION OF YOUR WEEKEND BE ON THE **TEST**?

You may think you have thoroughly explained something or meticulously prepared a proposal only to find that a Thinker poses ten questions you hadn't thought to cover.

Use Big Words—Many Thinkers have quite an extensive vocabulary. Having such a wide range of words to choose from allows them to be extremely succinct. They know that a single word can carry enormous expressive power when used correctly.

Communicates with Conviction—Persuasive and convincing, Thinkers use strong statements. They look for compliance, belief, or agreement in their listeners.

Wry Sense of Humor—One way that Thinkers like to entertain themselves (and sometimes others) is by being "funny." Sometimes they will carefully craft a joke and tease it to the surface at the right moment. Their favorite humor is when they leave others wondering if what they said was serious. They are not likely to care if something they say gets taken the wrong way. If the other person's mental capacity is that limited—their loss—no sense taking the time to explain it!

Zena took her daughter to a well-known, reputable medical center. Her daughter needed a physical exam so she could go to daycare. Zena was given a form that instructed, "If your child has a temperature do not send them to daycare."

Zena chuckled to herself and said wryly, "If my daughter did not have a temperature, then she would be dead! Of course I would not send her to daycare."

The medical assistant, not catching Zena's sense of humor, explained, "Oh, we mean 'fever' when we say 'temperature.'"

"Why not just say 'fever' then?" Zena questioned.

The assistant quipped, "Any intelligent person would know we mean 'fever' when we say 'temperature!"

"Actually," responded Zena, "any intelligent person would be irritated that you say 'temperature' when you mean 'fever!'"

How Thinkers Listen

Thinkers listen for information and want to know the purpose for the communication. Often, they assume the communicator has approached them to solve a problem or to exchange necessary or intriguing material. They tune out when there is redundancy, extreme emotion, and subjects that are of little interest to them. They seem to automatically click into data gathering and concept or strategy formation.

Many Thinkers focus so intensely on thinking about and processing (then reprocessing from several different approaches) the "data" presented that they regularly miss out on the additional messages supplied by non-verbal

communication such as tonality, body language and facial expressions.

You may be sharing to gain empathy and instead they are concentrating on solving your challenge, offering little or no outward signs of compassion, while all the while in their minds they are demonstrating the ultimate compassion by taking the time to solve your problem.

Tips for Communicating with Thinkers

When Linda first met Gary she was often perplexed at the long pauses she would get after asking a question. Being an extravert, she would blurt out thoughts as they hit her. She enjoyed fast-paced conversations and flitting from topic to topic. When she would pause to ask Gary a question about how he felt about a subject, silence ensued that made her very uncomfortable. Feeling perhaps he hadn't heard or understood the question, she would often repeat or rephrase it. Gary would assure her that he understood and was just thinking about how to answer her.

Linda would insist, "Just tell me your answer. Why do you have to think about it? Whatever is, is. What is there to think about? Just tell me your thoughts."

Gary would assert, "There are many ways to articulate what I am thinking."

Confused even further, Linda would urge, "What do you mean? Just say your answer!

Gary would further explain, "I am pondering the aspects that would be the most relevant to you."

Linda had an uneasy feeling that Gary was trying to hide something because he was very careful to monitor every word that came out of his mouth. She thought about her own way of communicating and concluded, "If I were taking that long to respond, I'd be making something up!"

After attending a Personality Lingo® workshop, Linda learned that Gary is an introverted Thinker.

She now understands that what might seem like a playful conversation starter to her is interpreted by him as a serious request for information. And, because Thinkers pride themselves on being accurate, he takes his time to ponder the question at hand before answering.

Gary, on the other hand, is now able to detect when Linda is flippantly talking off the top of her head, just making conversation, or is really asking a serious question.

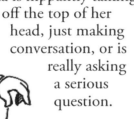

Following are some ways you can help open lines of communication with Thinkers.

Give Them Time to Think—Thinkers like to ponder the subject at hand. They like to weigh many possible options before responding. They are not only thinking of the content of their message, but also what would be the most accurate method of conveying it. Sometimes the most succinct response for them is complete silence.

Don't Misinterpret Their Request for Information—Realize they have a need to question and explore. If they ask "why" or "what do you mean" realize that they are seeking more specific information, not trying to read between the lines or interrogate. Be logical and factual.

Give the Big Picture—Provide an overall context, outcome, or purpose for the discussion. Do you need a problem solved? Are you just sharing information? Give the big picture or end results first, then fill in the details. Remember, don't insult their intelligence by stating or restating the obvious, especially if they know more about the topic than you do.

Stick to Logic—Unless Connector is a very strong second style for them, Thinkers are not usually influenced by emotional appeals. Although they feel their emotions deeply, they usually do not show it. Furthermore, they are not swayed when you show your emotions. Thinkers appreciate accuracy. You are better off using logic and facts. Emphasize an opportunity to learn and gain wisdom.

Watch Your Vocabulary—If you use large words, make sure you know what they mean and how to pronounce them properly or Thinkers may get annoyed and stop listening.

Notice Their Humor—Many Thinkers have a wry sense of humor that can sometimes be misunderstood. Give the benefit of the doubt. You don't have to laugh at their jest, but at least recognize it as humor instead of mistaking it for cruelty.

Debate with Them for Fun—If you have been deemed a worthy opponent by a Thinker, take the opportunity to dive into a healthy verbal exchange of ideas. Although they like to be straight to the point and appreciate it when you are too, they also enjoy arguing both sides of an issue. Be prepared to defend your position. Share with them the big picture and your global views.

Speak for a Purpose— Thinkers usually do not like small talk and are the least likely of the color styles to be up on the office gossip. However, once you have gained their trust and confidence, they can open up.

Understand and Heed—Their interests may vary greatly from yours so don't be insulted if they don't seem fascinated in what you have to share. They usually won't give things a high priority unless they see the value, logic, or intrigue. Don't continue insisting they listen to matters that only you find satisfying.

If You Are A Thinker

If you are interested in facilitating smoother communication with others that do not embrace a similar style as yours, the following are techniques for further understanding their language and style.

Ease up—Notice whether your "why" questions are being misperceived as interrogation or as doubt of another person's intentions. If this is the case, use softeners to gain your answers, such as, "Please say more about…."

Allow Emotions—Just because others want to show their emotions does not mean that you are obligated to act or help them in any way. Let others express their feelings. Understand that's how some people process.

Pay Attention to Other People's Needs—Before charging ahead with your own agenda, take some time to gain rapport. A few minutes at the start of a conversation can save much time and frustration later for both of you. Notice the effect your behavior has on others. Is your body language sending signals that you don't want to be approached?

Add Some Detail, *or Not*—When asked to describe an experience, be aware of what the other person is requesting. Do they want just the big picture or some details? Some Thinkers have a tendency to give only the big picture, while others may go into an in-depth explanation. Avoid "data dumping"–the spewing of specifics about subjects when others aren't interested. Determine the appropriate strategy for relaying information according to the person you are communicating with. Pay attention to cues of captivation. Are they actually intrigued and fascinated by your facts? Or are they starting to shift in their seats, look at their watches and trying to avoid eye contact? It's okay to occasionally miss signals that others aren't interested, we've all mistaken politeness for interest at some point but it is important to notice if

you've gone past politeness and actually started irritating them. You can discuss the topic at another time with others that truly get it.

Learn to Listen without Fixing—Many times people just want to be understood and heard—not every "problem" needs to be "fixed." Before the communication gets too far, politely ask them if they are seeking solutions or just a listening ear. This way you will know whether to listen for details or filter for feelings. Simply listening and empathizing is a worthwhile activity in itself.

Recognize What's Right—Thinkers have a phenomenal gift for spotting flaws or inconsistencies. From the simple use of a word in a sentence to the faulty implementation of a system or discrepancy in someone's idea. As valuable of a gift as this may be, in communication with other styles, it can come across as harsh criticism, instead of objective feedback if not prefaced properly. Although many Thinkers may expect this type of straightforward critique and find it refreshing, other styles can be put off and degraded by it; feeling as though they can never measure up. If you know you have the habit of always pointing out mistakes first, practice pausing and finding something positive to genuinely appreciate before trying to help them improve.

Save the Debate—Although you may derive entertainment from playing "mental chess" with others, not everyone appreciates an intense discussion. Achieving a goal while alienating others can burn some bridges you may want to cross later.

Make Time for Your Relationships—Notice what the people in your significant relationships need and appreciate. When feasible to do so, figure out what you can do to accommodate them, even if it does not seem practical or logical.

Inform Others—When you need to think, instead of immediately fading into your head to figure things out, let others know this is what you are doing. Notify them that you are not tuning them out, you simply would like some time to think. If you really want a challenge, allow others in on your processing. If your nature is to be introverted, experience what it is like to examine externally by speaking your thoughts out loud, as they occur. Let others in on your analysis of the data.

Chapter 14

COMMUNICATING IN STYLE

I wish I could tell you that learning to communicate "in style" is remarkably easy. Truth is, it takes some practice. But the payoff is tremendous! Not only will it improve your interactions, it changes your effectiveness in virtually everything you do. It is surprising how many people experience better results in communicating after just a few adjustments to their approach.

If you are serious about bringing your communication skills to the next level, the following steps will offer you further direction.

165

Step #1 IDENTIFY
Pause and Pay Attention

To avoid hearing communication as only black and white (this style or that one), pay attention to broad themes. For example, anyone can be caring, kind, and considerate–not just Connectors and Planners. If you listen for the overall tone and motivation behind the interaction, you'll notice communication patterns emerging. Study the chapters describing the various characteristics, needs and communication approachs of each personality style so you are familiar with them. Because we all have differing amounts of all four styles in our personality, notice how often people communicate with their first and second style, switching back and forth almost seamlessly. Extraverts usually lead conversations with their top style communication patterns and back them up with their second style traits. Introverts tend to communicate internally with their top style, so externally they lead with their second style. If you listen closely you can hear them interweaving hints of their most dominant style.

Step #2 CLARIFY
Look for the Intention

Although you may not understand some people's behavior because it is not the way you would act in the same circumstance, know that the individual has a "good" reason for acting that way. For example, if someone is acting stubborn, selfish, or even hurtful (by anyone's standards) we could look behind the behavior and discover that they have a positive intent or motivation, perhaps to stand behind what they think is right or to gain respect. Standing firm for what is right or gaining respect are positive aspirations.

It is interesting to note that people may even admit trying to inflict misery, and perhaps if you asked the person why they were doing it they may not realize what is underneath their actions right away. But if you kept asking, "...and what would that do for you?" you would discover the underlying reason would boil down to a positive one (perhaps only beneficial or positive from their perspective or to them, but positive nonetheless).

Try this and see: when you dig deep enough you'll find the positive intent. Looking for the positive intent of others will reduce negative judgments and allow you to open your mind to dealing with the situation at hand instead of focusing on whether the behavior is appropriate or not.

Step #3 MODIFY
Adjust Your Approach

Have you ever been frustrated with others who have a different communication style than yours? Did you ever wish they would make life a little easier and just adapt to your style? Some people wish they could just "tell it like it is" without people getting their feelings hurt. In contrast, others might wish that people would "slow down, show some consideration, and take the time to listen." Both parties wish the other would accept their way as the right way.

Think about those individuals in America that speak only French. Of course, they wish that others spoke their language fluently. This would help ease their struggle with English. If you had coworkers who spoke only French, wouldn't you think it was nice if they learned English to be able to communicate with you? On the other hand, they would probably appreciate any attempts you made to learn French to help communicate with them while they tried to learn English.

As in any successful relationship, there is always give and take. The important thing is how flexible you can be to get the result you are seeking. If you take the stand of "it's up to them to learn my language," be ready for some challenging times. In addition, as you can guess, the way you say things in any language can make all the difference in the world in meaning.

Learning new ways to communicate can be like learning a new language. It takes some getting used to it before you feel really comfortable and natural.

How can you meet them in their world momentarily to establish rapport? As you begin your conversation, pace your communication so it reflects their preferences and style. Notice how receptive the other person is and modify your body language, tone of voice or choice of words to put them at ease and let them know you understand their approach. Remember Steven Covey said, "Seek first to understand, then to be understood."

Step #4 APPLY
Practice for Success

When we first learned to drive we had to consciously remember to look, steer, work the pedals, and probably even shift too. We may have over-compensated and driven rather unsteadily. We may have had to remind ourselves to check the rearview mirror or to remember to use our turn signals. But now driving is so automatic to most of us that it seems the car practically drives itself. It is this way with communicating. When you use the communication techniques in this book, you will start to experience results. It may be more transformational than you realize, and you may or may not already be aware of how quickly this transformation has taken place. You probably have already noticed that as you read, your mind began to use the information to apply it to the circumstances and people in your life.

At first you may feel more comfortable with some of the methods than you do with others. Go ahead and experiment; have fun! You could drive along in life in first gear and get where you want to go. However, when you learn to smoothly shift into other gears you will get there more effectively with less stress.

Step #5 VERIFY
Double-Check and Try Again!

Learn to recognize the difference between occasional occurrences and actual patterns. To avoid jumping to conclusions, find people with different

167

styles with whom you can communicate
to bounce your ideas off. When practicing
different ways of communicating, make
sure you are clear about
the purpose of a
conversation. Are
you looking to
share data and ideas, solve
a problem, make a decision, or
perhaps just share an interesting story?
What about the other person? If you are
busy trying to reestablish a relationship
with someone and his or her main goal is
to get information, chances are you will
be more effective if you switch gears into
information mode.

Remember that every time you try
something that does not happen to
work as favorably as you had hoped,
you are just that much closer to finding
a way that will! Even if you dislike your
initial results, the knowledge you gain is
priceless in making distinctions for better
decisions in the future. Try something else
until you find what you are comfortable
with. Keep trying until you find a strategy
that works for you. As with driving, the
more you practice, the more natural it
becomes.

Part IV
THE STYLES
UNDER
STRESS

How we handle stress in our lives depends upon a lot of things: workload, time constraints, the people we interact with, our past experiences...yet there is something more–our personality style. What is stressful to one person or style may be exciting or motivating to another. Most people are not consciously aware of their stress patterns and coping behaviors.

In this section we will take a closer look at the different personality styles and their relationship to stress. We'll identify common causes of stress, characteristic behaviors when stressed, as well as tips for reducing stress.

Most of us have experienced a time in our life when we've felt overwhelmed. When people and circumstances are

169

not cooperating with our plans, we instinctively turn to behaviors we believe will bring us relief from our stress.

Typically we try to cope by amplifying the natural tendencies of our dominant style. If we haven't gained control of our stress levels through these means, we become even more determined to take hold of the situation and increase our efforts even further by taking these normally positive traits to the extreme. Under these circumstances, our otherwise constructive behaviors shift to potentially destructive actions which can work against us and end up increasing our stress instead of reducing it.

When the stress still doesn't let up or becomes even more severe, we abandon our dominant style behaviors and start to try out our lesser preferred style traits. The thing is, we usually have less practice using these traits effectively so they show up as immature, uncivilized, underdeveloped versions. For instance, those folks who typically don't exhibit their emotions readily, their otherwise self-contained demeanor can give way to awkward, uncharacteristic emotional outbursts.

We may not recognize these behaviors as part of our character and negatively judge ourselves. When this occurs it accelerates a downward spiral of stress.

What's Personality Got to Do with It?

To find out more distinctions about how each style reacts to and deals with stress, I worked with Dr. Ed Redard to create an online stress survey. By the end of two years we had collected over 10,000 responses. Sifting through the data it became abundantly clear that although there were general categories of stress that each style had in common (work, money, relationships), there were also very specific differences.

The following chapters integrate these newfound insights with previously established facts about the connection between stress and personality. The stories and lists depict typical behaviors one might see for each particular style when stressed. Any one of the styles could possibly demonstrate any of these behaviors. They are not restricted to the particular personality style for which they are written; they are just the most common for this style. Many of the suggestions for stress management as well as tips for reducing the stress of others can be applied across all the styles.

Being able to recognize when you or someone you know is stressed is the first step to turning things around. Pay close attention to your most dominant style stress behaviors so you can put your personality strengths to work for you instead of against you. Understanding the stress signs and triggers of other styles will help you identify more clearly what might be going on behind their behaviors. The tips provided not only help you reduce or manage your stress, they supply tools to assist you in finding the compassion and patience to encourage others styles when they are under stress.

Chapter 15
CONNECTORS
UNDER
STRESS

When Connectors are feeling good about themselves, they appreciate everything and everyone. They behave with honesty and integrity. They like teamwork and cooperation. Usually, Connectors are contagiously enthusiastic and express their feelings readily. They can be very encouraging. They strive for peace and harmony and enjoy creating things to make life better.

However, when Connectors are not getting their needs met, it can bring out another side in them. It is essential for this style to be able to express their authentic self and feel they are making a contribution. Because Connectors find great pleasure in contributing to others, they can become overextended. Everyone has their limits to how much stress they can take before becoming immobilized. If they spend too much time on other people's problems, too much energy doing for others, and constantly putting their own needs last they can get overwhelmed and start feeling like a victim or door mat. If Connectors find themselves in relationships or environments where there is constant conflict, rejection, or negativity, their emotional reserves can get drained to the point that they can begin to shut down. Afraid to let themselves "feel", they possibly will try to "numb-out" by binge eating (especially sugar), pull back from social interactions, or wall up in their bedroom or house.

A Disconnected Connector

Tammy is a single mother with two teenage sons. Her father's illness was getting increasingly worse, and she had just moved to a "fixer-upper" home. At work, there was a bit of restructuring

happening. Her direct supervisor, Vanessa, accepted a position in another department. Tammy had really enjoyed working for Vanessa. She felt that the two of them had a friendship as well as a good working relationship. "Who knows who will be replacing Vanessa?" Tammy thought apprehensively.

Tammy tried not to be upset with Vanessa for leaving, but she felt abandoned and unappreciated. When Vanessa would try to talk to Tammy about her new position, Tammy found it hard to listen. She would plaster on a smile and nod her head, acting like she was interested, while on the inside, she did not want to hear about it. Tammy found herself avoiding Vanessa as much as possible. Yet when confronted, she gave no verbal clues about her real feelings.

Instead, Tammy felt the need to vent about other issues to her coworkers. She would lament that "no one" noticed the hard work and extra effort she was putting forth at home or work. Her workload was overwhelming, she was not getting enough sleep at night, and to top it off–she was gaining weight. Her coworkers eventually grew weary of listening and started avoiding her.

Tammy's venting soon turned into emotional tantrums–drawer slamming, crying, and even yelling. The slightest conflict would bring her to tears. Her outbursts would catch everyone off guard. Practically the entire staff would tiptoe around her, trying not to set her off. Tammy soon began questioning her coworkers' actions. She started getting mad at them too, accusing them of sabotaging her or gossiping behind her back. She would take general comments overheard out of context and act as though they were aimed specifically at her.

When Vanessa's birthday arrived, Tammy refused to help decorate Vanessa's new office or pitch in to buy a card. In the past, Tammy would have been the organizer of such activities, so when Vanessa discovered her office decorated and read the thoughtful card, she assumed that Tammy had arranged it all. Vanessa waited until she could have a moment alone with Tammy. She thanked Tammy profusely and told her how much it meant to her to have her office decorated and to receive such a nice, thoughtful card.

Not wanting to admit that she had done nothing to help, Tammy simply said, "You're welcome. It was nothing."

What Brings Out the Worst

Some of the obvious reasons Tammy was stressed had to do with her overwhelming responsibilities at home. Compounding her challenges in her personal life were the changes at work. She felt rejected by her supervisor and left out when her coworkers tiptoed around her. She also experienced a sense of isolation by not being able to vent and share. There were a few actions others could possibly have taken, such as Vanessa including her a bit sooner in some of her decision making or her coworkers giving

her an empathetic audience in private.

Because Connectors place a high value on positive interactions, they get stressed if they are feeling a "disconnect". Whether they feel left out of decisions, are required to work alone without collaboration, or sense a mismatch in rapport—rejection, isolation, and lack of inclusion can be triggers for this style. Connectors also have a concern for the welfare and wellbeing of others. It is stressful for them to say "no" and feel like they have let someone down, so they can get overwhelmed taking on the concerns of others and putting their own needs last.

Connectors are passionate about all the possibilities life has to offer. They seek to understand themselves and the purpose for their life. It can be stressful when they are operating out of alignment with their values, especially at work or in personal relationships. In addition, it is disheartening when they feel their work or life lacks "meaning", or their wellbeing is off balance.

Common Stressors

Conflict

Overloaded, overwhelmed

Isolation or being left out

Rejection

Lack of trust, being "back-stabbed"

Lack of acknowledgment

Lack of tolerance

Aggressiveness

Negativity

Not able to express genuine self

Not able to share

Not being appreciated

Lack of caring

Insincerity

Lack of romance or touch

Lack of cooperation

Unsure or unsafe environment

Rigidity

Saying "No"

In attempts to maintain harmony and protect their true feelings, Connectors may portray the opposite of what they are feeling. They may not want to let on that they feel hurt, inconvenienced, or unappreciated. They can withdraw their love, concern, or listening ear on the inside, yet still appear like everything is fine on the outside. Some Connectors will cry, scream, or lash out in an attempt to divert their own attention, as well as the attention of others, to a different problem altogether. Keep in mind that this is not something they do on a conscious level, but rather subconsciously. They may even fantasize about running away or having someone or something rescue them from their circumstances.

Following are some of the behaviors you might see when Connectors are stressed, experiencing low self-esteem, or not getting their needs met for an extended period.

Characteristics Under Stress

C'mon Baby and Rescue Me—Indulges in melodrama. Acts out to test love, devotion, commitment or friendship. Can end up in difficult or dangerous situations that require serious attention.

Passive-Aggressive—Brandishes the "silent treatment". Dispenses put-downs veiled as compliments. Begrudgingly follows through with a commitment while harboring resentment.

Flash Floods—Damned up emotions come gushing out through tearful downpours. Victim mentality. Requests viewed as unreasonable and limiting. Crying in response to minor demands.

Masquerades—Puts on a happy face/ false front to hide the truth of their pain. Disguises their genuine feelings. Offers reassurances but harbors secrets to protect relationships and perceptions.

Flat Tired—Exhausted, drained, weighed down by inertia, overly fatigued, joyless, lack of enthusiasm, apathetic, numb, quits caring, retreats socially.

Flees Into Fantasy—Withdraws from reality into an imaginary world. Seeks distraction and relief from unpleasant situations. Mind spins with endless improbable negative possibilities.

Eats Their Emotions—Develops a devoted friendship or relationship with food. Attempts to fill emotional void with chocolate, sweets, carbs. Soothes wounded spirit with comfort food.

Many times Connectors try to suppress their intense emotions around a painful situation and may even "go numb" to escape the stress. Remember, feeling good about yourself, although influenced from the outside, comes from the inside. When individuals have stable self-esteem they are more able to ask for what they need. So, what can you do to help boost your self-esteem, lower your stress levels, and get your needs met? Read over the following suggestions and decide which ones would be the most helpful to you.

If You Are A Connector

Have you ever noticed that sometimes it is easier to spot the behaviors of others than to notice the same behavior in yourself? If you have a high amount of Connector characteristics in your personality, the preceding list will most likely depict some of the most common stressors for you.

Check the above list of "Characteristics under Stress" and take an honest inventory. Do you recognize yourself resorting to these behaviors? Because we are all unique individuals with different experiences and situations, we will, of course, have variations in the ways we react to stress. In general, though, many of the reactions that Connectors have will be manifested in these kinds of behaviors with their other styles blended in.

Since the world of a Connector revolves around relationships, it is easy to think that if others would just change the way they behave, it would lessen our stress levels. Although this may be true in some respects, you are the one that has the greatest effect on your own attitude, self-esteem, and stress level. By adopting the following behaviors you can gain a new positive perspective.

Learn to Accept "Negative" Emotions— Some people express themselves in assertive ways that can seem rude or mean. Others need space to be sad, grumpy, or alone. Although you may not enjoy feeling "down" and feel it is your job to cheer everyone else up, some people need a period to be alone and process. It's okay to try to redirect the focus of others, but pay attention to whether you are being effective or not. Also, some people enjoy a little conflict or argument. When you try to create

harmony out of a situation when others are actually trying to stir things up a bit, it can cause frustration for everyone. Notice when it would be appropriate to allow others the freedom to debate, even if they are loud and boisterous. Sometimes the best action to take is to remove yourself from the situation.

Take a Stand—Notice if you perceive that a conflict exists when it really does not. Many times you have control over a situation and don't even realize it. Stop and notice! It really is okay to take charge. Examine your own needs. Pay attention to what you really want instead of repeatedly basing it on what others want or need. If you spend so much time doing for others, you risk losing track of what would best serve you, as well as them.

Note: Expressing your needs and asking for what you desire does not equate with yelling, screaming, or being "mean."

Many times Connectors wait until they are at the point of being steaming mad before they will stick up for themselves. Then when they finally express themselves it comes spewing out with aggressive, defiant indignation.

Instead of getting mad, get assertive. Assertiveness is clear, direct expression of feelings.

This expression of feelings does not include stomping on the other person in the process. Feelings can be expressed firmly and honestly with respect for the feelings, opinions, and rights of others. Know the difference between your true feelings and the feelings you convey because they seem more appropriate. It is much better to let people know what you want than to expect them to guess.

Foster Growth in Others by Doing Less—Because of your tremendous drive to contribute, the lines of knowing just how much and how long you should continue to give and do for others may begin to get fuzzy. It's admirable to contribute, but not to your own demise. Notice when others can do for themselves and when some things just do not need to be done at all. Be careful not to promote others' dependence on you. Sometimes we dig ourselves in so deeply doing for others that we don't leave them any other option but to depend on us. Do them and yourself a favor and let them grow and achieve on their own. The following story is often passed around at self-help groups to help participants recognize that sometimes it is the struggle that allows us to grow.

Recognizing the Importance of Life's Struggles

A young student found a cocoon one day and brought it to his home-room, which was in the biology lab. The teacher put it into an unused aquarium with a lamp to keep the cocoon warm. About a week went by when a small opening began to appear on the underside of the cocoon. The students watched as it began to shake. Suddenly, tiny antennae emerged, followed by the head and tiny front feet. The students watched this unfold, and would run back to the lab in between classes to check on the progress of the cocoon. By lunchtime the creature had struggled to free its listless wings; the colors revealed that it was a monarch butterfly. It wiggled, shook, and struggled, but now it seemed to be stuck. Try as it might, the butterfly couldn't seem to force its body through the small opening in the cocoon.

Finally, one student decided to help the butterfly out of its difficulty. He took scissors from the table and snipped off the cocoon's restrictive covering. Out plopped the insect-like thing. The top half looked like a butterfly with droopy wings; the bottom half, which was just out of the cocoon, was large and swollen. The butter-pillar or cater-fly never flew with its stunted wings. It just crawled around the bottom of the aquarium dragging its wings and swollen body. Within a short time, it died.

The next day the biology teacher explained that the butterfly's struggle to get through the tiny opening was necessary in order to force the fluids from the swollen body into the wings so they would be strong enough to fly. Without the struggle, the wings never developed and the butterfly could not fly.

As it is for the butterfly, so too, it is for us. We cannot violate the laws of creation. Without struggles a lot of things in life never develop.

Let It Go—Most people already like you. It is a given. You are a wonderful person with terrific talents. You may believe you have evidence to the contrary, but why focus on that? Instead, if someone does not pay attention to an idea you contributed, or fails to respond when you say "hello," or multitasks in your presence without making eye contact, accept that they are doing the best they can at the moment, given the circumstances. You may perceive their actions as rude, when in reality they are just different. It doesn't mean that you should fail to acknowledge others or purposely ignore them to "give them a taste of their own medicine." Relinquish grudges. Be yourself and don't hold it against them for doing things their way. Don't punish others for not being a Connector.

Validate Yourself—Have you ever experienced a time when you felt that you did a hundred things right, yet the one mistake you made is what others noticed? Keeping in mind that feedback is good and useful, take into account the comment about the "mistake." Set aside your judgments about the person, the way the feedback was delivered, and the "meanings" you attached to it. Notice what is useful about the feedback. Focus on how you can incorporate and use it for improvement in the future. If you think about it, they cared about you enough to want to help you improve!

Pay attention to whether you have developed the habit of putting yourself down or focusing on your own shortcomings. You can learn from what did not turn out the way you wanted by taking mental notes about what needs to be done differently in the future. Then, purposefully shift your focus to everything you did "right" instead. Focus on what you want to happen instead of what you do not want.

You naturally desire to experience and express your feelings. Validate yourself for your helping, caring, and contributing. You are blessed with the gift of loving and caring about others. Acknowledge your friendships, your sacrifices, your successes. Let your inner light glow. Be yourself.

Use Your Talents—Once I was talking to a very stressed Connector in a computer class I was attending. She had taken a different position at her job because she needed the five percent increase in salary that came with it. Before, she had been working with victims of violent crimes and their families. She facilitated groups, answered a hotline, and organized events. She really enjoyed working with people and seeing the progress they made in the programs. Currently she was working with computers, entering data. She had recently been given an assignment to design a new database for her organization, something in which she had no background or experience. She really was in over her head but did not want to

give up. Thus, the computer class. She expressed how miserable she was in her new job but she needed the extra money to take care of her family.

If you find yourself in a situation where you are dissatisfied with your job, it usually comes down to two choices: (1) change your mind about your job, or (2) change something about your job. A great book to help you discover the type of work that uses the natural preferences for your personality style is *Follow Your Inner Heroes to the Work You Love* by Carolyn Kalil.

Set Boundaries—"Give 'em an inch and they'll take a mile" was probably first muttered by a Connector. Those with this style pride themselves on being empathetic and not taking advantage of others. They are skilled at noticing when others are overwhelmed. They are careful not to overstep the boundaries of others. However, others are not always as perceptive in these areas. Therefore, it is up to you to set boundaries for yourself and take total responsibility to see that they are honored.

If you continue trying to be everything to everyone, chances are, someone is going to get let down, and often that someone is you. If it has become a chore and is causing you stress to try and keep up with things that seem to go unappreciated or are taken for granted– drop it! Keep the things in your life that give you the most satisfaction.

Remember, it is not "mean" or "harsh" to set and maintain a boundary. It is actually courteous, informative, and beneficial. Contrary to what you might expect, people will respect you for it if you do so with caring firmness.

To find out more about how to set and announce your own boundaries, survey people you respect and find out how they set and announce theirs. Use several techniques until you find one that suits you. Who knows? It may be the first one you use!

Look Before Leaping—Being a "possibility person," you may have a tendency to project idealistic qualities on others or have high expectations for outcomes. When circumstances don't meet your expectations, use your innate ability to pick out the positive intent behind someone's behavior or see other opportunities in the situation. As much as you might wish that people would reciprocate the love, friendship, or contributions you provide them, it is not always going to show up in the form you would desire.

I remember a cartoon I saw in a calendar published by the Hope Heart Institute (Seattle, Washington). It was of a little bunny that was staring at a small door that had a sign on the doorknob that read, "Closed." The bunny had a sad look on its face. What the bunny was not noticing was a big door right next to the other one. This door had a huge "Welcome" mat in front of it. The door was wide open and you could see a gigantic carrot garden inside. There were signs posted amongst the carrots, "Jumbo Carrots–Free!" The bunny was too busy focusing on the closed door to see the

wide open one. What are you focusing on that is preventing you from seeing other possibilities?

Take Care of Yourself—Again, remember to pay attention to your own needs. Many times we are so busy doing for others that we let our own health and well-being suffer. Are you getting enough exercise, sleep, and nutritious foods? What do you do for stress relief? When was the last occasion you had a massage or took time for yourself? When taking a plane ride, the flight attendant explains that in an emergency, the oxygen masks will fall from an overhead compartment. If you were with a small child, who would you put the oxygen mask on first–yourself or the child?

Although as a parent your instinct might be to "save" your child first, then yourself, the flight attendant always instructs the adult passengers to put their own masks on first. This is because if anything were to happen to the adults, the child would have little chance of surviving without them. If you don't take care of yourself, how will you ever be able to authentically express yourself or fully contribute to others?

Meditate—If you haven't discovered the benefits of deep breathing, meditation or other relaxation methods, now is the time. Although you could meditate while standing, it is beneficial to sit in a comfortable position. You can decide to close your eyes, or at least relax them so they partially close. Begin to concentrate on your breathing. Slowly inhale then

179

exhale as you feel yourself relax and release. Without trying to control the pace or depth of your breath from here forward simply be aware of your breathing. Notice as your thoughts flit in and out, letting them flow without judgement. Observe your thoughts and emotions, not hanging on to them but instead keeping your awareness on your breath and the sensation of breathing. Taking this mini vacation from your busy day helps clear your mind and restore your equilibrium.

Express Your Unique Self—Find ways to express yourself. Do you need to dance, draw, or sing? What is it you have been putting off?

When Connectors are not expressing their true selves they can get confused, depressed, and frustrated. It is so emancipating to be able to release the pent-up desires at last. Although many times Connectors will gauge what they do upon the approval they get from others, ultimately they are much happier when they follower their bliss. One way to do this is to seek out other Connectors. If you find yourself surrounded by others that don't appreciate or bring out the best in you, you still have choices. One would be to have them read this or other books on personality styles. This will help them gain an appreciation for your gifts. Another choice is to join clubs or attend classes where other Connectors are likely to be. Try yoga, meditation, a dance class, or whatever else you are interested in.

How to Help Reduce Stress for Connectors

If you happen to have some Connectors in your life that you think may be stressed, there are some things that you can do to support them in regaining their equilibrium. These suggestions work best when they are actively putting in the effort to address their own needs. However, these tips are still very effective in helping you help prevent Connectors from getting stressed in the first place.

Some of the following suggestions may be out of your comfort level just now. But if you have a genuine desire to learn and grow, they will quickly become a natural part of your behavior. To help reduce stress for Connectors, offer them:

Validation—Connectors try hard to make sure they are not letting anyone down. They definitely appreciate the acknowledgement when they have gone the extra mile. They flourish when they know they have made a difference in the life of another. However, Connectors can get overwhelmed taking on the concerns of others and constantly putting their needs last. They can be so good at supporting others that they can sometimes be taken for granted. Pause to complement the creative way they accomplished something. Let them know you value them. They especially appreciate gestures of a personal nature such as a handwritten note or card, a voicemail message, or making terrific eye contact and saying "thank you for being you."

Kindness—Be positive. Connectors can be upset by criticism. Discern what they are going through or experiencing. Show sensitivity; give personal support and empathy. Save negative comments or stories for others who appreciate them. Connectors are most comfortable in environments that are warm and friendly, and allow for personal interaction, individual creativity, and expression. Allow them to express their feelings.

Avenues for Growth and Creativity—If they do not have a way to express their creative energy, Connectors can experience a dull depressive ache. They yearn to express their genuine self and find pleasure in the process of creating. Whether it's drawing, painting, acting, singing, dancing, talking, the way they dress, or

communicate—going too long without an outlet may make them burst! Let them release their creativity, uniqueness, and individuality. This outlet can be as simple as using brightly colored pens when working on a chart, leaving an uplifting message on their answer machine, or decorating their cubicle, room or notebook. Subtle or splashy, it boosts their mood to decorate, design, and discover their artistic selves.

Acceptance—Don't brush off their concerns. Practice tolerance, patience, appreciation, and reassurance. Offer opportunities for them to "fess up" without being rejected. Include them. Involve them in teams, relationships, and friendships. Provide ways for them to obtain support systems and social contacts.

Harmony—Connectors have an innate urge to make everyone around them happy. If others are sad, Connectors feel it is up to them to cheer them up. If two people are arguing, the Connector will find the positive points of each. Connectors really can put themselves into the shoes of others and empathize. Therefore, if you know Connectors that are under stress, keep arguments with others out of their vicinity. Even if it has nothing to do with them, they will still feel obligated to try and make it better.

A Listening Ear—Sometimes Connectors just need to vent without others trying to "fix their problems". Refrain from telling them to calm down which can negate their feelings. This is the time to listen without judgment. Let them know you care by keeping them company. No matter the urge to share similar stories; do not add to their stress by voicing your complaints. Keep the focus on them, not you.

Warmth and Human Contact—Connectors crave human contact and companionship. When they go too long without it they can feel left out, unappreciated, and invisible. During times of stress, they may withdraw or sulk. Hang in there. Allow them space but don't abandon them altogether. They appreciate you being accessible when they are ready to talk. A simple hug can soothe a stressed-out Connector and smiles are a welcome sign of acceptance.

Limited Requests—Connectors are prone to overcommit themselves and can become overwhelmed or exhausted doing everything for everyone around them. Limit the number of requests you make of them during times of stress. Pay attention to their needs and priorities. Offer your help to lighten their load.

Love and Romance—Connectors welcome compliments and intrigue. Instead of seeing them as a mushy romantic or fantasizer, appreciate their love of the dramas and nuances of life. If you are in an intimate relationship with a Connector, think of something they would personally enjoy. For example, tuck a "love" note somewhere for them to find unexpectedly.

Trust—Keep confidences. They need a confidante, friend, or someone they can tell their deepest secrets to without worrying they will tell someone else or judge them for their actions. One way to earn their trust is to share something personal about yourself.

CHAPTER 16
PLANNERS
UNDER
STRESS

COULD YOU PLEASE NOT
SWALLOW SO LOUD?

When Planners are at their best, they are task and structure focused as well as serious and hardworking. They like to plan ahead and keep things organized. They care for their health and are dependable, reliable, and conscientious.

This style is known for being respectful, responsible, and cooperative. And ordinarily, they place traditions and family time high on their priority list.

However, when Planners are fatigued, stressed, or otherwise pushed to their limits they can dig in their heels and become overly rigid, self-righteous, and possessive. Normally productive, their helpful attitude can turn pessimistic, negative, and highly opinionated. They may worry about things they have no control over and get compulsive about the things they can control. They may get physically sick and are prone to complain about their symptoms in explicit details to others.

A Pooped-Out Planner

One semester, when I was teaching health classes at California State University, Stanislaus, we had just returned from a short Thanksgiving break. We were addressing the topic of stress management. I had asked my class what kinds of things caused them stress, and had already written several responses on the board, when one woman, Betty, called out, "My husband!" The class laughed as I added it to the list of other stressors. After a few other students contributed their responses, Betty yelled out again, "My husband!"

We all laughed even louder this time as I acknowledged her humor and underlined "My Husband!" on the chalkboard. Wanting to finish getting all of the class's thoughts on the board before getting any details or explanations about them, I encouraged the class to continue sharing the rest of their stressors. For a third time, Betty yelled out, "My husband!"

We all laughed again. This time there was no moving on. Burning with curiosity and still smiling with the rest of the class, I turned to Betty and asked. "Please share with us, what is it about your husband that stresses you out?"

Betty braced herself on her desk as she struggled to stand. The smiles of amusement shifted to concern as she turned around to address the class. "I have fibromyalgia," she explained. My body aches constantly and I can't sleep well."

Everyone gave their full attention to Betty as she continued. "For Thanksgiving, I made it quite clear to my husband that all I wanted to do this year was rest. It is a tradition in our family to make a huge turkey dinner with all the trimmings but I was just too darned tired. I have a hard time getting out of bed and moving around the house, let alone cooking a feast, so I told him, 'I am not doing Thanksgiving this year!' But do you think he understood? Do you think he had any sympathy for me? Oh no! He whined, 'But we always have Thanksgiving dinner; it just won't be Thanksgiving without it!'

I'm telling you, the man stresses me out! What did he expect from me? I try to keep the house clean, take care of the kids, hold down a part-time job, and go to school. I can barely get to my doctor appointments I'm so busy and in so much pain. So I told him, 'If you want Thanksgiving dinner you'll just have to cook it yourself. I need some rest!' With that, I turned and went upstairs to rest.

Do you think he was quiet so I could sleep? Oh no! I should be so lucky. I couldn't believe the noise the man was making! I could hear pots and pans clanging, cupboard doors banging, and him rustling around downstairs. Why me, I thought? Why can't he just be quiet so I can sleep? I pulled the pillow over my ears to try and drown out the noise. I tossed and turned, growing more irritated with every sound. Finally, I had just drifted off to sleep and guess what happens? Yep! My husband! He comes knocking on the door.

'Honey, wake up. Dinner is ready.'

Did the man not understand me? Did I not tell him all I wanted to do was rest? The man stresses me out. So still sleepy and aggravated more than ever, I got up to see what he was fussing about. I dragged myself downstairs and into the dining room.

Much to my surprise–he had dinner all spread out on the table. There was turkey and potatoes and even candles lit. I was impressed. I started to feel a bit guilty about all my complaining, that is, until I went to sit down and saw my kitchen!

I could not believe it! What a mess! What was he thinking? Do you think I can eat when my kitchen is dirty? No way! How could he do this to me? How dare he make more work for me! All I wanted to do was rest. And now I've got hours more work to do. So he offers to help. And you know what he does next..? (We were hanging on the edge of our seats in anticipation.) He takes the rag and gets it wet in the sink and he sloshes the water all over the counter. Then he takes the rag and sloshes it all over the stove. (At this point Betty noticed the blank stares on our faces.)

"Don't you get it?" she said making hand motions in the air in demonstration. "You're supposed to take the wet rag and wring it out. You wash one little section. Then you wet it and wring it out again and wash the next section. You don't slosh water everywhere! You complete one section before moving on to the next! The man drives me crazy! I told him to get out of my kitchen. I spent three hours cleaning up the mess. Dinner was cold, and I never got my nap! I'm telling you... THE MAN STRESSES ME OUT!"

What Brings Out the Worst

Planners are responsible by nature and usually take on a lot. It can be stressful when they or others are running late. It's also a stress when people try to pile more on their plates when their schedules are already jam-packed with priorities. Spur of the moment decisions can throw them off balance.

Once they set their goals and agenda, they typically have a clear picture in their minds of how the project, day, or event is going to unfold. If things change without warning–although out of their comfort zone and definitely stress inducing–they can usually figure out a way to adjust accordingly. However, when Planners are already extremely stressed and exhausted, unexpected changes and unmet expectations can overwhelm them.

Remember, for Planners, there is a right way and wrong way of doing things. Especially in times of stress, they want to maintain a sense of consistency and rely on their routines. They like a place for everything and everything in its place. Chaos, waste, things left undone (or done the "wrong way") are frustrating and having to repeat instructions they thought were clearly articulated can be exasperating.

Common Stressors

- Lack of follow through by others, when others don't do as they promised

- Taking on too many responsibilities

- Irresponsibility in others

- Untrustworthiness

- When things are not put back where they belong

- Not adhering to schedule or plans

- Lack of closure; having to switch what they are doing without completing it first

- Schedule conflicts; several things going on at the same time

- Indecision; leaving options up in the air for too long

- Frequent or unanticipated change

- Unclear expectations; lack of rules, instructions, or guidelines

- Not knowing where they fit in; lack of membership or belonging

- Lack of consistency, leadership, or master plan

- Lack of cooperation; when others don't carry their own load or do their part

- Not being appreciated

- Neglect of family time or traditions

- Waste

- Disorganization

- When someone lacking necessary skills is left responsible

- Missing deadlines or not enough time to complete tasks

- Rule breakers; rules or policies not being enforced

- Tardiness; self or others

- Interruptions

Planners normally thrive on responsibility. Usually, it is a source of strength for their self-esteem. However, this internal drive to be dependable and do the right thing, along with their desire to belong, can at times result in them taking on an overwhelming amount of duties. The feeling that they are the only ones that can carry out the duties can be so overwhelming that their body shuts down from the overload and they can become physically sick. In essence, if they will not take a break, their body does it for them. During times of stress and tremendous challenge, Planners' already existing need for consistency can intensify to an inordinate demand for control and excessive resistance to change. When the environment around them lacks rules, organization, and clear expectations they can become narrowly focused and overly system bound. They may complain that others are not doing their part or are doing things "wrong". In their own way, they are trying to relieve their stress while at the same time bring order to chaos, remain loyal to their families, organizations, and communities, and above all, be responsible.

Characteristics Under Stress

Finger Wagging—Complains, blames, and scolds. Gets irritable, edgy, blunt, critical, dispenses hurtful comments. Feels resentful and exasperated when expectations are not being met.

Supreme Court Justice—Imposes *their* uncompromising rules, standards or viewpoint. Self-righteous, increasingly intolerant and controlling. Rationalizes their insensitive behaviors as honorable.

Conducts Covert Missions—When extremely worried and overwhelmed they will take things into their own hands and may go behind peoples' backs to make decisions and get things done.

Scatterbrained—Forgetful and disorganized, lacking concentration. Unable to focus, second guesses self. Anxiety attacks, racing thoughts. Becomes unglued.

Eviction Notice—Writes off people, organizations, and ideas that they see as lacking appropriate standards or ethics. Like closing a door, they can shut people out and not give them a second chance.

Martyr—Sacrifices health by pushing beyond physical and emotional well-being needs. Continues forward with little sleep, food, or support to fulfill responsibilities for the sake of principle.

Physical Ailments—Headaches, upset stomach, body aches, and tense muscles. Chest pains, palpitations, insomnia, colds and infections. Accidents. Clenched jaw and grinding teeth.

Not surprisingly, Planners seek to maintain a certain equilibrium of responsibility. Too much or too little can cause them stress. Their mood can plummet when they are unsure of their roles or do not feel they are useful.

Sometimes lack of closure on projects or even issues from the past can cause them to worry or disturb them in the present. They can become frazzled by situations where they feel they have lost control.

The following suggestions are ways for Planners to reinforce their self-esteem and lower their stress levels. If you have Planner as your most dominant style, determine the underlying cause of your stress. Is it lack of closure on a past issue? Not feeling needed? Too many responsibilities? Keep looking beneath the surface to figure it out. Once you realize the cause of your stress, it will help you choose which areas you will want to concentrate on. Try the following suggestions that apply to your circumstances to discover which strategies work best for you.

If You Are A Planner

Enough Is Enough—Set realistic limits. Go home when your shift ends, leave your work at work, call in sick when you

are not feeling well. The house doesn't have to be "clean-clean" all of the time. Realize that you will never be absolutely 100% caught up to your own high standards. It's okay. Sometimes the best use of your time at the moment is to rest and recuperate.

Validate Yourself—Acknowledge all the things you accomplish and all your contributions. You are respectful, responsible, and loyal. You try very hard to do a good job. Know that your efforts are appreciated even if it isn't always expressed in a way that you recognize and value.

Get Involved—Find a place to belong. Volunteer for a hospital, retirement community, or school. Join a service organization, support group, church, etc. Take a class on something that you enjoy and contribute to the success of the class.

Focus on What You Can Control—When things around you seem to be unraveling, notice the areas that you do have control over. One of them is your perception of the event. Pay attention to the words you are using to describe a situation. Do you label it as a disaster or an opportunity to learn something?

Start New Traditions—Are some of your traditions adding more stress than pleasure? Maybe it is time to enlist some help or modernize a tradition. Just because it's always been done a certain way does not mean it is still the best way. Embrace change and explore new ideas.

Give Yourself a Break, Delegate—Be aware of trying to drive others as hard as you drive yourself. Learn when things are good enough. If you are able to let go of having things accomplished in a certain manner, you open up all kinds of possibilities for delegation of responsibilities. This will leave you more freedom to focus on other matters. Realize that sometimes others are eager to pitch in and help.

Be Responsible...For Yourself—Take the time to take care of yourself. You have an obligation to spend time nourishing your health and well-being. How can you possibly perform your duties if you yourself are in no condition to do so? It is of utmost importance that you explore and find avenues for self-preservation. Set aside time for yourself and place as much value and priority on it as you do on your other responsibilities. Spend this time doing things you enjoy.

Bring Closure to Past Issues—Because Planners honor tradition and ceremony, sometimes that is just what it takes to bring a past issue to completion. Eve Delunas, Ph.D. describes in her book, *Survival Games Personality Play*, some creative ways to perform a ceremony. She writes, "These ceremonies can be formal or informal; they can take place in or out of the therapist's office. They may involve writing, speaking, announcing, presenting, eating, drinking, building, creating, burning, burying, planting, cleaning, gifting, or journeying—and even flushing a toilet."

Lighten Up—Enjoy the process, not just the success of completing a goal. Inform others of your needs without nagging. Although it is always a good idea to let others know what your expectations are, let go of what they "should" or "must" do.

Leave Leeway—All of your time does not need to be scheduled with productive activities. When scheduling, leave some wiggle-room for unexpected events. Reframe your ideas of what is responsible and include relaxation.

How to Help Reduce Stress for Planners

Some of the very same suggestions for relating to Planners from the earlier chapter are excellent ways to help them keep stress levels to a minimum. Following these tips will help ensure that you are not adding to their pressures.

Be Responsible—If you said you would do something, honor your commitment. Do what it takes to follow through in a timely manner. Be as thorough and accurate as you can. Planners are dependable, and they expect that others will be too. If you have an appointment with a Planner, be on time or even early. They interpret it as a sign of respect and responsibility when you are on time and, as disrespect and irresponsibility when you are late.

Acknowledge Them for Their Contributions—Planners work hard to be responsible above and beyond the call of duty. When they perceive that they are being taken for granted it can be disheartening for them. Let them know how much you appreciate their contributions. Comment on their planning, organizing, thoroughness, efficiency, and assistance to the organization or family as a whole. Hold a recognition ceremony to acknowledge their accomplishments. Give them gifts, cards, plaques, or other awards. Although they may not admit it or request it, they enjoy tangible recognition.

Be Consistent—It is very stressful to almost anyone and especially Planners when they are treated inconsistently. For example, if they are respected one day and treated negatively the next. Knowing what is supposed to happen or what is expected is a very secure feeling for them. Once a rule, norm, or procedure is established they want to be able to count on it. If a rule is not enforceable, then change it so it can be. Making exceptions all the time can undermine the efforts of Planners who are trying to abide by the rules and do their best to see to it that others abide, too. Also, stick to the schedule. As mentioned, Planners flourish with predictability. They appreciate it when things start on time and end on time. Keep with your agenda if at all possible. Planners usually have their own time planned in a fairly tight schedule. If you don't stick to yours, it can throw theirs off tremendously.

Show Respect—Demonstrate respect for them, for authority, and for the organization by not gossiping or complaining unless you have suggestions for improvement. Clean up after yourself and put things back where they belong. When you leave messes it can be very irritating and frustrating to Planners, who just cannot leave it that way. If something is out of order, they feel compelled to make it right. If you know Planners who are under a lot of stress, remember to at least not create more work and frustration for them.

Provide Clear Expectations—Planners appreciate knowing where they stand and what is expected of them. To leave them guessing is one of the most stressful things you can do to a Planner. If they do not know the rules or procedures, they will take the initiative to try and establish some for themselves. And, if they have guessed wrong and violated some unspoken rule, they can be crushed. After all, they were doing the best they could under the circumstances, and now their attempt to be responsible has been stained by the feeling that they have done something "wrong." They try at all costs to be "right" and appropriate.

Conserve, Don't Waste—Planners find it very irresponsible to throw away things that feasibly can still be used, to order things in greater quantity than needed, and to consume precious time in inefficient ways. If too much time is spent doing things that could be done more efficiently if others were more conscientious, responsible, or organized, it can be draining to a Planner. Notice how things can be reasonably done differently to save time, energy, and resources.

Plan Ahead—Be especially careful not to wait until the last minute to make requests or changes with Planners who are already under a great amount of stress. This may cause them to become overbearing and rigid, even snappy or bossy. It's always a good idea to give

191

Planners the time they require to be thorough in completing a project. This becomes even more important if they are already pushed beyond their limits.

Give Them Responsibility—Planners can feel worthless and bored without some kind of responsibility where their efforts contribute to the family, organization, or community. Many times people make the mistake of not wanting to impose on others by asking for their assistance. Well meaning friends and relatives may avoid delegating tasks, especially around holidays. But responsibility can be just what a stressed out Planners is actually seeking. Planners enjoy doing their part to pitch in. With this in mind, pay attention to whether the Planner you are dealing with is stressed from boredom and lack of duty or because they are overwhelmed. If it's lack of participation that is causing them to stress, invite them to participate. If they are overwhelmed, by all means give them some room to relax a little.

Honor Their Traditions—What is important to you? Planners place a high priority and value on their traditions. This can sometimes get in the way of other people's enjoyment who may want to do things differently for a change. Keep in mind that Planners find rituals and ceremonies comforting, a sort of solid foundation to stand on. Traditions help keep the past alive and are important for making transitions to the next year, season, relationship, job, or even task. If your intention is to reduce stress for the Planners in your life, embracing their traditions or supporting them by helping to create new ones are great ways to do it.

Encourage Them—Let them know you think it is equally important to their other responsibilities for them to schedule time to take care of themselves. Find out their interests and encourage them to pursue ways to get involved.

CHAPTER 17
MOVERS
UNDER
STRESS

When Movers are at their best they are versatile, spontaneous, self-confident, resourceful, and decisive. Their playful manner can brighten up a mundane chore and add fun to a workday. However, Movers can be very intimidating when they are stressed or low on esteem. They can become exceedingly pushy, overly aggressive, and confrontational—even physically violent. Placed in an overly restrictive environment, they will go to great extremes to gain their freedom or control.

A Depleted Mover

Roy is a talented carpenter. Using tools and figuring out how to build things comes naturally for him. He could build a house all by himself if he wanted to. His skills range from pouring the concrete for the foundation to tiling the roof. Knowing he is talented contributes to Roy's natural cockiness. He enjoys being the center of attention in most circumstances, and he loves to take charge.

As a subcontractor, Roy accepted a job putting up a new housing division. He enjoyed showing off his skills to his coworkers who were not as experienced. The crew looked up to Roy and would, almost without question, follow his lead. He was assertive and confident. He seemed to always know the quickest, most cost-effective way to get a job done. He would find ways to finish projects, even if he had to do it himself. He enjoyed the challenge. In fact, just to spice things up, Roy would cajole the men into making bets with him about who could do something faster or better. If they were reluctant, he would harass them until they did. Of course, when he bet, he never lost, even if he had to cheat just a bit to win.

Roy also had a habit of stretching his lunch hours, horsing around, and generally not following his foreman's directions. Leo, the foreman, was tired of Roy running the show. Roy would overrule Leo's decisions and practically take over projects, telling the rest of the crew what to do.

It wasn't long before Leo started taking verbal digs at Roy, downplaying his skills and denigrating his techniques as useless or idiotic. When Roy would recommend a better way of approaching a task, Leo would overrule it and insist the crew follow his instructions. If Roy made a clever joke or funny comment, Leo would immediately scold him and remark that he would never amount to anything if he didn't get serious about his work.

One day Leo reprimanded Roy in front of the whole crew. So the next morning Roy decided to be later than "usual." Instead of taking his coffee and donuts to the work site, Roy sat in the coffee shop and enjoyed a leisurely breakfast. "Leo isn't going to tell me what to do," he thought to himself. "After all, I always complete my jobs on schedule, if not ahead of time. Who cares if I'm a little late showing up?"

By the time Roy finally showed up at the construction site, Leo was fuming. Roy was pleased. He walked right past Leo with a smirk on his face and began his work.

"Good morning," Leo said. "Nice of you to finally show up."

"I thought you'd appreciate it," retorted Roy.

"This isn't funny, Roy," said Leo.

Movers Under Stress - Chapter 17

"Where is your sense of responsibility?"

"My responsibility is to show up and get the job done!" taunted Roy. By now the rest of the men on the crew had paused and started to gather around in anticipation of a show-down.

"Your responsibility includes showing up on time!" Leo shouted, losing his composure.

"On time is when I@!%# get here!" retorted Roy.

"You had better start showing up on time or you're fired!" threatened Leo.

"@!%# you, old man! You can't fire me 'cause I @!%# quit!" blasted Roy. "Who cares about this @!%# job anyway! I can find a job anywhere! I don't need this @!%#!"

Roy seized a large wrench that was lying nearby and hurled it at a huge bay window, shattering it on impact. He grabbed his tools and huffed off the site and into his pickup truck. He put a tape in his tape player and turned it up full blast. "Take this job and shove it!" the lyrics blared. Roy spun his truck in several circles in the dirt, blowing up quite a cloud of dust.

"@!%# you!" He yelled as he pulled away from the audience at the construction site. Of course, he made sure to wave his arm out of the window—complete with a one-finger salute.

What Brings Out the Worst

Movers are made to be on the go. If they are required to remain stagnant for long periods, they can get very restless. Rarely ones to sit on the sidelines, this style likes to be part of the action and they want to be able to act NOW! When opportunities arise, they want to be able to seize them in the moment. It's stressful when they feel they have missed out. Wanting to charge ahead, they can get bogged down by details and too much processing. Rules, protocol and obligations can be stressful and make them feel trapped without choice.

Because this style is "now" focused, they like to act swiftly. Waiting can be like slow death. This includes slow talkers, slow drivers, and indecisiveness.

Often energetic and physical, boredom and complacency are stressors. Whether they admit it or not, most enjoy the adrenaline rush of chaos or even an occasional crisis and get stressed if life seems too smooth and uneventful. Although they love their leisure time, it can cause them stress if they lack a challenge or don't have any clear goals.

195

They enjoy credit for accomplishing something with finesse and can get frustrated if their talents aren't recognized, even if it is only for a spit second!

Common Stressors

Lack of freedom or choices

Feeling trapped

Being forced to do something another person's way

Not being able to use their skills

Rigidness

Strict guidelines or rules

Forced to keep quiet or not participate

Insufficient attention

No sense of humor

Waiting; slow actions

Indecisiveness

Traffic or car problems

Routine

Lack of sex

Details; paperwork

Inactivity or restriction of physical movement

Lack of money

In the story at the beginning of this chapter, Roy was provoked quite a bit by his foreman, Leo. Instead of setting boundaries and providing enough wiggle room for Roy to express his own style, Leo stifled Roy when he tried to use his skills. He belittled him for being playful and minimized his talents as inadequate. This would probably be a tough situation for anyone to handle. However, the way in which Roy reacted was not very resourceful–coming to work late on purpose, swearing at his foreman, and throwing things. There are better ways to channel one's energy.

When feeling threatened, Movers will use their powerful confidence to instill fear in others–fear that Movers will lose their temper, neglect their responsibilities, otherwise embarrass, or even leave the person, job, or situation.

Characteristics Under Stress

Raging Rapidly—Quick to blow up. Throws things, belligerent, loud. Gets aggressive physically and verbally. Resorts to name calling and inappropriate, cruel comments.

Risky Business—Sex, drugs and rock n' roll. Indulges in substance abuse, cheating, gambling, speeding, driving out of control. Adrenalin behaviors: playing "chicken" with vehicles and people.

Hits Panic Button—Frantic, alarms others with "urgent" emergencies and fabricated deadlines. Makes situations seem critical needing immediate action. goes to "DEFCON 1, red alert".

Snark Attacks—Dismissive, sarcastic, derogatory, mocking, snippy, cranky, edgy. Plays mean practical jokes to make others look foolish.

Win at All Costs—Behaves unethically. Uses manipulative, illicit methods to achieve their goals. "Damns the torpedoes", oblivious to external realities and consequences. Rejects rational advice.

Blame Game—Faults other people, organizations, or society for their predicament. Proclaims "Not me, not my fault". Finger pointing, makes up excuses in the moment, condemns others "guilty".

Quits—Takes toys and goes home. Cuts off, breaks up, leaves, drops out, detaches, burns bridges. Behaves in an unconcerned superficial manner, blows people off, finds a new audience to entertain.

It's the times when Movers act before pausing to determine the consequences that cause the most trouble for themselves and others. For instance, they may not want to wait for the "go ahead" from a spouse or boss and may make snap decisions they later regret.

Add the criticism of others on top of this ill thought-out decision, and you are sitting on a powder keg.

Their urge for immediate gratification and action can get them into trouble if they are not careful.

To try and circumvent the drain that boredom, lack of money, time constraints, or other restrictions can cause, some Movers may turn to stimulants such as caffeine, nicotine, or other drugs to help them regain their energy or spark. They may defiantly break rules, challenge

others, and even stir up trouble just for entertainment.

If you are a Mover, use the following tips to help you get along with others and keep your playfulness an asset, not a liability.

If You Are A Mover

Your quick thinking and demand for action can get you ahead of yourself. Since you usually enjoy operating in a rush of adrenaline, you might have a tendency to arrange your life so you are constantly on the edge and perhaps putting others on edge as well. What you may find fun and exhilarating, others may perceive as stressful. In fact, the people in your life that are depending on you may not find your behavior very fun at all.

So how do you get your own needs for freedom, spontaneity, and attention met without trampling others in the process? The following are some suggestions.

Go Have Some Fun—Filling up your fun tank will fuel your tolerance and multiply your motivation to cooperate with others. Instead of trying to get a majority of your needs for fun and games met at work, where it could be detrimental to your employment status or even the health and safety of yourself and others, find other avenues. What do you like to do for fun? Get out. Go motorcycle riding, visit amusement parks, attend concerts, or venture out for some camping. Joke around, sing, play in the rain, splash in the mud. It is important to your overall wellbeing to include play in your life. Do it safely and legitimately.

Start Your Own Business—If you are tired of conforming to the rules and procedures of others, why not be your own boss? It is important to either find ways to love what you are doing or do something else. If you are wise enough to research your options and plan ahead in your investments of time, money, and resources, owning your own business can meet several of your needs all at once.

WELL? WHATAYA THINK?

Make an Impression—You can be in the spotlight in a variety of ways. Choose inspiring, motivating ways. At work, be the best you can be. Let your actions speak for themselves. It is much more impressive than getting attention for breaking the rules. Capture the interest of others by sharing our triumphs at appropriate times. Display your trophies and be proud of your accomplishments. At play, practice your skills, pour yourself into your endeavors.

Get Hands-On—Use your love of tools to create. Build something–if not a house then a sand castle. If you want to develop your skills, take a class on auto repair, sculpting, landscaping, glass-

blowing...what are you interested in? Choose something and go for it!

Move That Body—Get some physical activity. Exercise: pump iron, jump rope, climb trees. When stressed, go for a walk, jog, or run to cool off–but do come back when your thinking clears. Get out and dance, roller skate, bike ride, something that will get you in action–*NOW!*

Find Other Movers—It can be very stressful to have to guard every word and action in order not to upset those around you. Having other Movers who will not take your complaining as insults and can hear your words through your colorful language is like breathing fresh air.

Reward Yourself—Be aware of any tendency to set high goals in the moment, then get overwhelmed and disappointed in the next. Remember to notice the things that you do accomplish. Pay attention to achievements along the way to the big one. Set up a system of immediate reward. For instance, if you are trying to quit smoking, instead of feeling like a failure for slipping and smoking one cigarette, reward yourself for all the ones you did not smoke.

Compete—Get involved in competitions and games. Take charge of arranging events if that's what it takes. Join a sports team, create a contest at work, challenge your neighbors to a cook-off. Find ways to compete that won't jeopardize your job, health, budget or relationships.

Focus—Concentrate on one thing and complete it before starting something else. Reduce distractions by turning off your phone or putting away projects that are not a priority at the moment.

Prioritize—Decide what is most important and what has to be addressed. Complete the most important project before moving on to the next one.

Keep Healthy Habits—Notice when you may be slipping into unhealthy, compulsive behaviors, such as:

Lacking sleep because of too much partying or "extracurricular" activities

Using drugs

Drinking too much

Smoking

Gambling or taking financial risks

Overeating

Taking physical risks (i.e., driving over the speed limit)

Overindulging in sex

Take Inventory, Then Take Action—Figure out what is most important to you and what is or isn't working in your life. Find out how others succeed at overcoming unhealthy habits. Then do it even better than they do! Grab hold of your life with the same enthusiasm that you grab hold of the moment.

How to Help Reduce Stress for Movers

Movers are generally optimistic and enthusiastic. If you are flexible and want to encourage them, little effort will be required to boost their mood. You can add a bit of excitement to your life by allowing a Mover to entertain or provide ways to create a contest or game. They love to perform and volunteer readily for leadership roles that involve taking risks.

When you understand their core needs and values, you can provide them with an environment that allows and encourages them to express themselves. Not only will you engender their respect and appreciation, you will ensure their future cooperation and support. They will comply with home and work rules when you allow them "time-outs" or private counseling instead of a public showdown.

The following are suggestions for preventing Movers from over stressing or burning out. These suggestions can also help Movers that are stressed or feeling down about themselves to lighten up. Some of them may fit with your values and rules of operation; others may not. The fact is, they do work. Only you can decide if they are right for you and the various relationships in your life. There is a big difference between encouraging Movers to shine versus allowing them to bulldoze over your needs. It may take a bit of fine-tuning to incorporate these changes into your relationships.

Allow Them Freedom and Choices—Movers want options, including doing nothing if they choose. Just knowing they can opt out of a situation or have other choices can give them a sense of comfort and lower stress levels. Do not impose unnecessary duties, schedules, or rules just for your sense of control or comfort. They will inevitably find ways to get around them anyway. Give them opportunities to offer solutions based on their experiences. Respect their relaxed ways. Leave room for spontaneity. Share your sense of humor.

Give Them Attention—Let them show off their skills. Recognize the impact of their presence. Validate their talents. You can stimulate Movers to greater achievement by providing tangible incentives for jobs well done; rewarding their cleverness, creativity, and ingenuity; and praising their ability to accomplish things.

Be Consistent, Not a Bully—Movers often rebel against discipline and will resist an order if given too rigidly, without any leeway for creativity or flair. It threatens their self-esteem and puts them down. Be firm and direct with them, but not challenging or threatening. Formulate ground rules for behavior with their input "up front." Enforce the rules consistently. Discuss options. That way, before they take any liberties, you give them permission to do what they love doing.

Make It a Game—Appeal to their sense of adventure by making a bet, dare, or contest. If it feels like a "have-to" it is not fun. Do the unexpected. Tell them they can't do something. For example, "I'll bet there's no way you can have this done by Monday—only an expert could do that. It's just too much." Chances are they'll prove you wrong.

Supply Immediate Feedback—Give them recognition and straightforward critiques. Let them know immediately when they violate a rule. If you let it slide, most likely it will happen repeatedly. Equally, give them instant acknowledgment for a job well done.

Note their quickness of action, their flair and skillfulness.

Get Out of Their Way—Movers are concrete problem solvers who need hands-on activities. The thought of sitting for hours doing one thing seems like a slow death-sentence to them. Give them the freedom to demonstrate their ideas verbally and physically. So many people unknowingly stifle the flair and productivity of Movers by bogging them down with rituals, routines, and personal rules. Although this is not the way to inspire them, Movers do like to be efficient. You may be surprised at the proficiency they can achieve. If they are given the freedom to develop their talents, they may feel more compelled to pay attention to the ground rules. This is because they can focus their attention

of doing a good job rather than the perceived restrictions placed on them.

Be Confident—Speak and move with confidence. If you are too wishy-washy, some Movers get an irresistible urge to walk all over you. However, be careful to recognize the difference between assertiveness and aggressiveness. The latter can trigger a fight with an out-of-esteem Mover. Be direct and clear on what you expect.

Move With Them—Movers find predictable routine tedious and boring. Frequent change of pace and variety will help eliminate much of their stress. Don't make them sit still while they talk with you. Be willing to walk from room to room or conduct business while playing a sport.

Appreciate Their Directness—Allow them to be open and expressive. Of course, this does not mean that it is okay for them to swear at a board meeting or do similarly inappropriate things. What it does mean is to give the benefit of the doubt. Remember that most Movers are looking for the shortest route to reach their goals. They may not take the time to say "good morning," "please," and "thank you". They will sometimes leave these words and rapport-building rituals out of their vocabulary because they are looking straight at their target and aiming to get there quickly.

Some people may think they are doing Movers a favor by trying to "train" them to pause and say "hello" before allowing them to continue with their agenda. Although this may work when trying to train children, if you have not had much success or are aggravating the situation, skip it. Movers find it condescending and controlling.

Respect is relative anyway. Watch two Movers interact. Notice if either one is insulted by the other's bluntness. Usually, it is a relief to them to be able to cut to the chase.

Understand Their Need to Multitask—Recognize their desire for variety and for accomplishing more than one thing at a time. One of the biggest complaints about Movers' behavior is that they do not pay attention or make good eye contact. If you want to bring out the best in them, quit expecting them to sit still. They really are able to work on other things while talking to you. Waiting to get their full attention seldom does much good. They may indulge you by looking at you but their mind will be elsewhere.

CHAPTER 18
THINKERS
UNDER
STRESS

When Thinkers are at their best, they are some of the most fascinating people to be around. Their passion for improvement and visionary ideas can be awe-inspiring! Their tenacity for creating solutions and their expansive knowledge base are a magical combination for seeing concepts brought to fruition and introduced to the world. They have natural abilities for decision-making, being objective, and weighing the data to be considered. They are envied by those that wish they were able to stand their ground and express their point of view with conviction and confidence.

203

Thinkers' love of their work and high expectations are admired by those stuck in jobs they hate. Although they may not be very involved socially in the mainstream, they are pleasant to be around. If you earn their trust, you can experience their deep, caring feelings and lasting friendship.

However, when Thinkers get stressed, their patience wears thin and things that may have only slightly irritated them previously can become unbearable. Like Dr. Jekyll and Mr. Hyde, Thinkers can shift from an otherwise intelligent, rational person to someone who is critical, uncompromising, condescending, and harsh. Their typical wit and amusing sarcasm can become intentionally caustic ridicule. Their composure may switch from their usually objective demeanor to judgmental, demanding, and controlling. Or, they can become withdrawn, ritualistic and detached—not interacting with others, refusing to take part.

A Stressed-Out Thinker

Jack slouched in his chair with his legs extended straight out in front of him. His arms were crossed in front of his chest. Instead of sharing in the smiles and laughter of the other audience members, he sat in obvious defiance with a deadpan look of boredom and irritation on his face.

This was the last workshop of the two-day staff retreat. Not being given any other choice, he had already attended the required workshops on team building, collaborative change, and appreciating diversity. His mind was stagnant and bored. His comments had been met with impatience, and his questions with exasperation. How else was he supposed to keep his mind from going comatose if he couldn't give or get any decent input? He was almost trembling inside at the thought of having to sit through this last workshop.

The facilitator was one of those smiling "rah-rah cheerleader" types. She had started an interactive exercise activity. It was a version of the old "telephone" game. Several people were given a cartoon illustration to view. After looking at the picture, they would tell the person next to them what they saw, that person would tell the next one, and so on down the line until the last person in the row was told the story. When all groups were finished, the last person in each row stood up to tell what their story turned out to be. The participants were bursting with laughter as they listened to story after story.

Rolling his eyes, Jack let out a deliberately loud groan. "What the heck do these people find so amusing?" he thought to himself. "This is such a waste of time and brain cells. This is stupid."

Suddenly Jack stood up and stormed his way to the front of the room, abruptly snatching the microphone from the instructor's hand. "EXCUSE ME, PEOPLE!" he yelled aggressively, scowling first at the instructor, then at the audience. "We all learned this in the second grade," he barked. "I know I did! Can we just get to the point? You guys are all acting like a bunch of idiots! Why do we have to endure these touchy-feely games to make a point? 'A message can get misconstrued if you do not get it straight from the source. Check your facts to make sure they are accurate.' There, that is the point. Now can we get on to some information that we don't already know?"

What Brings Out the Worst

Often referred to as "heady intellectuals", Thinkers seek knowledge and information. Intellectual stagnation, redundancy and having to "dumb down" to interact with others can be frustrating. This style craves competence and finds situations that would have them look foolish very stressful. The also get stressed over the stupidity of others. Lack of data or equipment failure get in the way of them being able to be competent. Thinkers can be tenacious in figuring out how to solve a problem or design an efficiently functioning system. Lack of progress, equipment failure and limited vision of those surrounding them are all stressors.

Independent by nature, Thinkers are usually quite comfortable working on their own, unencumbered; so micromanaging and unessential input are unwelcome frustrations. They don't like the expectation that they should want to participate in social functions out of obligation or ritual and have a disdain for "chit chat". If a Thinker is resorting

to emotional outbursts such as Jack displayed, you know he has been pushed beyond his limits.

Common Stressors

Impositions on their ability to display their intelligence

Overly sensitive people

No flexibility

Being limited to standard curriculum

People who don't try to solve their own problems

Not understanding or knowing something

Equipment failure

Incompetence, stupidity

Not enough time to gather data

Unfairness

Boredom

Lack of independence

Rules that block progress

Redundancy, routine

Nothing new to look forward to

Emotional outbursts

Mistakes

Ignored recommendations

No system in place or failure of others to use system

Made to look stupid or incompetent

From the preceding story and list you probably can understand what triggered Jack's response. He had no choice but to sit through workshops that he was not interested in. His questions and comments were met with irritation instead of attention, and he did not enjoy the invasive nature of the "touchy-feely" activities. However, had his self-esteem been strong in the first place he would have figured out a way to be more resourceful. He could have made up his mind to support those around him in their growth, knowing strategically that it would not only be an investment in *their* future but *his* as well.

Characteristics Under Stress

Analysis Paralysis—Over-scrutinizes a situation so much that a decision or action is never taken. Overwhelmed with too many details, fears making any decision could lead to flawed results.

Wanders WebMD—Excessively preoccupied with worry and convinced they have a serious illness. Perceives aliments and afflictions despite the absence of any actual medical condition.

So Misunderstood—Feels no one understands them. Gets trapped in a "brain asylum" of always having to "dumb down" their complex thoughts so the "commoner" can comprehend. Becomes cryptic, enigmatic, and ambiguous.

Obstinate—Once convinced of their logic they refuse to alter their course, change their opinion or plans. Views commitments as entrapments. Goes against rules believing they don't apply to them.

Disappearing Act—Retreats to their cave or fortress of solitude. May be physically present during conversation but doesn't actively listen. Tunes outs, withdraws, ignores. Shuts down, refuses to interact.

No Fault Guarantee—Quick to blame circumstances, people, or technology for their situation. Comes up with a plethora of facts and conspiracies which "explain" the reasons for their state of affairs.

Tongue Lashing—Sarcastic, biting, angry outbursts. Uncharacteristically harsh criticism, personal attacks. Exaggeration of faults, everything is "the absolute worst". Condescending, insulting, demeaning.

Not all Thinkers lash out when their fuse runs short. Some won't speak at all and will withdraw their cooperation, input, support, or even their love. They've been known to cut off a relationship or friendship and not look back. Others refuse to make decisions or may get overly obsessed with unrealistic expectations; pressuring others through intellectual arguments, requiring things be absolutely accurate, correct, and perfect. Or, quite the opposite, some Thinkers drop their standards, fail to implement ideas, become apathetic, and retreat into their "cave" (as author John Gray puts it).

If You Are
A Thinker

If you are a Thinker and feel yourself getting stressed, it is time to shift your focus outward. You are a big-picture thinker in many areas, so use this ability and apply it to your personal situations. What you focus on is what becomes real for you, so relocate your focus to more empowering thoughts and ideas. What possibilities are you not noticing? Expand your thinking to include empathy for others and their journey in life.

Balance Your Critiques—Refrain from "punishing" or getting irritated at others for not living up to your expectations and high standards. For each drawback or mistake you notice, find a positive point. Pay attention to how much control you really have over a given situation. If you are stuck in a situation where you have to sit through a boring lecture, discover what you can learn or find ways to support others. Take action to change the things that you can and recognize the things that you simply cannot so you can channel your energy into other pursuits that are higher on your priority list.

Honor Your Independence—You are not anti-social, a misfit, or unfriendly just because you prefer independent activities. Don't force yourself to get involved with activities you are not interested in just because of social pressures. If you are involved in activities to stretch your comfort zones and are growing from the experience–that is one thing. But if you find that you are feeling less alive and fulfilled, lacking somehow, because you are not enjoying it, shift your attention to the things you do like. You have the unique ability and nature to be content and savor solo activities. Enjoy them!

Validate Your Interests—Browse the web; visit universities, museums, and research centers; take classes. Feed your hunger for knowledge. Many Thinkers mention that people have called them "weird" because of the topics of conversations and endeavors they choose to involve themselves in. There are plenty of others with similar interests. It's just a matter of finding them.

Pay Attention to Your Physical Condition—If your health goes down the tubes because you are not taking a break to exercise and eat well, how do you expect to have your full capabilities to work at your potential? Design a strategy for maintaining your health. Investigate programs and create one that fits your particular needs. For fun, chart your progress.

Smile—Interacting with others in a friendly manner can open up worlds. If you are not used to smiling and relating with others on a "personal" level, try an experiment. Make it a point to notice others, not just the people that you know and like. Smile at them as you pass them. (Seriously, a simple smile can change the way that others perceive and relate to you.) Notice the effect that it has. Shifting your focus outward in the presence of others can help you establish rapport, gain cooperation, and open doors of opportunities that otherwise would have been closed.

Reach Out to Others—It may be a habit of yours to try to solve your problems all by yourself. Although this is resourceful in many situations, there are times when it is beneficial to seek answers with the help of others. Who can you confide in or turn to for personal, not just work-related, assistance?

Prioritize—Learn to discern the difference between things that really do need to be perfect and those that just need to be done. Spend your energies perfecting the important ones. Weigh the investment versus the payoff. Is it more useful to you to have someone behave according to your standards and be unhappy or to have someone be happy at the sacrifice of perfection?

Invite Yourself to Make Mistakes—It is a required criterion for success to be able to adjust and make refinements. Think about what you feel that you cannot do and give yourself permission to try. Allow for results that are less than perfect the first time out. Challenge yourself to see how well you can do an average job on something. If you do an average job, you win! If you end up doing a better than average job, you still win.

Recognize You Can Only Change Yourself—You can definitely have an influence on others. Though you may be able to help them change, they must be the ones to make the change. Realize that people are responsible for their own behaviors and attitudes.

Read—Pick up a copy of *A Guide for Rational Living* (1997), by psychotherapists Albert Ellis, Ph.D. and Robert A. Harper, Ph.D. It offers a revolutionary approach that "can teach any intelligent person how to stop feeling miserable about practically anything." This book contains no-nonsense methods, backed by hundreds of research studies, for changing self-defeating behaviors. It set new standards in the field of psychology, providing answers to help people deal with their lives more effectively.

How to Help Reduce Stress for Thinkers

Most Thinkers want understanding and their own space, not a whole lot of emotional attention and doting. Typically, Thinkers will not confide in anyone when they are having difficulties. If they do, it would only be with a choice individual or two. If Thinkers do confide in you, they are usually to the point of seeking solutions or suggestions, otherwise they would not bother to mention their problems at all.

To cope with challenges Thinkers have a tendency to isolate themselves or bury themselves in their work. They may even turn to mind-altering alternatives, such as drugs or hypnosis, fringe organizations, or the metaphysical realm, to find solutions to whatever it is that is bothering them. You might not be able to tell when they are under minor stress, but if you pay attention, you can tell when they are majorly stressed. Sometimes there is little you can do besides understand and not take things personally.

The following are ways that you can support Thinkers in reducing their stress. If you follow these suggestions on a regular basis in relating to the Thinkers in your life, it can help prevent them from getting stressed out in the first place (at least by you).

Notice When They are Being Affectionate or Complimentary— Thinkers can have covert or subtle ways of showing affection or giving a commendation. It may appear in the form of a joke or even a nod of the head accompanied by a smile. Sometimes they are disappointed when people miss their intended recognition, yet they usually will not turn up the volume to make it more obvious. Instead they will just let it drop. Pay attention to their unique style of demonstrating approval or affection. You may be surprised to discover what you've been missing has been there all along. You just didn't recognize it.

Recognize the Value and Usefulness of Their Endeavors—Accept their futuristic, idealistic nature and quest for perfect performance. Provide opportunities for them to choose tasks that are difficult and challenging. Although Thinkers like acknowledgment for their ideas, creativity, and competence, they will not seek it out as readily as others. Let them know their contributions are important and their work appreciated. However, take heed not to pretend you know something about their project when you don't. This will only irritate them more! Don't go overboard with the emotional displays and stick to the specifics of why you find their work so valuable.

Understand Their Emotions are Deep— And that's where they like them–kept down deep, not on their sleeve. Quit expecting the Thinkers in your life to display emotion in the same way that you do. They may not want to say "I love you," or show a lot of affection. For many Thinkers it is just not in their nature. Those with this style can be a lot like cats. Some cats love to give and receive affection; others will run away if you approach them. Some come to you at their own pace. And, some won't accept or show affection altogether, no matter how hard you try. Thinkers have their own way of showing ardor. Usually, it does not include public displays like holding hands and kissing in front of an audience.

However with that said, there are numerous variations and of course there are always the exceptions. Some Thinkers show plenty of affection, especially when their second style is Connector and they like it when you do, too. The key is knowing the difference between your needs and desires and theirs.
If both parties respect the wishes of the other then they can get along without compromising their own needs.

Honor Their Privacy—Unless you know them really, really well, when they are reluctant to share personal anecdotes, don't pry. They will share when you have earned their trust. If they don't eventually open up, that's okay too. Many times they prefer to talk about ideas and events, rather than relationship or personal issues. If you enjoy discussing personal issues, find someone else who does too, and give the Thinkers a break.

Allow Them Independence—Thinkers have the ability to be content with solo activities. Just because you may need to be surrounded by people does not mean that they do. Don't label them as antisocial or pressure them to get involved in activities that simply are not of interest to them. Yes, it is beneficial to experience a variety of things, but just because you enjoy an activity does not mean they will. If you are in a personal relationship with a Thinker, negotiate for a balance of independent and together time. Thinkers like to feel included but not coerced.

Demonstrate Logic Behind Rules—Their need to understand the reasoning behind rules and procedures, and their reluctance to obey them blindly, comes from the fact that they are usually thinking of a better way of doing things. Make sure you have a valid explanation of why things need to be done a certain way. Be open to listening to their ideas for improvement. Perhaps it is time for a change in the rules.

Consider Their Ideas—Sometimes people are so intimidated by Thinkers' imaginative concepts or style of explanation that they may simply avoid listening to their ideas. Hear them out. Ask them for the research that backs up their suggestions – you just might learn something. Open your mind to new options and ways of looking at things. Allow them the freedom to get "out of the box" with their ideas. If a Thinker presents you with an idea, odds are they have already done the "inside" work – considered the problem, worked through the possible solutions and selected the statistically "best" method to arrive at the desired outcome. Use this vast reservoir of intellectual brain power. While their solution may not be immediately practical to implement, it may spur some creative solutions you had not yet considered.

Provide Information When They Request It— Thinkers aim to be accurate and competent in their endeavors, so before they decide on a direction for action they like to have all the data. Don't dismiss their questions or scold their requests for proof. Just remember: "inquiring minds want to know."

Realize that Love of Their Work Does not Mean They Love You Less—Don't try to force them to make you their priority. Learn to live in conjunction with

their fervor for their work. Allow them opportunities to increase their knowledge and demonstrate their competence. How many ways can you find to be interested in their work?

Understand Their Sense of Humor— Thinkers' minds can conjure comedy from most any situation. They have an exceptional wit for word play and to imagine things in other contexts. They also enjoy the covert communication of sarcasm and the ambivalent state it can leave the receiver. If their humor is a bit too much for your taste, simply let them know without placing a lot of judgment and drama around it. If they get a rise from you, they are likely to do it again just to get your goat. Be aware that most Thinkers are not trying to harm others by their cynicism, they are simply pointing out the incongruity of life–which they find amusing. Don't take their humor personally.

Pay Attention to What They Need and Want—Your idea of showing how much you love them might be to give them a hug or cards and candy. They may want you to show your love for them in a different way. Be open to their needs and desires.

Beyond Personality

By using the personality concepts there is much you can contribute to reduce stress, solve conflicts, open up lines of communication, and understand the actions of others. However, sometimes a person has more going on underneath their stress that is definitely outside your area of influence.

On occasion, you may run across someone with mental illness, on heavy medications, abusing drugs, or who has serious psychological issues. Although following these guidelines is useful, it is not enough to overcome the influences of these circumstances. When a person's emotional well-being or self-esteem is extremely low, they may need to seek professional help. Use your common sense to know the difference between things over which you have some influence and those over which you do not.

Because this book is meant as a guideline, not an in-depth study of the personality styles, it is not a substitute for personal counseling. Remember to take advantage of other resources also available to you. If you or the people in your life are under a significant amount of stress or suffering from extremely low self-esteem or depression, check out the variety of books, tapes, classes, and self-help groups in your community and on the Internet.

PART V

Chapter 19

TURNING UP THE INTENSITY

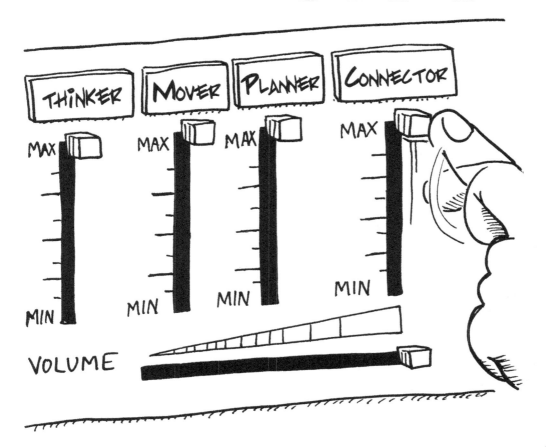

Strengthening Your Other Style Traits

Learning about the different personality styles has given us a deeper understanding of the motivations behind behaviors. We know that every style and combination has something of benefit to offer. Some individuals recognize the benefits so much that they favor the characteristics of another style over their own.

Jake, (a Mover), shared with me that he wishes the other traits in his personality were stronger. "I am constantly stressed, I seem to just always operate that way. I am so driven that I can't not be productive. I wish I wasn't bugged by the tiniest imperfection, or feel I have to constantly achieve. My Planner friends don't seem to have those problems. They seem to have their lives together and are so content. They are satisfied with their secure 9-5 jobs and love raising their families. Sometimes I feel like they can't relate to me and vice versa."

Jake is not alone. There are Connectors that admire Thinkers, wishing they too could maintain their emotions and composure in more situations. Planners have shared with me that they wish they didn't always feel compelled to complete work before feeling comfortable enough to play. Thinkers sometimes confide that they wish their intentions of making another person feel special wouldn't get side-lined because a fascinating project captured their attention instead. And, Movers yearn to be able to stay more focused and operate within guidelines,

without the irresistible urge to seize the opportunity of the moment, or use a shortcut.

Admiring the traits of others is healthy as long as you aren't feeling that it is wrong or bad to be who you are. As we grow and experience different aspects of life, we are constantly evolving. It is of great benefit to be able to operate in a variety of modes by strengthening our other style traits. The great thing is—it isn't necessary to wait for a life experience to push you to your next level of development. You can start practicing now to enhance the characteristics you desire.

For a simplistic example, let's say that Jake is right-handed or right-hand dominant and wants to get better at writing with his left hand (a less dominant trait). He doesn't have to wait until he breaks his right arm and is forced to write with his left to start practicing. If he begins writing with his left hand now, and continues to do so on a regular basis, he can become really good at it.

He will remain right-hand dominant, but now he'll also be good at writing with his left hand too!

On the other hand (pun intended), some of us may be so proud of our strengths and gifts that we may not take the time to consider what we are missing out on by not developing the other styles in our personality.

Zeke's top style happens to be Mover with a strong second style of Thinker just like Jake. However he expressed a totally different sentiment, "I love my style, the other styles suck! I am glad I am not ruled by my emotions or stuck in a rut."

Although it is fun to be validated for being the unique individuals that we are, remember that our strengths magnified can become liabilities. Desiring structure is admirable. Becoming extremely demanding and rigid is not. Flexible is fine, flaky is frustrating.

It is the individual contributions of each different style that make up the personality combination needed to get projects finished, keep organizations operating, and societies functioning. Since we are all evolving and our potential is limitless, we are all able to expand the other style in our personality.

Ideally, this process starts with embracing and appreciating our own top style then progresses to expanding our other styles. It is in being able to access an assortment of modes that gives us the greatest flexibility and thus the most personal power in situations. Personal evolution thus becomes a choice within one's control, rather than some random occurrence influenced by the circumstances we find ourselves in.

Take a look at the various suggestions for expanding the different style traits. Pay particular attention to the ones that are currently the less dominant traits for you. What ways can you increase each of the styles in your unique personality combination?

Increasing the Connector in You

If Connector is not your top or second style, these suggestions might appear a bit strange or uncomfortable to you at first. You don't have to try them all. Choose ones you think will assist you in opening up areas that you feel are not yet developed. This is not to say that we must change. Many of us expand our comfort zones and acquire new skills naturally over time. These tips are offered only to those interested in speeding up the process of expanding the other styles in their personality.

Foster Feelings— Cry, laugh out loud, express a range of emotions, and use the following list to "try on" an emotion a day. Distinguish between a whole range of emotions, just to experience what it feels like. It will also polish up your positivity. Discover how many ways you can express your "emotion of the day." Notice any physical cues in your body that will help you distinguish your feelings. Pay attention to the subtle differences between similar emotions, as well as the

215

drastic differences between the dissimilar ones. See if you can actually get in touch with the emotion, although "fake it till you make it" is fun too.

"Try on" Positive Emotions—

affectionate	invigorated
amazed	compelled
curious	interested
delighted	joyful
elated	lucky
enthusiastic	marvelous
excited	motivated
exhilarated	pleased
fabulous	refreshed
glad	phenomenal
gracious	spectacular
groovy	invincible
hilarious	terrific
intrigued	unstoppable

Of course you can always choose to express a plethora of negative emotions too. However, these usually come quite easily to many of us and therefore it's not typically necessary to practice them. Practicing negative emotions can be uncomfortable or in some circumstances even dangerous, and those who choose to might want to do so in the company of a good friend or under the supervision of a mental health professional.

Seek Harmony—Be nice. Before speaking, put yourself into the other person's position. Notice how they might feel receiving your message (not how you might feel, but how they might feel). Use softeners when making requests or giving directions. Use words such as "excuse me," "please," and "thank you." While you might not care much about certain rituals, others often do. Think of a very nice person you know, someone that seems to get along with everyone. Ask yourself, "What would they do in this situation?"

Listen—Experience what it feels like to give your undivided attention. Make as much eye contact with others as they are comfortable with. Pay attention to the feelings behind the words. Allow them to finish their sentences without filling in words or thoughts for them. Let go of trying to "fix" the problem, and just listen.

Take Care—Before diving straight into your agenda, pause to notice the needs of others. What could you do to assist them? It could be as simple as offering to take their coat or offering a drink of water.

Practice Positivity—Focus on what is good or beneficial about a situation or person. For each negative thought or comment you come up with, counter it with three positive points. For example, if you think someone is a jerk, three positive counter-thoughts could be "How can I help this person? What can I learn from this situation? What is good about this right now?"

Join a Cause—Volunteer to assist a human betterment movement such as passing out gifts to the needy at Christmas, volunteering your time at a local hospital, or visiting a senior living center.

Get Esoteric—Just for fun, get your palm read. Visit an acupuncturist, join a yoga class. Learn how to use creative visualization and enhance your intuition.

Rev Up the Romance—Say "I love you" out loud. Write a love note. Buy a gift or even better yet–do something for someone that isn't necessarily practical, logical, or responsible. Instead, give them a bubble bath, massage, or whisper in their ear something that fits their taste and desires. Set the atmosphere by playing soft music, lighting candles, and preparing a special meal. Stop and think. What unique gesture would show them that they are special?

Touch—Give or accept a hug. Read the book, *Vitamin T Is for Touch* by Bob Czimbal and Maggie Zadikov (Open Book Publishing, Portland, Oregon). It is a terrific guide to enjoying and increasing the amount of appropriate touch in your life.

Acknowledge—Pay attention to others and cultivate the habit of expressing the positive things you notice or validating people for just being human. Everyone has intrinsic value, whether you can recognize it or not. "Nice job!" "Great haircut!" "Thank you!" are all wonderful ways of expressing acknowledgment. Sometimes we think other people know how much we appreciate them and so we don't verbalize or otherwise demonstrate it. Another way to show appreciation is to write notes or thank you cards, or buy small gifts.

Seek Self-Expression and Exploration—Write in a journal, sing, dance, compose some poetry. Have discussions about the meaning of life. Explore self-help resources. A great place to start is to search for the term "self-help" on *Amazon.com*. You'll find topics such as creativity, self-esteem, happiness, spirituality and personal transformation.

Stir up the Spirituality—Get out in nature. Learn to meditate. Pray. Attend a religious service. Visit a retreat center. What will it take to release your spirit and connect with the Universe?

Refresh Relationships—Make a phone call, write a letter, get in touch with friends and family. Join a team. Keep in mind that how you work together as a group is as important as what you accomplish.

217

Increasing the Planner in You

If Planner characteristics are not very dominant for you, the following are some ideas to increase your Planner style. Enhancing your Planner traits can increase your professionalism as well as lower your stress by helping you improve in the areas of time management and organizational skills.

Get Organized—One of the best books I have ever read is *Clutters Last Stand* by Don Aslett. It is a guide for de-junking your life. It gives instructions for cleaning out closets and sorting through drawers, boxes, medicine cabinets, garages, etc. It is one of the most emancipating feelings to be rid of the stuff that is constantly getting in the way. If you have a tendency to misplace items such as your keys, establish a routine.

Have a designated, convenient place to put your keys. Always put them there.

Go shopping for organizers for your closet, office, or cupboards. For fun, color-code files, computer disks, or even the clothes hanging in your closet!

Respect Time Lines—Be on time for meetings and appointments. Plan to be there early to give yourself enough leeway to at least make it on time. If you are not comfortable leaving a lot of latitude because you get bored easily with the extra time, bring a book or other project to work on in case you end up waiting. Usually, though, you'll find the extra time is a welcomed gift. It helps calm nerves and allows space for extra preparations that you may not have had time to address in the past.

Follow the agenda in meetings as much as possible. Jot down ideas that pop into your head if it is not the proper time to share them at the moment. Usually, ideas presented at the proper time in the agenda are given more precedence than those that are announced out of turn. When people are able to stick to an agenda, usually much more progress is made. Just for fun, practice watching the clock or being timekeeper for a meeting.

218

Stick to Decisions, Plans, and Commitments—After making an arrangement or choosing an option, stay with it and follow through. Do the research ahead of time so you aren't compelled to change your mind after the data comes in. Go the extra mile to ensure you can stick to your word. Honor the plans of others and experience what it is like to have some structure and predictability. It's fun to be able to count on decisions.

Multiply Your Manners—Pick up a book on etiquette and read the sections that apply to your life and circumstances. Notice what other highly respected individuals say and how they behave in situations. Interview others to find out if you have any habits that you are not aware of. You may be surprised to find that you have a few slang words in your vocabulary or habits such as nail biting, fidgeting, or playing with your hair that might come across as unprofessional. Perhaps the way that you dress or your grooming could use a few adjustments. Start by asking family members and close friends, then move on to coworkers. Reassure them that you will benefit from their feedback and won't take comments and

suggestions personally. Tell them how much you appreciate their contributions to improving your decorum.

Prioritize Your Time—If your time management skills are not meeting your needs, attend a class on how to use a daily planner system. Just purchasing a planner does little good unless you know how to use it properly and then do so. Planning can cut down on wasted time and open up opportunities for you to accomplish more of what you really want to be doing. Classes on project management are also useful.

Plan Ahead—Think of what you will need to take care of before an event arrives. Don't wait until the last minute. Instead, mentally rehearse what will be occurring and notice what you will need to do to prepare. For instance, if you are heading on a trip, think of the days you will be gone and what leads up to your departure. Pay attention to the preparations required and make a list. Use the list as a guideline and reminder of what needs to be

MAX

Max —
Back in
a week

accomplished. Prioritize your list so the important and time-dependent items get completed first. Add to the list as new ideas come up. Keep track of your list and keep it handy. As you complete each item check it off the list. Create a budget and stick to it. Knowing how much money you have to spend ahead of time reduces the stress of trying to figure it all out later.

Determine Details—Pay attention to the style and needs of the people you are relating with. If you are used to giving big picture, ambiguous answers to individuals seeking specifics, practice honing in on some details. When giving directions or answering a question, offer some specifics. For instance, one time my friend was pulling into a gas station and asked, "How close am I to the pump?" I answered, "You're fine, you've got plenty of room." A more precise answer would have been "about three feet."

Think before You Speak, Act, or Interrupt—Pause before responding and think to yourself momentarily, "Would this be appropriate? Is this politically correct?"

My mother has a saying: "When in doubt, leave it out." She taught me to think of this phrase whenever I wasn't sure if something was proper or not. If I were thinking of pointing out the pitfalls of someone's idea that they were very enthusiastic about, I would pause and think "when in doubt, leave it out." I would readjust my thinking and focus on the positive point of the idea first. If you are contemplating "speaking your mind"

and it really will not contribute anything but hurt feelings, anger, or ego, leave it out. If what you have to say will forward the action on a matter, by all means go for it!

Rediscover Tradition— Investigate your family tree or look into other traditions and customs. Discover the heritage of your organization or community. Read up on a little history. Discover the pleasure of participating in a traditional meal or custom. Revitalize old traditions or establish some new ones for your family and repeat them year after year. It gives family members something to look forward to.

Check Procedures—Be aware of any tendencies you may have to take shortcuts. Circumventing lines of authority can threaten your credibility as well as your livelihood. It can also end up jeopardizing your safety and the safety of others. Although you may have the agility to get yourself out of a tight spot, others may not.

Get informed. Find out what the rules are in the variety of circumstances you find yourself. How many times have you repeatedly driven down the same street and wondered what the speed limit was or some other traffic question? If you are on the other side of the street going the opposite direction and a yellow school bus has its flashing red lights on, are you required to stop? If you live in California the answer is yes! Pay attention when the laws change. Look it up on the Internet. Try browsing the Department of Motor Vehicles site for information. It is free and could save you lots of time, money, and emotional turmoil.

What are the regulations in your neighborhood? Is it lawful to play your stereo loudly at 7:00 a.m.? How about at work? Do you know where your policies and procedures manual is? Do you know the safety guidelines?

Belong—Join an organization, club, guild, or association and participate fully. Take on the responsibility of facilitating an event or being responsible for some duties.

Increasing the Mover in You

If you are looking for ways to increase your flexibility, spontaneity, and enjoyment of the present moment, the following will help you turn up the intensity on your Mover characteristics. Of course, some of these ideas may seem far-fetched if Mover is not one of your top styles. Usually, it's beneficial to stretch your comfort zones, as long as you are not putting yourself at any physical or psychological risk or compromising your integrity. These suggestions are meant to nudge you in the direction of enjoying the moment and going with the flow—not to encourage you to break rules or make you look silly. Whether you feel silly or not, as you incorporate these methods into your days, you'll get increasingly pleasurable results. What you enjoy may be quite different from what others enjoy, and there is no reason you have to incorporate new behavior into your repertoire. But if you are like many people, all you need is a little jump-start to open up more avenues for intensifying your zest for life! So here are some possibilities.

Do Something for the Fun of It— Dive into an activity with abandon. Forget about schedules and duties for the moment and allow yourself to fully participate. Instead of questioning whether the activity is productive, logical or responsible, ask if it would bring you joy. Worry less, live more. The deadlines and responsibilities will still be there when you are finished. Why drag them with you into the moment? Let go, have fun, giggle.

Activate Your Body—Exercise, get yourself moving! Turn on some music and sway, swing, or bounce to the rhythm. Sing. You don't have to know the words to a song to belt out a tune–make up some goofy lyrics! Go for a walk, dance, hike, swim, or sail. Roller skate, jump rope, ski, or find an exercise class. However you can find a way to get some movement, do it.

Express Yourself Openly—To start, find a safe audience, such as a good friend or coworker that would be willing to hear you out with no holds barred. Share openly your opinions and comments. Let go of the fear of being judged or of not being politically correct. Vent, share, talk about whatever you'd like to at the moment.

Stretch Your Comfort Zones—Follow an impulse. Get some variety. Try new ways. For example, drive a different route to work in the morning, try a new restaurant or something new on the menu. Jump in and troubleshoot in a situation without planning. Take a vacation and leave half a day open with no schedule–just follow a whim, or do whatever activity comes up at the moment. What is it that you have always wanted to do (within reason, of

course) but have hesitated to do because of lack of skill or confidence? Just as an experiment to see what it feels like, take on a challenge or charge forth with a desire. Do so without any expectations for the outcome, and you may even double your pleasure.

Negotiate—The next time you get a "no" or "can't be done" answer, and you really feel there could be a way–don't give up. Come up with alternatives and back them up with evidence of how they would be viable. Extend your imagination. Visit a flea market and haggle with the vendors for a better deal than the price that is marked. If you really want to stretch, venture onto a car lot and negotiate for a low price on a car. Just for fun. Leave your credit cards and cash at home. This way you have nothing to lose. The time you spend will be like taking a crash course in negotiating skills. Observe the tactics or techniques the sales people use to try to get you to buy.

Take an Acting or Public Speaking Class—This is an excellent way to experience the fun of using big gestures,

loud voices, and variations of energy levels, intensity, and enthusiasm. Not only can it increase self-confidence, it can also provide avenues for discovering and experiencing a variety of personality styles.

Lighten Up—See the humor and fun in situations. Share a joke, get playful. Depending on the situation, let yourself get casual and comfortable. Leave a few things undecided. Keep some options open and go with the flow.

Play to Win—Have you ever participated in an activity and stopped short of your potential? I once attended a seminar in which we actually played a game of "Simon Says." There were 2,000 people in attendance, and I figured I'd play until I got out—no big deal. It only took about three minutes before I was out of the game. After about fifteen minutes there were only ten participants left standing. The seminar leader asked the audience how many had said something like this to themselves before they started: "I'm going to win this. I'm going to play

223

full out. I'm going to participate with my whole heart and soul. I'm going to go for it!" Out of the 2,000 people, only 12 raised their hands, and 10 of them were standing on stage!

My friend John often repeats a phrase that his father would tell him as a child: "There are those who make things happen, those who watch things happen, and those who wonder what happened." Which are you?

Savor Your Senses—Most of us already enjoy plenty of good food. But do you stop and savor it? Do you pay attention to the way it smells, feels in the mouth, or its texture? Do you make noises when you eat, such as "yummmm"? When you eat, slow down and appreciate the sensations of the whole experience. Enjoy the experience of a mud bath, or just relax in a bubble bath at home while you listen to soothing music. Get a massage. Savor the smell of fresh cut flowers. We have at least five senses: taste, touch, sight, hearing, smell. What ways can you find to experience them more fully?

Create an Adventure—When you find yourself in a situation that is starting to cause stress, look at it through a child's eyes. For instance, if you are getting tense because it's raining and you are getting muddy, go with it–play in the rain, get muddy! Or if you are waiting in an airport and have just found out that your plane has been delayed, instead of groaning and waiting in your seat, reading a book or making some phone calls–create an adventure! What would an eight-year old do? Go exploring. There are usually stores and restaurants to investigate and even airplanes to watch. Take a long time in the bathroom. Eat popcorn by tossing it in the air and catching it in your mouth. If you are traveling with others, it can be even more fun. What games can you play? Try "I Spy." For instance, you look for something red and say, "I spy something red." Everyone looks for and tries to guess the red object you have spied. Whoever guesses gets the next turn. The possibilities are endless.

Accept Attention—When you do something funny or awkward, instead of being embarrassed, relish the attention. Laugh with your audience; play with the situation. If you did something wonderful and people have not noticed, call it to their attention. If they did notice, accept their praise. Enjoy it and know that it brings great pleasure to others when you accept the gift of their compliments.

Increasing the Thinker in You

How easy would it be for you to find the ultimate lowest price on a car, design a blueprint for developing a new product at work, teach a child about the rotation of the planets around the sun, or search the Internet for a little known fact? If your initial reaction is anywhere from "huh?" to overwhelmed, you may benefit from expanding your Thinker traits. Being able to say "no" with firm conviction, to stay calm in the face of conflict, or to make more objective decisions are aspects of Thinker behavior we all admire. Use the following suggestions to turn up the intensity of your Thinker traits.

Exercise Objectivity—If you have a habit of taking things personally, it's time to learn how to pause and mentally step out of the situation to get a more objective view. When you noticed you've been triggered, instead of quickly spiraling into an emotional reaction, stop and take a deep breath. Thank your emotions for giving you a signal to pay attention.

Now put your "Thinker" cap on and imagine in your mind's eye that you can observe yourself and the other person, as if you were watching a scene in a movie. What do you notice? Is the other person

tired, angry, or insecure? Could they be joking, have poor communication skills or feel threatened by you? What state are you in? Are you receptive to the other person's feedback? What frame of mind would you need to be in to be able to decode their perhaps sloppily delivered message? Notice if the content of their message was packaged in a different way, how you might gain a new understanding. Frequently, it is not what a person said that gets us triggered, it's how they said it. Taking this movie-watching, observer perspective helps you to listen more objectively to feedback without being emotionally triggered.

"It's a fool who takes offense when none is intended, and a bigger fool who takes offense when one is."
–Brigham Young

Check Your Facts—Instead of taking something at face value, investigate it further. Do your homework. For instance, did you know that the famous "7-38-55" statistic that virtually everyone uses to support the notion that our communication is only 7% verbal, 38% voice qualities and 55% body language— is a misinterpretation? For decades, people have been using this quote, assuming that since they read it or heard it from a respected source, it must be true. Go ahead and look it up. This commonly misquoted "fact" is the result of only two studies conducted in 1967 on thirty participants, all females. No one, not even the researcher who conducted the studies, can quite figure out how that formula came to be so widely used because *he claims he never published it!*

Get Techie—The mind of a Thinker is irrevocably tied to technology in its myriad of forms and applications. Technology is, in fact, often used as an extension of their brains to a much greater degree than the other styles. Instead of shying away from that new gadget or program, unleash your inner geek to harness some of the awesomeness that technology has to offer.

There are endless possibilities: learn to blog, make your own web site, watch a DIY video and fix something yourself, listen to a podcast, learn the computer shortcut keys for your favorite word processing or other program, load some new apps on your cell phone, make your own QR code, make a Wiki, create a personal playlist of your favorite music, learn how to download and edit a MP3, submit a word to Wikipedia or Urban dictionary, learn how to back up your computer, take a course at the Apple store, make a screencast lesson to teach someone else what you learned!

Practice Being Precise with Your Words—Challenge yourself to learn a new word a day to expand your vocabulary. If you encounter a word you don't know, look it up.

Record Ideas—Document your discoveries and thoughts. Actually take some steps to implement them, even if it is sharing your idea with someone you trust. Create a graph or chart to explain your inventions. Design models and schematics for further clarification.

Think Long-Term—Look at the big picture instead of dealing with the most pressing issue at the moment. Slow down enough to prioritize the important versus the urgent. Speculate as to what effects today's actions will have on tomorrow's objectives.

Solve a Problem for Yourself—Before turning to others for assistance, try to figure out a challenge on your own. Read instruction manuals, try various alternatives, get creative.

Explore—Look up something on the Internet. Visit a library, museum or other resource center. Ask yourself, "What else can I find out about this subject?" Then look for it. Read something about math, science, magic, philosophy, or technology. Watch the Learning Channel. Take a journey to a distant place.

Stop and Contemplate—Instead of making a quick decision or response, pause to think. Gather some data and scrutinize the facts. What are the pros and cons? Actually write out a chart or list and give points to which data weighs the heaviest and is the most important. Before acting or answering, consider several options. Give yourself time to think about different ways to express or

do things. Make a decision based on what would be the most logical, as well as how you feel.

Ask "Why?"—In college, I was taught analytical reasoning. We were told to look at a research paper and see beneath the obvious–what the author wanted us to think, and find the facts beneath. It helped me to ask more questions in order to delve for hidden facts or even manipulation. Just as with analyzing research papers, it can be beneficial to explore beneath the surface. When you are presented with something that you are unsure of, instead of just taking the person's word for it–ask. Get curious and get your questions answered.

Debate the Other Side of an Argument Just for Fun—The dual benefit; since you are not emotionally vested in winning, because you are arguing the opposite of what you really believe, if you concentrate, you can experience what it's like to argue a point without your emotions taking over.

Stretch Your Sense of Humor—See how well you can recognize word puns in people's speech throughout the day. You'll be amazed at how much you hadn't noticed before. If you really want to have some fun with this, comment creatively with your own new words. Start simple. For example, when your husband tells you he is going to "hop in the shower," you might respond, "You're not going to skip or jump, just hop?"

Accessing Your Other Styles

Notice that as you expand your capacity to access the personality traits of your less preferred styles more easily, you are still able to access your most dominant style when you want to.

As we develop various aspects of ourselves, we gain an appreciation for the ways others operate.

The executive director for an insurance company shared with me that to assist in helping his staff strengthen their different personality styles he purchased several brightly colored shirts in four different colors. Each color represented a personality style. He used yellow shirts for Planner, red shirts for Mover, green shirts for Thinker and blue shirts to represent the Connector style. In meetings he asks his staff to choose a color different from their most dominant style and "operate" in that color or personality style for the meeting.

"It is fun to watch the staff transform into operating from a different style. Those wearing red shirts were full of energy, playfully tossing out ideas. The "Thinkers" in green logically explained their projects using big words and diagrams. The ones wearing blue shirts were patient, kind and compassionate and the "Planners" wearing yellow kept bringing order to the meeting and attention back to the agenda. We all have a great time expressing ourselves in creative ways.

As we continue our evolution through the stages of our lives, we naturally strengthen the different styles in our personality. This balancing enables us to operate in a variety of situations with more ease and confidence. Knowing your personality and expanding other parts of it are great ways to accelerate your journey and gain the desired flexibility to understand and relate to yourself and others at a whole new level.

Part VI
NAVIGATING
LIFE
WITH PERSONALITY

Shifting Your Course

As you stop and think about the insights you have gained by reading about your personality and the style of others, you'll realize how knowing this information can transform the way you interact with the people in your life. You'll notice that although every person is unique in many ways, the values, preferences, and motives you are able to recognize can give you clues as to what a person may think, say, or do in certain situations. It can also help you understand the intentions behind their actions. Instead of resentment you'll find compassion. Animosity will be replaced

229

with understanding and potential conflicts with cooperation. You'll discover yourself applying the Personality Lingo concepts in virtually every aspect of your life.

From Animosity to Understanding

Ann was on a committee that was planning a statewide conference. The committee had only met twice and chaos and animosity were already rampant. Several members seemed to consume the meeting time by suggesting ideas, ordering pizza, and bantering with each other. Other members were irritated at the "time-wasting" and attempted to gain control by confirming tasks to be completed and giving orders. Ann tried her best to facilitate harmony in the group by taking on tasks and giving her attention to everyone, not just the outspoken. She was extremely uncomfortable with the conflict between members and although she knew she was making positive contributions, thoughts of quitting the committee ran through her mind. It was at this point, thank goodness, they had a guest speaker in their general meeting. The woman conducted a presentation on the personality concepts! Ann found the information about the different styles fascinating and immediately began thinking about how she could apply the information in her own life.

A week passed and the committee met at a hotel so they could take a look at the facilities. The group was interested in obtaining several small rooms for "break-out" sessions and was told by the hotel to look at the El Dorado Room. As they were walking into the room, they noticed there were about five people already there. Ann, not wanting to be rude or intrude upon the people, said in a loud whisper, "Wait! There are people in the room. Let's come back later."

Jules, one of the most outspoken of the committee, darted to the front of the group, waving them on. "Oh, who cares? Let's go in; we'll only be a minute."

Ann stood dumbfounded as the group filed past her into the room. She felt that her opinion had been negated and overruled. Her mind started heading into a direction of hurt feelings and misunderstood intentions, when suddenly she clicked out of it. "Wait a minute," she thought to herself. "Jules is a Mover. She didn't mean to negate me as a person. She simply was trying to 'just do it.' She just wanted to charge forth with her agenda." Ann was able to immediately let go of the angst she had started to feel and instead appreciate the "charge-ahead character" of Jules. What could have possibly turned into a slow-burning grudge instead had dissipated because of the understanding that her knowledge of personality styles provided. Much to her surprise, on the way out of the room Jules acknowledged Ann for her politeness and apologized. "Sometimes my directness gets a bit ahead of me. Thank you for being such a team player."

During the conference, because the committee recognized the caring concern for people that Ann consistently showed, they chose her to monitor each room to make sure the speakers and participants were comfortable. She made more handouts if needed or asked the hotel to adjust the heat when necessary. She did a fantastic job of anticipating people's needs. For instance, if she saw a speaker clearing his throat repeatedly and looking around, she would appear with a freshly poured glass of water.

During lunch, several attendees wandered around looking for places to sit. Wanting to make sure they were comfortable but not interrupt those that were already seated, Ann asked the hotel personnel to bring out more chairs. This way, if she saw people unsuccessfully searching for a seat, she could offer to place chairs at any table they would like. This seemed to be a good system—until the bill came at the end of the conference. The catering captain stood with Ann explaining that he would have to charge her for the twelve extra chairs that were brought out.

"We charge for lunch by the chair," he told her.

Had she known this, she would have never asked for more chairs. She would have gone around to the tables and found the existing chairs. "But we did not have twelve more people for lunch," she told him. She tried several ways to communicate to him that they should not have to pay the extra charges because in actuality there were no extra people eating lunch. But he was not budging.

"We charge by the chair," he repeated firmly.

Getting more uncomfortable by the minute, Ann suddenly recalled that Wendy was a Thinker. Maybe she could explain the situation to the catering captain in a way he would understand. Wendy was quickly brought into the conversation, clip-board in hand.

"Look," Wendy said to the man, showing him the figures she had tracked and calculated on her clip-board. "This is how many people attended the conference; this is how many people paid for lunch. This is how many people actually showed up for lunch. I know. I took their tickets. I counted them as they came in the door. This is the number of people that ate, and this is the amount of money we are paying you."

The man looked at Wendy and said, "Okay."

We Are Not Tied to Our Type

It is important to realize that knowing your personality style does not give you

231

free reign to behave in unacceptable ways. It is ridiculous to think that it is okay to be late for work and say to your boss, "Oh I'm just a Mover, this is the way I am." It's just as ridiculous as thinking that all Movers have a tendency to be late. We all have preferred ways of operating. Preferences do not necessarily equate to skills or competencies. Be careful not to stereotype or bind yourself into your personality style. Although your temperament remains in your nature throughout life, we are all evolving and changing with each life experience.

Use this knowledge to unlock your self-expression and to validate yourself for your preferences. And remember—you can always strengthen the less dominant styles of your personality.

Recognize what you can gain by expanding your less dominant styles.

I was conducting a personality style presentation for an elementary school staff that had just finished establishing a policy regarding interdistrict agreements. These agreements govern when a child who lives in one school district can be allowed to go to a school in another district. The policy was needed because in the past decisions were based more on who begged the most to get into their school than on any clearly designated criteria. It had caused a tremendous amount of stress for Wanda, the secretary, who was the one to have to deal with parents seeking an application. It was her job to fill out the paperwork and let the parents know if their child was accepted or not. Wanda was relieved to finally have something in written form that she could rely upon. Included in the policy was a deadline date for applications.

Three weeks after school had been in session for the new year, and two days after the deadline date for interdistrict agreement applications, a mother came into the office and requested an application for her children. Wanda informed her that she had missed the deadline date, but that she could try applying next semester. The woman was furious! She had been in Europe over the summer and had just returned home. How was she supposed to know there was a deadline date? She had counted on getting her kids into this school. School was already well into session, and they had missed enough already. She accused Wanda of being to blame for her children not being in school yet.

Wanda held her ground. She was glad to have the new policy guidelines to stand behind and gave the woman a copy of the policy. Wanda apologized for any inconvenience and again suggested that the woman could apply for her children to attend next semester. The woman would not have it. She insisted on seeing the principal. Wanda told her that it would not do her any good. It was policy.

Hearing all the commotion, the principal appeared. He ushered the upset woman into his office. After about half an hour, the two emerged from his office. The principal handed a completed application to Wanda and said, "Please process this for me and see that her children are admitted to the school as soon as possible."

The woman glared smugly at Wanda, as if to say, "Nah-nah-nahnah-naaah-nah!" Of course, Wanda was embarrassed and humiliated. She was only doing her job, and now she was being made out to be the "bad one." She was angry with the principal for not supporting her and the new policy.

The principal was Connector-Mover. After training in Personality Lingo, he realized his contribution to the problems created by not sticking to policy and why it was so important to Wanda, who was Planner-Connector, to have his cooperation and support. Her needs for consistency and fairness were being sabotaged by his "quick to accommodate and keep the harmony" attitude.

Recognizing his own tendencies was the first step in adding the necessary skills to still honor his Connector-Mover

desires while embracing and supporting policy.

A Little Insight Goes a Long Way

It is important to make accommodations for others whose style happens to be your least dominant preferences. Put yourself in their shoes. Ed is a family practice physician. His patient load is overwhelming. He sees an average of thirty patients a day. From the moment he arrives at work he is ordering charts, diagnosing conditions, and writing prescriptions, as well as stacks of other

CONGRATULATIONS ON YOUR NEW ARRIVAL!

duties. He moves steadily from room to room, dealing with whatever challenge is presented to him. He is constantly concentrating on what he needs to do to serve each patient's needs, so when he walks through the hallway to the next room he does so without stopping to connect with his co-workers. They used to think Ed was antisocial or mad at them. They would say "hi" to him, and he would respond, "hi" and continue straight to his next patient without pause. He rarely, if ever, attended any social events such as Christmas parties or luncheons. One time his staff asked him to sign a card for a coworker's baby shower and he didn't even know the woman was expecting– and she was eight months pregnant!

His staff explained that before they understood about personality styles (Thinkers in particular) they always mistook his seriousness for being mad, his not paying attention to social events as being antisocial, and his lack of acknowledgment as being pompous. Now they understand more about his natural tendencies. So if they want him to know something, they call it to his attention. When he is jolted out of his concentration for the task at hand, he can recognize their needs more readily and does so. His staff has a new understanding and admiration of his skills and vice versa. He actually enjoys the pleased responses he receives when he surprises his staff with gifts during the holidays. He has taken up the habit of using an expressive word for the day. When people greet him with the usual "Hi, how are you today?" he responds with something like "sensational" or "golden."

Dramatic Transformations

Many of you probably have already noticed some subtle changes in your relationships and level of acceptance of others as a result of learning Personality Lingo. You can recognize more easily

when you are, or are not, getting through to someone. Now you have some vocabulary and insights at your fingertips. You'll continue day by day to discover ways to use this information in many situations–to reduce antagonism, confusion, and conflict and increase compassion, understanding, and cooperation.

After determining that her ex-husband, Sam, had predominantly Mover characteristics, Cindy decided to try a new motivational strategy with him, one that would appeal to his sense of adventure and challenge. It had been a sticky divorce and many of Cindy's, as well as the children's, items were still at their old house where Sam was living. If Cindy asked Sam to please bring an item with him when he picked up the children for visitation, he would inevitably forget or refuse. Because she was not welcome at his house and she wanted to keep the peace, she had to find another way to motivate him. Being a Thinker, Cindy was willing to devise a strategy. Instead of asking him to bring the items, she appealed to his Mover personality style by making a game out of it. "I'll bet you can't guess what I need you to bring," she would challenge.

"Your bike!" he would guess. "No, guess again."

"The tea kettle."

"Wrong room, try again."

"The rocking chair!"

"Yes! You're right. Can you guess what else?" She would continue with the guessing contest until he determined all the items. The amazing thing was that he would remember to bring every single item, without fail. Cindy admitted that sometimes she felt weird or even manipulative playing this game, so she would occasionally just straight out ask him to bring something. Of course when she did this, he would inevitably forget. Anytime she created a contest, game, or challenge he would come through with flying colors!

Respect vs. Manipulation

The interesting thing about communicating with others in their "Personality Lingo" is that to those who do not understand the benefits, it may seem manipulative at first. It is such a sad disservice when people misinterpret respect for manipulation. When you learn to speak another language to be able to talk to your neighbor, colleague, friend, or loved one—are you being manipulative or respectful? Of course it depends on your intent. If your intent is to open up lines of communication, then you are being respectful.

Through the Eyes of Others

Another terrific way to show your respect and consideration for others is to notice what they need and value. Sometimes in our aim to please, we don't notice that we are contributing in a way that would make us happy, but not necessarily in a way that would make others happy. Our intentions may be very honorable, yet the results might not be as good as they could be if we had looked at a situation from more than just our own perspective.

Colleen absolutely loved holidays, especially Christmas. She had always derived such pleasure from upholding the traditions of decorating the house, making a home-cooked meal, and opening presents around the tree. When her three children were not yet in school, her husband worked outside of the home and she stayed at home to take care of them. Because she was at home, she took on the sole responsibility for making sure the holiday was a memorable occasion. She would pull out her grandmother's recipes and make homemade apple pie. She helped the children make ornaments, and they decorated the house together.

However, when the children were old enough to go to school, Colleen took on a part-time job. By the time the last child graduated from high school, Colleen was working full-time outside of the home as well as taking on some bookkeeping clients for a home business she had started. As the Christmas season approached, Colleen became increasingly stressed. Now her days were spent at work and her nights doing bookkeeping. Her children were married and had children of their own. Instead of cooking and buying presents for her family of four, she now cooked the holiday meal and shopped for fourteen! Because she had always been the one to prepare all the festivities, she tried her hardest to continue the tradition. Although circumstances had changed tremendously, she never asked for any help. Her children tried to volunteer a few times to assist her but she always turned them down. She felt it was her obligation to come through as she had always done in the past. What once had been her favorite time of year had now become the most stressful.

In early December, Colleen attended a personality workshop at her office. During the session she discovered she had many Planner characteristics. It helped to explain why she felt a driving sense of duty to uphold traditions. She also learned the values of the other personality styles. She recognized many Connector as well as Planner traits in her children. Knowing this, she realized that her children were being respectful in allowing their mother the honor of carrying out the traditions, while at the same time probably yearning to contribute. Only a few days after the workshop, Colleen had the opportunity to ask her children to pitch in for the upcoming holiday. They were delighted! They knew how much joy it brought their mother to prepare for the holidays so they didn't want to rock the boat by insisting that she accept their help. They figured it might come across as rude or make it seem as though they did not appreciate her efforts. But they wanted greatly to be part of the preparations and were relieved to have her finally accept their help.

Colleen shared with me that it was one of the happiest holidays she ever had. She had started a new family tradition of everyone pitching in and preparing together!

Validation for Your Own Style

You are a unique combination of characteristics. And, although society may try to force its opinion on us about the way we should be, through the media and other pressures, we recognize how unrealistic that really is. Take weight management for instance. It's one thing to want to watch your weight for health reasons; it's another to try to lose weight because of the feeling that you don't measure up to some imaginary "ideal." You are an awesome individual with your own set of values, likes, and dislikes. Deep down we know what is right for us. When we behave with integrity and are able to express ourselves, it is a freeing experience. I remember one time recently in a personality workshop that I was conducting, a young woman motioned for me to come over to where she was sitting. "I'm a Mover!" she beamed.

"Good," I said, "then you are sitting at the right table."

"No," she said, "you don't understand! I AM A MOVER! All my life I was trained to be a Planner. I did not think there was any other way to be. I thought there was a 'Gold Standard' the way everyone should be. I had no idea that there were other people that felt the way I do or valued the same things. I have gone to counseling over the guilt and inadequacies I have experienced. I have never felt more validated than at this very moment. Thank you!"

She continued, "The greatest thing is that I know I have choices. I still can choose to behave as a Planner, but I know I don't have to. If I feel like letting a little of my Mover show, it is not wrong, bad, or better—it is just different."

Chapter 20
LIVING
WITH
PERSONALITY!

New Perspectives

After reading this book and applying the concepts you've learned, you are now better able to recognize what energizes you and how it may differ from what energizes those with other top styles and combinations. Enter interactions with a willingness to learn. Notice that their reality is as valid as yours and keep an open mind so you can gain something by interacting with them. People are constantly sharing with me how after they learned about personality styles they attended a family or community event and watched people's behaviors in a new light. They were tickled to be able to recognize the personality style characteristics various individuals were displaying.

Speaking the Lingo of Personality

Many people that have been exposed to the personality concepts are amazed at how quickly and easily–even spontaneously–the language is brought into so many of their conversations. They find themselves saying things like, "Oh, it's the Connector in me..." or "You seem to be in the Planner mode today..." Listen to notice how much this happens. The next time you are in a conversation with someone who has enthusiastically chosen a subject you are interested in, or especially ones you are not, become aware of what style is motivating them. You'll be surprised and delighted to discover your world has personality!

Traveling in all Directions with Personality

Those who really embrace the personality concepts will find themselves applying the insights in virtually every area of their lives. One time a coworker approached me and said she was going on a blind date and knew that the man had a lot of Connector traits. She wanted to know what I could tell her about Connectors! I was surprised that she was aware of the many Connector traits in the man's personality. I was further intrigued as to how she knew this information if it was a blind date and she had never met him before. She told me that a friend of hers told her he was a Connector. How did the friend know? Personality Lingo is contagious!

It is fun to recognize the Personality styles and combinations in the people around us. The next time you watch a movie, pay attention to the characters and see if you can determine their personality styles. This is fun to do with TV shows and storybook characters as well. Take The Wizard of Oz, for instance. Can you guess the styles of Dorothy, the Tin Man, the Scarecrow, and the Lion? How about the Wizard?

Everyone Adds Value

There is no "best" type of personality style, and everyone is a different combination. Keep in mind that you are more than just your most dominant style. The whole is greater than the sum of its parts. Be proud of your personality style and allow others enjoyment of theirs. Think of ways to bring out the best in people by recognizing their needs, values, and talents. See how many ways you can bring out the best in their style while maintaining your own.

Share Personality Lingo with Others

More and more people are experiencing the benefits of knowing their personality and sharing the concepts with the people in their lives. The more people around you that know the lingo of personality, the easier it is to communicate, understand behaviors, and solve conflicts. Share this book or spread the benefits by visiting our website at *www.PersonalityLingo.com* and getting a workshop or presentation at your school, work site, or community event. In the meantime, keep these key points in mind:

"Do unto others as they would have you do unto them."

As you know, some people don't want to be treated the way you like to be treated. Take hugging, for instance. I love to hug! When I was younger I used to assume that because I liked receiving hugs as much as giving them that others would also like to be hugged. Wrong! As you may have already discovered, some people do not always appreciate a hearty hug–especially from a stranger. I also like to speak loudly and directly and enjoy it when others do the same. Still, I meet people that prefer softer tones as well as a softer approach. When we treat people only our way, it can increase tension and resistance levels. Our willingness and ability to balance our behaviors with the circumstances, as well as the people we relate to, is essential for our personal effectiveness. Learning the language and preferences of others not only lowers tension and resistance levels, but also demonstrates the utmost respect. It helps to build collaboration and strengthen relationships.

Personality Lingo is only a model; it takes real life to validate it.

Although discovering your personality and ranking your styles can give you tremendous insights into the behaviors of yourself and others, it certainly does not explain or solve everything. Through training and reading this book, you can learn the guidelines. Life is where you learn to apply them. There are variations within all styles; personality theory is only one filter through which to view human behavior. Use this as a powerful tool to combine with other methods that work for you.

Do you have some stories to share?

How has knowing your personality style affected your life? How has it validated your desires or allowed you more self-expression? What have you learned about relating to and connecting with others? Would you like to share your story with others that are interested in enhancing their relationships and increasing their understanding? Would you like to see your story appear in a future book or article about personality styles? Write to me and let me know your adventures and discoveries! How are you speaking Personality Lingo?

Mary Miscisin
7485 Rush River Drive, suite 710
Sacramento, CA 95831
www.PersonalityLingo.com

Resources

Baron Renee. (1998) *What Type Am I?* Harmondsworth, England: Penguin Books.

Baron, Renee. (1994). *The Enneagram Made Easy: Discover the 9 Types of People.* New York, NY: HarperCollins.

Birkman, Sharon (2013). *The Birkman Method. Your Personality at Work.* San Francisco, California: Jossey Bass Wiley.

Blatny, Mark. *Assertive toddler, self-efficacious adult: Child temperament predicts personality over forty years.* Personality and Individual Differences. 43(8):2127-2136.

Bouchard, Thomas (2001). *Genes, Evolution, and Personality.* Behavioral Genetics, 31(3): 243-247.

Cain, Susan. (2013). *Quiet: The Power of Introverts in a World That Can't Stop Talking.* Portland. Oregon: Broadway Books.

Cloninger, C. (1994) A *psychobiological model of temperament and character.* Archives of General Psychiatry, 50(12):975-90.

Congdon E, et al. (2012) *Early Environment and Neurobehavioral Development Predict Adult Temperament Clusters.* PLoS ONE 7(7).

Cyphers, L. (1990) *Twin temperament during the transition from infancy to early childhood.* Journal of the American Academy of Child & Adolescent Psychiatry 29(3):392-7.

Delunas, Eve. (1992) *Survival Games Personalities Play.* Carmel, California: Sunlink Publications.

Dick, Danielle M. et al, *Adolescent Alcohol Use is Predicted by Childhood Temperament Factors Before Age 5, with Mediation Through Personality and Peers.* Alcoholism: Clinical and Experimental Research, 2013.

Fisher, Helen. (2000) *Why Him? Why Her? Finding Real Love by Understanding Your Personality Type.* New York, NY. Holt Paperback.

Freidman, Howard. (2010). *Personality: Classic Theories and Modern Research (5th Edition).* Old Tappan, NJ. Perason.

Gonda, X. (2009) *Towards a genetically validated new affective temperament scale: A delineation of the temperament phenotype of 5-HTTLPR using the TEMPS-A.* Journal of Affective Disorders, 112: 1–3, 19–29.

Huszczo, Gregory. (2000) *Making a Difference by Being Yourself: Using Your Personality Type to Find Your Life's True Purpose.* Boston, MA. Nicholas Brealy Publishing.

Jung, C.G. (1955) *Modern Man in Search of a Soul.* Orlando, Florida: Harcourt, Inc.

Jung, C.G. (1976) *Psychological Types - The Collected Works of C. G. Jung, Vol. 6.* Princeton, NJ: Princeton University Press.

Kang, Jee, et al. *The association of 5-HTTLPR and DRD4 VNTR polymorphisms with affective temperamental traits in healthy volunteers.* Journal of Affective Disorders, 109 (1-2): 157–163.

Keirsey, David & Bates, Marilyn. (1984) *Please Understand Me.* Del Mar, California: Prometheus Nemesis Book Company

Keirsey, David. (1998). *Please Understand Me II.* Del Mar, California, Prometheus Nemesis Book Co.

Kroeger, Otto, & Thuesen, Janet. (1992) *Type Talk at Work: How the 16 Personality Types Determine Your Success on the Job.* New York: Dell Publishing.

Matheny, A. (1983) *A longitudinal twin study of stability of components from Bayley's Infant Behavior Record.* Child Development , 54(2):356-60.

Miscisin, M. (2005) *Showing Our True Colors.* Santa Ana, California: True Colors Inc. Publishing

Myers, I.B. (1998) *Introduction to Type.* Palo Alto, California: Consulting Psychological Press, Inc.

Myers, I.B. (1980) *Gifts Differing - Understanding Personality Types.* Palo Alto, California: Davies-Black

Nigg, J. T., and Goldsmith, H. H. (1998). *Developmental psychopathology, personality, and temperament: Reflections on recent behavioral genetics research.* Human Biology 70: 387–412.

Pinker, Steven. (2003) *The Blank Slate: The Modern Denial of Human Nature.* New York, NY. Penguin Group.

Quenk, Naomi. (2001) Was That Really Me? How Everyday Stress Brings Out Our Hidden Personality. Palo Alto, California: Davies-Black Publishing.

Rettew, David. (2008). *Latent profiles of temperament and their relations to psychopathology and wellness.* Journal of the American Academy of Child & Adolescent Psychiatry, 47(3):273-8.

Reynierse, James . (2012). *Toward an Empirically Sound and Radically Revised Type Theory.* The Journal of Psychological Type, 72: 1-25.

Saudino, Kimberly (2005) *Behavioral genetics and child temperament.* Journal of Developmental & Behavioral Pediatrics. 26(3):214-23.

Made in the USA
Coppell, TX
30 June 2022